# Table of Cor

MW00465274

# An Introduction to Software Engineering

Software engineering is concerned with all aspects of software production from the early stages of system specification through to maintaining the system after it has gone into use. In this chapter, we will explain the following:

the definition of computer science and software engineering and how the two are different

how software engineering is similar to other engineering disciplines and what that means for software engineers

the unique challenges of software engineering

software development models and processes and their component parts, software development practices

> *Software systems are perhaps the most intricate and complex . . . of the things humanity makes.*      *– Fred Brooks [8]*

As a discipline, software engineering has progressed very far in a very short period of time, particularly when compared to classical engineering fields (like civil or electrical engineering). In the early days of computing, not much more than 50 years ago, computerized systems were quite small. Most of the programming was done by scientists trying to solve specific, relatively small mathematical problems. Today we often build monstrous systems, in terms of size and complexity. And, the visibility of the software has transitioned from mainly scientists and software developers to the general public of all ages. "Today, software is working both explicitly and behind the scenes in virtually all aspects of our lives, including the critical systems that affect our health and well-being." [20] Essentially every person encounters software throughout their day – from cars to phones to television to the Internet.

Despite our rapid progress, the software industry is considered by many to be in a crisis. Some 40 years ago, the term "Software Crisis"[1] emerged to describe the software industry's inability to provide customers with high quality products on schedule. "The average software development project overshoots its schedule by half; larger projects generally do worse. And, some three quarters of all large systems are "operating failures" that either do not function as intended or are not used at all." [15] While the industry can celebrate that software touches nearly all aspects of our daily lives, we can all relate to software availability dates (such as computer games) as moving targets and to computers crashing or locking up. We have many challenges we need to deal with as we continue to progress into a more mature engineering field, one that predictably produces high-quality products.

## 1    The Engineering of Software

Until this point in your academic career, you have likely focused on being a computer scientist. Consider the definition of computer science developed by an ACM[2] Task Force [11]:

*The discipline of computing is the systematic study of algorithmic processes that describe and transform information: their theory, analysis, design, efficiency, implementation, and application. The fundamental question underlying all of computing is, "What can be (efficiently) automated?"*

Likely, the main focus of your studies and programming thus far have been to get the computer to do what you want it to do (i.e. transform information), as efficiently as possible. Professionals in the computing industry today must consider many other issues in using computer science to <u>engineer</u> software-intensive. Consider this definition of engineering proposed by Robert Baber (emphasis added) [2]:

> *. . . the systematic and regular application of scientific and mathematical knowledge to the design, construction, and operation of machines, systems, and so on of <u>practical use</u> and, hence, of <u>economic value</u>. Particular characteristic of engineers is that they take seriously their <u>responsibility for correctness, suitability, and safety of the results</u> of their efforts. In this regard they consider themselves to be responsible to their customer (including their employers where relevant), to the users of their machines and systems, and to the public at large.*

Computer science is one of the disciplines that provide a theory basis for the profession of software engineering. (Some others are psychology, economics, and management.) The above definition of engineering lays out two important issues involved in transitioning from computer science to software engineering. The issues underlined in the above definition of engineering are further discussed below:

> *Practical use, economic value.* Engineers need to produce products that customers actually want and are willing to pay real money for. These products need to help people do the things they need to do. Listening to the customer is of prime importance. Engineers also need to produce these products the customer wants as economically as possible. The best product in the world won't sell if it's too expensive. And, if we develop products using inappropriate practices and processes, our products will be too expensive. As engineers, we need to build valuable product for our customers.

> *Responsibility for correctness, suitability, and safety.* Engineers are ethically obligated to ensure their programs are correct and suitable for their customers. In fact, the software engineering code of ethics [1] authored by professional society ACM[2] states that software engineers shall commit themselves to making the analysis, specification, design, development, testing and maintenance of software a beneficial and respected profession for the benefit and protection of the health, safety and welfare of the public. In some

instances, our programs have safety critical implications, where people might die if a program has errors. In other cases, whole businesses could be at risk if a program is not correct or contains security vulnerabilities that enable attackers to steal or delete data. We are sure that you have always tried to get your programs to be correct and suitable in the past. The new dimension now is that you must always consider your responsibility and obligation to your customer. The work you do could impact their safety, their business . . . and their well being!

## 2    Software Development

In addition to the ACM professional society, our field had a second professional society IEEE. IEEE[3] defines *software engineering* as *the application of **a systematic, disciplined, quantifiable approach** to the development, operation, and maintenance of software; that is, the application of engineering to software* [17]. The "systematic, disciplined, quantifiable approach" is often termed a software process model (in the general sense) or a software development process (in the specific sense). Specific software development processes consist of a particular set of software development practices, which are often performed by the software engineer in a predetermined order. Software development practices, models, and methodologies will be introduced in the next two subsections.

### 2.1    Software Development Practices

Engineers adopt a systematic and organized approach to their work. As you learn software engineering, you should be exposed to many specific practices (or techniques) for developing software. By *software development practice* we refer to *a requirement employed to prescribe a disciplined, uniform approach to the software development process* [17], in other words, a well-defined activity that contributes toward the satisfaction of the project goals; generally the output of one practice becomes the input of another practice. As a software engineer, you should learn as many different types of software development practices as possible. Then, based upon the project and the people on your team, you can decide the right set of practices to take out of your "practice bag" to use on that particular project. In this book, you will learn practices you can "deposit" in your bag and about selecting an appropriate set of practices for a project and a team.

First, we provide one list of software development practices (but this list may vary depending upon the process and its associated terminology):

Requirements engineering
System analysis
High-level design/architecture
Low-level design
Coding
Integration
Design and code reviews
Testing

Maintenance
Project management
Configuration management

Each of these practices can be done in multiple ways. For example, you will see that requirements can be developed as traditional statements, as use-cases, or as user stories/features. The project and team decides how to perform each of the practices.

Most disciplines come to recognize some practices as *best practices*. A *best practice* is a *practice that, through experience and research, has proven to reliably lead to a desired result and is considered to be prudent and advisable to do in a variety of contexts.* Over time, we accumulate information on whether new practices are good or not. This information might be just stories of people succeeding with the practice, generally called anecdotal or qualitative evidence. Ideally, someone has done a controlled experiment that shows that a new practice is better than some other practice. This is called empirical or quantitative evidence. For example, before the damages of smoking were quantitatively assessed, there were physicians who recommended their patients not to smoke because there was some sort of evidence that the smoke was bad. Ultimately, structured empirical analysis backed up these physicians advice. Then, more people heeded their doctor's advice. Numbers talk! Similarly, software engineering practitioners often like to see a study that supports the benefits of a new practice before they change the way they engineer systems.

Those of you familiar with music will understand the concept of an etude. An etude is a musical composition written solely to improve technique. At the XP Universe conference in 2001, Kent Beck, the originator of Extreme Programming (XP) [3] likened learning software best practices to etudes in music. When he was learning to play a musical instrument, he was given etudes – short scores of music – to play over and over and over again. He said these short scores were not pleasing to the ear. The purpose of learning to play them was to really engrain in him how to play that kind of a combination of notes. Then later, when that sort of combination of notes appears in the midst of a larger beautiful composition, the notes will just flow off his fingers. Learning each etude was fairly painful, but the practice led to beautiful music.

So, how does this relate to software development? As you study software engineering, you will learn about many software development practices. You'll learn each individually, and (hopefully) you will "play" them over and over again. You will come to understand and appreciate when a certain practice is very rigorous and probably good for safety-critical software while a similar practice is not so painstaking and perhaps better for small, less critical projects. Engineering is all about selecting the most appropriate method for a set of circumstances – the right tool for the job. The goal is that when you are faced with a project, you will understand what types of practices are appropriate for that kind of project. You will then be able to include these practices into a suitable process just as an etude in incorporated into a classical musical score. Then, you will be making beautiful software!

6

## 2.2 Software Process Models and Methodologies

In simplistic terms, if you string an appropriate set of specific software practices together and if this set accomplishes all the fundamental activities listed in 3.1, you create a software development process. A *software development process* is t*he process by which user needs are translated into a software product. The process involves translating user needs into software requirements, transforming the software requirements into design, implementing the design in code, testing the code, and sometimes installing and checking out the software for operational use. Note: these activities might overlap or be performed iteratively* [17].

A software process model is a *simplified, abstracted description of a software development process.* The primary purpose of a software process model is to determine the order of practices in software development and to establish the transition criteria for progressing from one practice to the next [5]. Because of the simplification, several software development methodologies may share one process model – the differentiation is in the details of the process itself. Software methodologists incorporate the general characteristics of software development **models** into specific software development **processes** that adhere to the spirit of these models. While software development models have general characteristics, such as "having strong documentation and traceability mandates across requirements, design and code" [6], software development methodologies have *specific practices* that need to be followed, such as code inspection.

Process models can be characterized as plan-driven or agile [4]. The *plan-driven models* generally have an implicit assumption that a good deal of information about the requirements can be obtained up front and that information is fairly stable. As a result, creating a plan for the project to follow is achievable. A long-standing tenet of software engineering is that the longer a defect remains in a product, the more expensive it is to remove it. [7, 16] An overriding philosophy of plan-driven software models is that the cost of product development can be minimized by creating detailed plans and by constructing and inspecting architecture and design documents. As a result of these activities, there will be significant cost savings because defects will be removed or prevented. Plan-driven models can be summarized as "Do it right the first time." These models are very appropriate for projects in which there is not a great deal of requirements and/or technology changes anticipated throughout the development cycle. Plan-driven models are sometimes considered more suitable for safety- and mission-critical systems because of their emphasis on defect prevention and elimination. [4] Some examples of plan-driven methodologies are the Personal Software Process [16], the Rational Unified Process [18], and Cleanroom Software Engineering [19].

Alternately, *agile models* are considered to be better suited for projects in which a great deal of change in requirements or technology is anticipated [4]. Because of the inevitable change, creating a detailed plan would not be worthwhile because it will only change. Spending significant amounts of time creating and inspecting an architecture and detailed design for the whole project is similarly not advisable; it will only change as well. The methodologies of the agile model focus on spending a limited amount of time on planning and requirements gathering early in the process and much more time planning and gathering requirements for small iterations throughout the entire lifecycle of the project. Some examples of agile methodologies are the Extreme Programming (XP) [3], Scrum [21], Crystal [10], Feature Driven Development (FDD) [9], and Dynamic Systems Development Method (DSDM) [22].

However, there need not be a dichotomy between the two models; hybrid models that have both agile and plan-driven characteristics have been used successfully in many projects.

## 3    Software Engineering Challenges

There are some unique and pressing issues to deal with in the software industry. Several of these are now discussed:

*Tractable Medium.* We are engineers, yet what we engineer is a logical and tractable, not physical medium. The constraints of physical medium can serve to simplify alternatives. For example, in a house design you can't put a kitchen and a bathroom in the same place; batteries have standard voltages. Frederick Brooks, notable software engineer and author of the legendary book *The Mythical Man Month*, expresses an analogy,

> *The programmer, like the poet, works only slightly removed from pure thought-stuff. He builds his castles in the air, from air, creating by exertion of the imagination.* [8]

This tractability has its own pros and cons. On the positive side, as programmers we have the ultimate creative environment. We can create grandiose programs chock full of beautiful algorithms and impressive user interfaces. And we can completely change this functionality or the look of the interface in mere seconds and have a new creation! Conversely, because we are only dealing with "thought-stuff," our profession has a limited scientific and/or mathematical basis. In other fields, the scientific and mathematic basis of physical, intractable mediums constrain the solution to a problem -- only certain materials can withstand the weight of a car, only certain paints can take the intensity of the UV rays on the top of a mountain, etc. But, with software, the sky's the limit!

Quite often programmers are also asked to fix hardware product problems because people think that it is cheaper to fix the problems in the (tractable) software than it is to re-design and re-manufacture physical parts. Therefore, software engineers can be asked to make design and coding changes to compensate for hardware changes, sometimes at the last minute.

The software industry has been trying to formulate a scientific/mathematical basis for itself. Formal notations have been proposed to specify a program; mathematical proofs have been defined using these formal notations. The software community is also establishing analysis and design patterns [13, 14]. Patterns are general solutions to recurring analysis and design problems; the patterns are proposed and documented by experts in the field. Engineers can become familiar with these general solutions and learn to apply them appropriately in the systems and programs under development.

*Changing requirements.* Adapting for hardware changes is only one source of requirements churn for software engineers. Unfortunately, requirements changes come from many sources. Customers often have difficulty expressing exactly what they want in a product (software is only thought-stuff for them too!). They often don't know what they want until they see *some* of what they've asked for. Requirements analysts may not understand the product domain as completely as they need to early in the product lifecycle. As a result, the analysts might not know the right questions to ask the customer to elicit all their requirements. Lastly, the product domain can be constantly changing during the course of a product development cycle. New technology becomes available. Competitors release new products that have features that weren't thought of. Innovators think of wonderful new ideas that will make the product more competitive.

*Schedule Optimism.* Software engineers are an optimistic crew. In most organizations, the software engineers estimate how long it will take to develop a product. No matter how many times we've taken longer than we thought in the past, we still believe "Next time, things will go more smoothly. We know so much more now." As a result, we often end up committing to a date we have no business committing to, giving the software industry a "never on time" reputation.

*Schedule Pressure.* We often make these aggressive commitments because of the intensity of the people asking us for commitment. It seems that every product is late before it's even started, every feature is critical or the customer will go to a competitor. Products need to be created and updated at a constant, rapid pace lest competitors take over the business.

## 4.    Summary

There are some keys ideas to remember as you begin your study of software engineering. These ideas are summarized in Table 1.

Table 1: Key Ideas for Software Engineering

| | |
|---|---|
| 🔑 | Computer science is concerned with getting the computer to do what you want it to do, as efficiently as possible. |
| 🔑 | Software engineers use their computer science skills to create products of practical use and economic value. Software engineers are ethically responsible for the correctness, suitability, and safety of their projects. When possible, software engineers apply scientific and mathematical knowledge to their work. |

| | |
|---|---|
| 🔑 | A software development process is a process by which user needs are translated into a software product. Software development processes are comprised of specific software development practices. |
| 🔑 | A software process model is a generalized abstraction of a family of software development processes. |
| 🔑 | Plan-driven processes are more suitable for projects with a low degree of change or those with critical safety and security needs. |
| 🔑 | Agile methodologies are more suitable for projects with a high degree of change. |
| 🔑 | Software engineering is especially challenging because software is a tractable medium, requirements often change, and competitive pressures cause schedule pressure. |
| | |

## Glossary of Chapter Terms

| Word | Definition | Source |
|---|---|---|
| best practice | a software development practice that, through experience and research, has proven to reliably lead to a desired result and is considered to be prudent and advisable to do in a variety of contexts | |
| computer science | A discipline that involves the understanding and design of computers and computational processes. In its most general form it is concerned with the understanding of information transfer and transformation. Particular interest is placed on making processes efficient and endowing them with some form of intelligence | [12] |
| engineering | the systematic and regular application of scientific and mathematical knowledge to the design, construction, and operation of machines, systems, and so on of practical use and, hence, of economic value. Particular characteristic of engineers is that they take seriously their responsibility for correctness, suitability, and safety of the results of their efforts. In this regard they consider themselves to be responsible to their customer (including their employers where relevant), to the users of their machines and systems, and to the public at large. | [2] |
| Software development practice (or technique) | a disciplined, uniform approach to the software development process | [17] |

| Software development process (or methodology) | The process by which user needs are translated into a software product.  The process involves translating user needs into software requirements, transforming the software requirements into design, implementing the design in code, testing the code, and sometimes installing and checking out the software for operational use.  Note:  these activities might overlap or be performed iteratively. | [17] |
|---|---|---|
| Software process model | simplified, abstracted description of a software development process | |
| software engineering | the application of a systematic, disciplined, quantifiable approach to the development, operation, and maintenance of software; that is, the application of engineering to software | [17] |

## References

[1]     ACM/IEEE-CS Joint Task Force on Software Engineering, "Software Engineering Code of Ethics and Professional Practice," 1999, http://www.acm.org/about/se-code.

[2]     R. L. Baber, "Comparison of Electrical "Engineering" of Heaviside's Times and Software "Engineering" of our Times," *IEEE Annals of the History of Computing,* vol. 19, no. 4, pp. 5-17, 1997.

[3]     K. Beck, *Extreme Programming Explained:  Embrace Change.* Reading, MA: Addison-Wesley, 2000.

[4]     B. Boehm, "Get Ready for Agile Methods, with Care," *IEEE Computer,* vol. 35, no. 1, pp. 64-69, January 2002.

[5]     B. Boehm, "A Spiral Model for Software Development and Enhancement," *Computer,* vol. 21, no. 5, pp. 61-72, May 1988.

[6]     B. Boehm and R. Turner, *Balancing Agility and Discipline:  A Guide for the Perplexed.* Boston, MA: Addison Wesley, 2003.

[7]     B. W. Boehm, *Software Engineering Economics.* Englewood Cliffs, NJ: Prentice-Hall, Inc., 1981.

[8]     F. P. Brooks, *The Mythical Man-Month, Anniversary Edition*: Addison-Wesley Publishing Company, 1995.

[9]     P. Coad, E. LeFebvre, and J. DeLuca, *Java Modeling in Color with UML*: Prentice Hall, 1999.

[10]    A. Cockburn, *Agile Software Development.* Reading, Massachusetts: Addison Wesley Longman, 2001.

[11]    D. E. Comer, D. Gries, M. C. Mulder, A. Tucker, A. J. Turner, P. R. Young, and P. J. Denning, "Computing as a discipline," *Communications of the ACM,* vol. 32, no. 1, January 1989

[12]    CSAB, "Defining the Computing Sciences Professions," http://www.csab.org/

comp_sci_profession.html, no. 1997.

[13]  M. Fowler, *Analysis Patterns: Reusable Object Models*. Menlo Park, CA: Addison Wesley Longman, Inc, 1997.

[14]  E. H. Gamma, Richard; Johnson, Ralph; and Vlissides, John, *Design Patterns: Elements of Reusable Object-Oriented Software*. Reading, Massachusetts: Addison-Wesley Publishing Company, 1995.

[15]  W. W. Gibbs, "Software's Chronic Crisis," in *Scientific American*, 1994, pp. 86-95.

[16]  W. S. Humphrey, *A Discipline for Software Engineering*. Reading, MA: Addison Wesley, 1995.

[17]  IEEE, "IEEE Standard 610.12-1990, IEEE Standard Glossary of Software Engineering Terminology," 1990.

[18]  I. Jacobson, G. Booch, and J. Rumbaugh, *The Unified Software Development Process*. Reading, Massachusetts: Addison-Wesley, 1999.

[19]  H. D. Mills, R. C. Linger, and A. R. Hevner, "Box Structured Information Systems," *IBM Systems Journal,* vol. 26, no. 4, pp. 395-413, 1987.

[20]  S. L. Pfleeger, *Software Engineering: Theory and Practice*. Upper Saddle River, NJ: Prentice Hall, 1998.

[21]  K. Schwaber and M. Beedle, *Agile Software Development with SCRUM*. Upper Saddle River, NJ: Prentice-Hall, 2002.

[22]  J. Stapleton, *DSDM: The Method in Practice*: Addison Wesley Longman, 1997.

## Chapter Questions

1. Describe the difference between a software process and a software process model.

2. What are the challenges of today's SE? How do software engineers respond to these challenges?

3. Software requirements change is inevitable. However, the requirements of some software are not so volatile. Give three examples of such software. What are the characteristics of this kind of software?

4. For a commercial shrink-wrapped software product, what are the important goals the software developers seek to achieve? List at least 5 items, and rank them in order.

5. Search the web, and find three software process models. Give some description for each model.

6. Based on Baber's definition about engineering and your personal experience, do you think software is engineering? Why? How is software different from other kind of engineering?

7. As a software professional, we must take our ethical responsibility. ACM (Association of Computer Machinery) and IEEE (Institute of Electrical And Electronic Engineers) have produced a code of ethics and professional practice. Find it on the web, and describe in your word what ethical responsibilities we should take.

8. For more than 30 years, software engineers have been thinking how to improve the process of software development. Today, we can find an army of software processes, and new ones are being created. If you were a manager in a software consulting company, would you adapt new software practices? If you would, what would be the motivation? If not, what would be the concerns?

9. Why, in your opinion, are software engineers often over-optimistic?

# Software Reviews and Pair Programming

Software reviews are a quality assurance technique that helps us remove defects from our software programs and supporting documentation. In this chapter, we will explain the following:

the benefits of software reviews

the review technique of personal reviews, walkthroughs, and formal inspection.

the economics of software reviews

> *. . . three experienced engineers worked for three months to find a subtle system defect that was causing persistent customer problems. At the time they found this defect, the same code was being inspected by a different team of five engineers. As an experiment, this team was not told about the defect. Within two hours, this team found not only this defect, but also 71 others! Once found, the original defect was trivial to fix. [18]*

By this point in your life, we're sure you have written a paper and had someone else read it before you turned it in. Quite often, authors can be pleased with their own work and then quite shocked when others find mistakes or have excellent suggestions on how to make it even better. We're not the best judges of our own work, and to make matters worse, we're quite blind to our own mistakes. In the classic book, *The Psychology of Computer Programming*, Gerald Weinberg reminds us, "The human eye has an almost infinite capacity for not seeing what it does not want to see . . . . Programmers, if left to their own devices, will ignore the most glaring errors in their output—errors that anyone else can see in an instant [28]."

This chapter is dedicated to structured techniques for letting others look over our software development work. The techniques discussed in this chapter are called static techniques because they do not involve the execution of a program. Using these techniques, we can overcome our human shortcomings for finding our own mistakes, and we can brainstorm alternative approaches we wouldn't think of on our own. The first set of techniques for gaining this valuable input are various forms of periodic software reviews. The second technique is a more continual practice, pair programming. Even though the second technique is called pair *programming*, this technique is used on many phases of the software development process on many types of artifacts—requirements documents, design documents, implementation code, test cases, and so on.

We use these techniques to get defects out of our work as quickly and efficiently as possible. The longer a defect remains in our work, the harder and more time consuming it is to get out [6]. We also use these techniques to learn from each other. Each of us has our own skills, approaches, and techniques, and we have a lot to learn from each other.

## 1   Software Reviews

14

Software reviews are used for quality assurance. *Software reviews* are *a process or meeting during which a work product, or set of work products, is presented to project personnel, managers, users, customers, or other interested parties for comment or approval. Types include code review, design review, formal qualification review, requirements review, test readiness review. [20]* There are several varieties of software review; they differ according to the size of the review group and the formality of the review meetings. In this section, we'll learn about personal reviews (which are done solo by the creator of the artifact), walkthroughs (which are done informally with the artifact creator and one or two other people), and inspections (which are done formally with the artifact creator and up to four other people).

## 1.1    Objectives of Software Reviews

There are four explicit objectives for software reviews, as follows:

To detect errors in program logic/structure or inconsistencies from one artifact to the next. Harlan Mills' believes that "programming should be a public process" [7]. Exposing programs to others helps quality, both through the pressure by peers to do things well and because peers spot flaws and bugs [7] that an individual might not.

To make sure the intention of the artifact is clear (the more clear the better)
To verify that the design and/or software meets its requirements
To ensure software has been developed in a uniform manner, using agreed-upon standards

## 1.2    Beneficial Side Effects of Software Reviews

In addition to these explicit objectives, when reviews involve group participation, the reviews have additional beneficial side effects for the development group. First, reviews are an excellent means of learning about the overall system and about the techniques of teammates so as to improve communication within the team. Secondly, by working together several people on the team become somewhat familiar with the details of the artifact under review. This additional knowledge is helpful when the creator of the artifact is not available and the review participant must interact with the artifact. Finally, there's a psychological benefit for the creator of the artifact. When we know that others will be looking at our documents or code, we have more incentive to make things clear and simple. As a result, our work is generally of higher quality.

## 2    Types of Software Reviews

Some might think that if only we didn't make mistakes, reviews would not be necessary. But, even experienced programmers typically make about 100 defects per thousand lines of code [18]! Early discovery and removal of defects is vital so these defects do not propagate to the next step in the software process. We now describe three different types of software reviews for removing defects: personal reviews, walkthroughs, and software inspections.

## 2.1    Personal Reviews

On one end of the software review spectrum are *personal reviews*—here you privately review your own work. Think back to a time when you're asked someone to proof your term paper for you. You wouldn't give your reviewer your first draft, would you? You'd go through your term paper to polish it up and find the glaring errors before showing it to someone else. The same goes with software. Before others see your work, you should examine your own products via a personal review. Humphrey [18] reminds us that someone who inspects your work is making you a gift of time solely to help you improve the quality of your product. To show your appreciation, you should treat that time as important by ensuring your code is as clean as you can before submitting it for the inspection.

### *A Checklist for a Personal Review*

To prepare for a personal review, it is a good idea to create a checklist of questions designed to detect common errors. As you proceed through the review, ask yourself the questions on the checklist. For example, the following five sample questions could be on a checklist for a requirements document checklist:

1. Are all requirements traceable back to a specific user need?

2. Are any requirements included that are impossible to implement?

3. Could the requirements be understood and implemented by an independent group?

4. Are security requirements specified for each function?

5. Is there a glossary in which each term is defined?

### *Finding Defects with a Personal Review*

When you do a personal review, it is best if you print out the work you will be reviewing, such as a requirements document, a design document, code, or a test plan. Then, methodically, step through your work and through the checklist, trying to identify any possible errors. The objective of a personal review is to find and fix as many defects as possible before you implement, inspect, or test the design and/or the program. Research has shown that with practice you can remove between 50%-80% of your defects by doing a thorough personal review [18]. Every defect you remove from of your work on your own saves your teammates time in later inspections, testing, and field support and improves the quality of your product.

## 2.2 Walkthroughs

Going up the software review spectrum one step brings us to walkthroughs. A *walkthrough is a static analysis technique in which a designer or programmer leads members of the development team and other interested parties through a segment of documentation or code, and the participants ask questions and make comments about possible errors, violations of development standards, and other problems [20].* At least one other person attends a walkthrough with the creator of an artifact. Generally, no preparation is done before a walkthrough, and no formal follow-up is done after a walkthrough. This form of software generally follows a presentation format. The developer first makes an overview presentation of the software element(s) under review. Then, he or she traces the design or code step by step. [19] The developer also gives a detailed description of how the program handles a typical application. The audience, which can include customers/users and other team members, raises issues and asks questions. Errors, suggested changes, and improvements are noted as the walkthrough progresses. A walkthrough can therefore be effective at discovering omissions, and resolving misunderstandings; it can also be used to educate users or team members about an application.

There are three roles for walkthroughs [19]. These roles are defined below:

- *Author:* The author of the material presents his or her work.
- *Moderator:* The moderator handles the administrative aspects of the walkthrough, such as determining the schedule and distributing materials, and ensures it is conducted in an orderly manner. The moderator prepares a statement of objectives for the meeting.
- *Recorder:* The recorder writes down the comments made during the walkthrough. The comments pertain to errors found, questions of style, omission, contradictions, and suggestions for improvement and alternative approaches.

## 2.3     Software Inspections

Similar to walkthroughs, software inspections involve the author creator and several other people. An *inspection* is a *static analysis technique that relies on visual examination of development products to detect errors, violations of development standards, and other problems* [19]. Inspections are a more formal type of software than either personal reviews or walkthroughs. The style of software inspection we will describe is often referred to as Fagan-style [13] inspection, named after the software engineer who devised the practice, Michael Fagan. Software inspections generally involve three to six participants.

Organizations that include inspections in their development process generally have rules or protocols for carrying out the inspection meetings. Artifacts that will be inspected must be distributed to participants a set number of days prior to the meeting. Participants are required to review the artifact prior to the meeting so that they are prepared for an effective and efficient meeting. However, this pre-inspection preparation must not take more than two hours. Similarly, the inspection must also not last more than two hours lest the participants get too tired to provide useful input.

### *Roles within an Inspection*

Additionally, a Fagan inspection requires that several participants to be present, each with a particular role to play. For smaller reviews, participants may take on more than one role. The roles [19] are defined below:

- *Author:* To no surprise, the author is the person who created the document being inspected. However, as opposed to the authors role in walkthroughs, he or she is present at the inspection to answer questions to help others understand the work but does not step through the work; the reader does that. The authors listens to the input of the inspection team but should not to "defend" his or her work. The author does not take on any of the four roles defined below.
- *Moderator:* The moderator chooses the inspection team, schedules the inspection

meeting, ensures the artifact to be review are complete, and distributes the materials. In the inspection meeting, the moderator runs the inspection and enforces the protocols of the meeting. The moderator's job is mainly one of controlling interactions and keeping the group focused on the purpose of the meeting – to discover (but not fix) deficiencies in the document. The moderator also ensures that the group does not drift off onto a tangent and that everyone sticks to a schedule.

- *Reader:* The reader leads the inspection team through the software element(s) in a logical and comprehensive fashion. He or she calls attention to each part of the document in turn – paraphrasing or reading line-by lines as appropriate. The reader paces the inspection.

- *Recorder:* Whenever any problem is uncovered in the document being inspected, the recorder describes the defect in writing. After the inspection, the recorder and moderator prepare an inspection report.

- *Inspectors:* The inspectors raise questions and suggest problems with the document. Inspectors are not supposed to "attack" the author or the document but instead they should strive to be objective and constructive. Everyone except the author can act as an inspector. Often inspectors are chosen to represent different viewpoints, for example requirements, design, code, test, project management, quality management.

### *During the Inspection*

Everyone comes to the inspection prepared. The meeting is called to order by the moderator. The meeting proceeds by the reader paraphrasing the artifact section by section – the reader does not read the artifact line by line. When the reader is done paraphrasing a section, the inspectors identify possible faults in that section and/or pose questions about that section. The author can answer the question. If a question is not posed to the author, the author remains quiet and observes the meeting. The scribe records all issues discussed by the group.

### *After the Inspection*

Upon completion of the inspection, the team of participants decides if the artifact (1) can proceed to the next stage with minor changes; (2) needs to be fixed and re-inspected; or (3) needs to be scrapped and done over. It is very important that none of the participants is the supervisor of any of the other participants (especially the author) and that inspection data is in no way used in employee performance evaluations.

Organizations that have embraced inspections have often found that they have far fewer test defects [16]. Despite the advantages of these inspections, unfortunately, these reviews are often not done as much as they should be. There are several reasons the reviews are not done:

Developers simply don't believe that the reviews are worth their time—they've got a deadline to meet. Instead, these same developers spend endless hours in long, error-prone debugging sessions, finding errors that could have been efficiently found in a review. Developers might have ego problems in reviews. They might have trouble admitting their own mistakes and don't want a room full of people seeing their defects. However, we need to develop an egoless programming [27] culture where we each learn from each other

18

and benefit from each others' input so we can grow as software engineers and so we can produce higher quality products.

Some software engineers avoid inspections because they find inspections boring.

## 3 Pair Programming

Pair programming is a technique that can be used to complement software reviews or, sometimes, as as an alternative to reviews. Pair programming is a style of programming in which *two* programmers work side-by-side at *one* computer, continuously collaborating on the same design, algorithm, code, or test [29]. Pair programming has been practiced sporadically for decades [29]; however, the emergence of agile methodologies and Extreme Programming [4] has recently popularized the pair programming practice. Pair programming has been shown to have many of the benefits of reviews while also eliminating the programmer's distaste for reviews so that at least one form of review is actually performed.

### 3.1 The Driver and Navigator

One of the pair, called the *driver*, types at the computer or writes down a design. The other partner, called the *navigator*, has many jobs. One of these is to observe the work of the driver—looking for tactical and strategic defects in the driver's work. Some tactical defects might be syntax errors, typos, and calling the wrong method. Strategic defects occur when the driver is headed down the wrong path—what driver and navigator are implementing just won't accomplish what it needs to accomplish. The navigator is the strategic, longer-range thinker of the programming pair. Because the navigator is not as deeply involved with the design, algorithm, code or test, he or she can have a more objective point of view and can better think strategically about the direction of the work.

Another benefit of pair programming is that the driver and the navigator can brainstorm at any time the situation calls for it. An effective pair programming relationship is very active. In an effective pairing relationship, the driver and the navigator continually communicate. Periodically, it's also very important to switch roles between the driver and the navigator.

### 3.2 Pairing during All Phases of Development

The name of the technique, pair *programming* can lead people to incorrectly assume that you should only pair during code development. However, pairing can occur during all phases of the development process, in pair design, pair debugging, pair testing, and so on. Programmers could pair up at any time during development, in particular when they are working on something that is complex. The more complex the task, the greater the need for two brains.

### 3.3 Why Pair Program?

Some people think that having two people sit down to develop one artifact must be a big waste of resources. Managers are especially concerned about this since they think they will have to pay two programmers to do the work one could do. Even students are concerned about this because they think they might have to spend twice as long on their homework. However, some research results show that these concerns do not materialize.

### Higher-Quality Code

Previous research with senior-level undergraduate students at the University of Utah showed that pairs developed higher quality code faster with only a minimal increase in total time spent in coding. For example, if one student finished a project in ten hours, the pair might work on it for five and a half hours (for eleven total hours of time between the two). The code produced by the pairs in the study also passed 15% more of the automated test cases, demonstrating that the pairs produced code of higher quality. [30, 34]

At North Carolina State University, student pair programmers in beginning computer science classes generally performed better on projects and exams and were more likely to complete the class with a grade of C or better than did their solo counterparts. Results also indicate that pair programming creates a laboratory environment conducive to more advanced, active learning than traditional labs; students and lab instructors report labs to be more productive and less frustrating. [23, 32, 33]

### Enhanced Morale, Teamwork, and Learning

Pair programming offers additional benefits, including the following:

1. *Increased Morale.* Pair programmers are happier programmers. Several surveys were taken of pair programmers in the North Carolina study discussed above. Ninety-two percent of them indicated that they enjoyed programming more when they worked with a partner. Ninety-six percent of them indicated they felt more confident in their product when they worked with a partner. [34]

2. *Increased Teamwork.* Pair programmers get to know their classmates much better because they work so closely together. [11] It makes school more enjoyable when you can walk into a classroom or a lab and *really* know several of the people in the class. Classmates then seem more "approachable" when you have a question about the class.

3. *Enhanced learning.* Pairs continuously learn by watching how their partners approach a task, how they use their language capabilities, and how they use the development tools. [11]

## 3.4    How Does Pair Programming Work?

It may seem odd that two people can sit down at one computer and finish in about half the time, with higher quality code, and enhanced morale, teamwork, and learning. But studies have shown that pairing makes us work differently. As was done in [29], we will discuss six "hows" and "whys" that contribute to the great results of pair programming. They are pair pressure, pair negotiation and brainstorming, pair courage, pair reviews, pair debugging, and pair learning.

## 1. Pair Pressure

Pair programmers put a positive form of pressure on each other that functions as a time management strategy. Software engineers say they work harder and smarter on programs because they do not want to let their partner down. They are also less likely to read email, surf the web, or make a phone call. They handle interruptions more quickly so they can return to their primary task they share with their partner [9]. Engineers often pair for a few hours at a time during which they work intensely on their joint task without interruption. As such, the pair can work with a "pair flow" [5] state of mind in which the solution and the problem space are shared between the minds of the participants. The presence of a pairing parter helps an engineer recover the state of a primary task after interruption leading to more rapid interruption recovery [9]. Additionally, solo programmers can use interruptions as means for filling a need for social interaction; this need diminishes with pair programming [9].

Programmers say they work very intensively because they are highly motivated to complete the task at hand during the session. Pairing requires schedule coordination, which imposes explicit deadlines that motivate engineers to work intensively finish their tasks.

## 2. Pair Negotiation and Brainstorming

The term pair negotiation is used to describe how two pair programmers arrive at the best solution together. When pairing is working at its best, each person brings to the partnership his or her own set of skills, abilities, and outlooks and both partners share the same goal for completing the task. Each person has a suggested alternative for attacking a joint problem, and the partners must negotiate how to jointly approach the problem. In this negotiation, they evaluate more alternatives than either one would have considered alone, whereas, a person working alone tends to pursue the first approach that comes to mind. Together, the partners consider and include each other's suggestions and determine the best plan of attack.

Couched in effective pair programming is the phenomenon known as Beginner's Mind [5] wherein a person that is new to an area with no predisposition of a solution can see more possible solutions.

## 3. Pair Courage

Having a partner is a tremendous courage builder. Gaining affirmation from a partner gives programmers the confidence to do things they might be afraid to do alone When working with someone else, programmers can piece together enough knowledge to feel confident in what they are doing.

Working with a partner also gives us courage to admit when we do not know something. Developers by themselves tend to be embarrassed when they do not know something and will try to muddle through on their own rather than ask for help from their peers. When two people do not know something, there is a joint realization that it is time to seek help.

### 4. Pair Reviews

Pair programming functions as a form of continuous review and problem identification occurs on a minute-by-minute basis. Syntax or semantic errors and missing assumptions or unconsidered cases in algorithm design that may otherwise go unnoticed can often be observed by an attentive navigator before these problems gestate. This low-level review process complements that pair's strategic brainstorming by avoiding the small, subtle errors that a solo programmer may unknowingly inject and spend considerable time later trying to uncover and fix.

### 5. Pair Debugging

Every person has experienced problems that can be resolved simply through the act of explaining the problems to another person.

> . . . [an] effective technique is to explain your code to someone else. This will often cause you to explain the bug to yourself. Sometimes it takes no more than a few sentences, followed by an embarrassed "Never mind; I see what's wrong. Sorry to bother you." This works remarkably well; you can even use nonprogrammers as listeners. One university computer center kept a teddy bear near the help desk. Students with mysterious bugs were required to explain them to the teddy bear before they could speak to a human counselor. [21]

When explaining a problem to a partner, the partner will ask questions and will likely force the programmer to explain his or her potentially-flawed reasoning.

### 6. Pair Learning

Knowledge is constantly being passed between partners, from tool usage tips to programming language rules to design and programming techniques. The partners take turns being the teacher and the student on a minute-by-minute basis. Even unspoken skills and habits cross partners [10]. When pairs rotate to work with different team members, each programmer is then able to share new skills and knowledge with a new partner. As a result, switching pairs often is an effective strategy for spreading knowledge and information around a team [5]. As stated above, pair programming with frequent swapping also aids in indoctrinating and training new team members [5, 22, 31].

## 3.6    Distributed Pair Programming

Distributed software development is becoming common practice in industry. In education, students may also prefer to work from their dorm rooms or homes, rather than going to the lab to work with their partners. Furthermore, students enrolled in distance education courses may not ever be able to meet each other face-to-face. These distributed workers can practice pair programming through the Internet using a variety of tools. In the simplest of cases, programmers can use VNC[4] or Windows Meeting Space[5] (previously Net Meeting) to share desktops. These tools broadcast the display of the output of any application from a member to all the others, requiring sufficient bandwidth, trust, and security between the parties. Other tools, such as Sangam [17], xpairtise,[6] COPPER [24], or Facetop [25] have been designed to only transmits messages that are important for pair programming, such as the latest change made by the driver.

Distributed cognition expert Nick Flor stresses the importance of distributed pair programming systems to support cross-workspace visual, manual, and audio channels [14]. These channels allow pairs to collaborate and provide subtle, yet significant catalysts for on-going knowledge sharing and helping activities. For example, subtle gestures such as a headshake or a mumble can be the catalyst for an exchange between the pair. Transparent images of the partner shown in the screen by Facetop [25] can aid in the transmission of these channels. Additionally, Chong and Hurlbutt [8] discourage tools that have defined driver/navigator roles such as Sangam [17] because they inhibit the behaviors of more effective pair programmers who share the driver/navigator role throughout the session.

Some studies of distributed pair programming have been done with students at both North Carolina State University and the University of North Carolina -- Chapel Hill [1, 2]. These studies indicated that pairing over the Internet shows a great deal of potential when compared with distributed non-paired teams in which programmers work alone, and code is integrated later. In these studies, the students used desktop sharing software, NetMeeting, and Yahoo Messenger/headsets/microphones to communicate.

## 4    The Economics of Quality Assurance

How can we justify the time spent on pair programming and software reviews? It might seem faster to skip these steps and move right into software test.

### 4.1    General Research Findings

Research studies (including [3, 12, 15]) have been done to assess whether the time invested in software reviews is worthwhile. Researchers have found that reviewing was more effective and less expensive than testing in discovering program faults and that more than 60 % of the errors in a program can be detected using informal program inspection. As said above when pairs work, they produce higher quality code

### 4.2    Ease of Finding and Fixing Defects

In both reviews and pair programming, you find the defects directly and you deal with the problems that are identified. (In reviews, you should only identify problems, but not try to solve the problems on the spot. With pair programming, you solve problems on the spot.) By this, we mean that in a review, a fellow programmer could tell you, "On line 20, you put limit <= 100, but that should be < 100." You say, "Yes, you're right!" you correct your paper and fix it in your code later.

In black-box testing, however, you get only symptoms. For example, you run a planned test case and you get the wrong answer. The wrong answer is just a symptom of the problem in your code. Once you find that symptom, you must figure out why in the world you got the wrong answer – which line of code would cause such a symptom? The time you spend tracking down the exact problem that caused the improper behavior is called debugging. Depending upon the size of your program, this debugging time could be very time consuming. Most often there is no relationship between the size of the defect you find and how long it takes to find the defect (that <= sign in the example above could take hours or days to find.).

You should feel highly motivated to find and fix as many defects as possible before you head into your black-box testing phases. Consider that the review/pair programming form of defect identification and correction is fairly efficient, is quite predictable, and has been shown to be able to remove more than half of the defects in your project. You know that you and your four reviewers will sit together for two hours and you will find many problems. You know that you and your pairing partner will spend several hours together to write high quality code. However, once you start doing black-box testing, you enter the *chaos zone*. At this point, even the smallest defect could take many hours to find and fix —and these hours unpredictable and are often very frustrating. The relative ease of tracking down and fixing problems with reviews and pair programming when compared with the difficulties of tracking down and fixing symptoms with debugging sessions is why these practices are more efficient.

## 4.3    Garbage In, Garbage Out (GIGO)

As good as these reviews and pair programming are, any quality assurance practice (such as pair programming, reviews, and testing) cannot remove all the defects in a document or code. These practices are only imperfect *filters* that can remove a percentage of your defects. The percentage of defects removed by a quality assurance activity is called the *yield* of the practice. For example, if an inspection actually gets out 40% of the defects in the code, the inspection is said to have a 40% yield.

Because all of the quality assurance practices are imperfect filters, the more defects that are in the program, the more defects will escape to your customer. (Hence, the title of this section – Garbage In, Garbage Out.) Also, the more filters you have, the more defects you can remove. Consider three hypothetical programs (as shown in Figure 1) that would start with 100 errors in each of them (however, pair programming prevents half of these from being injected into the program at the coding stage). For the first program, the development team works solo and does inspection. For the second program, the development team also works solo but does not do inspection. Finally, the third program was developed by programmers working in pairs without inspection.

## 4.4    Economic Analysis of Reviews

Quality is certainly one concern we have in our development. However, if obtaining this degree of quality is exceedingly expensive, we may not be able to afford these quality assurance steps. We must analyze the economic feasibility of these steps. The previous discussion and Figure 1 show how having additional quality assurance activities can reduce the number of defects that are delivered to a customer. The top diagram in Figure 1 shows the case of solo programming *with* inspection. The middle diagram shows the case of no inspection. The bottom figure illustrates pair programming. Even more defects can be prevented from being "delivered" to a customer if both pair programming and reviews were used.

We consider two simple scenarios to explain the economics of quality assurance. The example makes two important but realistic assumptions.

> Experienced software engineers normally inject about 100 defects/KLOC (KLOC = thousand lines of code). About half of these defects are found by the compiler (the compiler has 50% yield).
>
> In industry, defects that escape from the compiler take on average eight hours each to find and fix in the testing phase. Eight hours/defect may sound like a lot, but it is realistic and actually quite low. It can be hard to find the defect. Sometimes a software engineer will have to get in their car or jump on a plane to go to a customer site to help find and fix the defect. All this time adds up!

### Scenario One:  Solo Programming, No Inspection

Consider the case of solo programming without inspection (middle diagram of Figure 1). For a 50 KLOC program, there will be (50)(100 defects/KLOC) = 5,000 defects. Half of these will be caught by the compiler and the rest (2,500) will escape to the testing phase, since the solo programmers do not perform inspection.

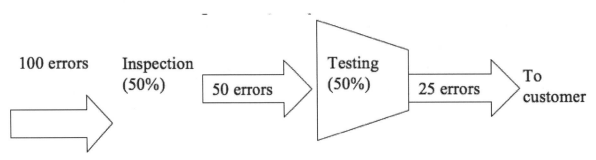

**Solo programming with inspection**

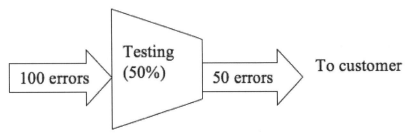

**Solo programming without inspection or pair programming**

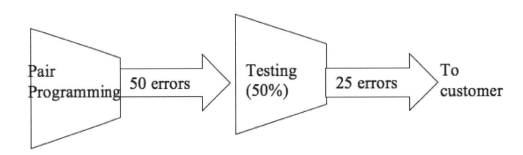

**Paired team without inspection**

**Figure 1: Quality Assurance Filters**

No practice is a perfect filter (it won't get out all the defects that are in the project.) Testing will generally identify only half of the defects that enter the phase. How many programmer hours will it take to find and fix this half of the defects?

(2,500 defects)(0.5 test yield) = 1,250 defects removed in test
(1,250 defects)(8 hours/defect) = 10,000 hours to find and fix those defects

How many weeks would it take 10 people to do this work, assuming 40 hours work/week each?

(10,000 programmer hours)/(10 people)(40 hours/week) = 25 weeks (or almost half a year)!

How many defects will escape to the customer?

2,500 – 1,250 = 1,250 defects escape to the customer

What would the impact be to the quality of the product if management said "You have three months (12 weeks) to test this product."

Unfortunately, this is what often happens. The testing phase comes right before the product is released. Often testers must compromise on the time so that the product can be released on schedule. At 8 hours/defect, each person can only remove 5 defects per 40 hour week). In 12 weeks, this team could only remove:

(12 weeks)(10 people)(5 defects/week) = 600 defects

This means that 2,500 – 600 defects = 1,900 defects would escape to the customer.


## Scenario Two: Solo Programming with Inspection or Pair Programming without Inspection

These cases are shown in the top and bottom diagrams of Figure 1. For the sake of this example, we will assume that pair programmers produce code of equal quality to reviewed code, though there are no research results to back up this claim. We do know of several industrial organizations that are beginning to offer employees an alterative to either formally inspect their code or to pair program; their anecdotes support that this alternative provides similar benefit. However, there are no research results that conclusively show that these alternatives are equal.

We again use the same assumptions as above (50 KLOC, 100 defects/KLOC, 50% yield from the compiler, 8 hours to remove each defect in test).

For a 50 KLOC program, there will be (50)(100 defects/KLOC) = 5,000 defects. For the solo programming group, half of these will be caught by the compiler and the rest (2,500) will escape to the inspection phase.

Inspections will generally identify only half of the defects that enter the phase. In industry, approximately 0.5 hours are spent to find and fix each defect in an inspection phase. (Defects might be found quite rapidly in an inspection. However, we must consider that four people might be attending the review. If 8 defects are found in an hour-long review, the average time is calculated 4 person hours/8 defects or 0.5 hours/defect).

How many programmer hours will it take to find and fix this half of the defects in the inspection?

(2,500 defects)(.5 inspection yield) = 1,250 defects removed in inspection
(1,250 defects)(0.5 hours/defect) = 625 hours to find and fix those defects

Now, 1,250 defects remain in the product as the product enters the test phase from either the solo/reviewed group or the pair programming group. We assume the pair programming group had not done an inspection, but instead had a continuous review as they worked. The test phase will still again only find half of the remaining defect.

How long will the test phase need to be?

(1,250 defects)(.5 test yield) = 625 defects removed in test
(625 defects)(8 hours/defect) = 5,000 hours to find and fix those defects

> How many weeks would it take 10 people to do this work, assuming 40 hours work/week each? (Would they be having fun?)
>
> (5,000 programmer hours)/(10 people)(40 hours/week) = 12.5 weeks
>
> How many defects will escape to the customer?
>
> 1,250 – 625 = 625 defects escape to the customer
>
> What would the impact be to the quality of the product if management said "You have three months (12 weeks) to test this product."
>
> Now, this deadline would not be a problem – the team would just need to work minimal overtime to complete test.

In summary, the solo/no review group needed to work 10,000 programmer hours in testing. The solo/review group needed to work 5,000 programmer hours in testing plus they had to dedicate 625 hours to inspect for 5,625 hours of quality assurance activity. The solo/review group saved 4,375 hours when compared with the solo/no review group and had higher quality code. We will also assume the pair programming group had similar results to the solo/review group – minimal increase in programmer hours due to doubling up, 5,000 hours in test, and high quality code.

To re-emphasize, often rushed development teams decide not to do any reviews and/or decide not to pair program because they "don't have the time." Remember the scenarios above when you are tempted to do the same. Finding, fixing, and preventing defects as early and efficiently as possible should be your goal.

## 5      Recommendations for Effective Reviews and Pair Programming

Reviews and pair programming can either be highly effective or a huge waste of resource, depending upon whether protocol is followed and whether the people involved contribute and are receptive. Below we give some recommendations for you to make your reviews and your pairing as effective as possible. We suggest that you take these recommendations and make them habits.

## Recommendation 1: Be Tactful, Patient and Respectful

Know how to *give* objective criticism. In both pairing and in reviews, remember never to infer (or blatantly say) that your partner or the author is inferior to yourself or has made a *stupid* mistake. Remember, to err is human, and we are all human and are always learning, particularly in the dynamic field of software development. Eventually (in a few minutes or a few days), you will be the driver or the subject of an inspection. At all times, treat others as you would like to be treated.

Respect your partner for who he or she is. He or she could be from another culture, an introvert, and extrovert, a global person, a detailed person, a good time manager, a procrastinator and so on. In this life, you will deal with all kinds of people – pair programming is a lesson in doing so. Remember – EVERYONE has something to offer.

## Recommendation 2: Respect the Protocol

Software reviews have protocols. For example, personal reviews rely on checklists, which need to be developed. In walkthroughs, authors present their designs and code in an informal way. In software inspections, there are specified roles for the participants, and all participants should come to the inspection prepared. Defects that are identified must be recorded.

Pair programming also has its protocols. The partners assume roles of driver and navigator. However, they swap these roles periodically. Pairs converse almost continuously. If you hog the keyboard, you will give your partner the impression that you want the power or that you don't have confidence in your partner. Don't be a keyboard hog!

## Recommendation 3: Know When to Stop, Take Breaks

Reviews are exhausting. Through many experiments it has been established that reviews should be no longer than two hours. If a review lasts longer than this, the participants start to get exhausted and the productivity of the review drops significantly. Over time, you will learn how much you can review in this period of time and will schedule the reviews accordingly.

"Pair programming is exhausting but productive. [26]" Because pair programmers do keep each other continuously focused and on-task, it can be a very intense and mentally exhausting.

Periodically taking a break is important for maintaining the stamina you need for another round of productive pair programming. During the break, it is best to disconnect from the task at hand so that you can approach it with freshness when restarting.

## Recommendation 4: Talk

In software reviews, you must feel confident to bring up the problems you have found when reviewing the artifact.

With pair programming, if the driver is doing all the work and the navigator is just watching, the pair is dysfunctional. A bored navigator is a sign of a problem too. A good rule of thumb is that the navigator should be ready to take the keyboard at any moment. If you are the navigator and the driver suddenly passes you the keyboard, you should be able to take over without asking any questions about what the driver is doing – you should be that engaged. If you are the driver, if you see your navigator getting bored or even starting to fall asleep – realize that is the PERFECT time to pass him or her the keyboard to be the driver.

The primary purpose of pairing and reviews are to work towards the best design possible, regardless of from where or from whom the design originated. While it's not good to argue over what to do all the time -- students who always agree with their partner minimize the benefits of collaborating. Your partner may as well be working alone if you are not willing to speak up and to take a position. For favorable idea exchange there needs to be some healthy debate and disagreement. Don't be afraid or too willing to give up on your idea if you believe it is best. Your joint goal is to make the best product possible.

## Recommendation 5: Listen and Practice Humility

"Ego-less programming," an idea surfaced by Gerald Weinberg in *The Psychology of Computer Programming* [28] a quarter of a century ago, is essential for effective pair programming. Excessive ego can manifest itself in two ways, both damaging the collaborative relationship and the spirit of a review. First, having a "my way or the highway" attitude can prevent the programmer from considering other's ideas. Secondly, excessive ego can cause a programmer to be defensive when receiving criticism or to take this criticism as an expression of mistrust. However, all must remember to put the team's progress above his or her own ego.

None of us, no matter how skilled, is infallible; all of us, no matter how skilled, can benefit from the input of another. John von Neumann, the great mathematician and creator of the von Neumann computer architecture, recognized his own inadequacies and continuously asked others to review his work.

> *And indeed, there can be no doubt of von Neumann's genius. His very ability to realize his human limitation put him head and shoulders above the average programmer today . . .. Average people can be trained to*

*accept their humanity -- their inability to function like a machine—and to value it and work with others so as to keep it under the kind of control needed if programming is to be successful. [28]*

Weinberg also shares [28] a true story about a programmer seeking review of the code he produced. On this particular "bad programming" day, this individual ego-lessly laughed because his reviewer found 17 bugs in 13 statements. However, after fixing these defects, this code performed flawlessly during test and in production. Think how much worse the programmer's life would have been if he'd been too proud to accept the input of others or had viewed this input as an indication of his inadequacies.

If you continuously think your partner is not a smart as your partner – than you are probably the problem. Be humble and you will learn.

**Recommendation 6: Be Prepared**

With software inspections, inspectors are to prepare by examining the artifact ahead of time and coming prepared to discuss the anomalies he or she has found. The idea is not to inspect the artifact "on-the-fly" during the meeting.

If you have an appointment with your pair programming partner or with a colleague to conduct a walkthrough, respect their valuable time. Do any preparatory work ahead of time, get to your appointment on time – or contact them to tell them you will be late or you have to cancel. Come to your appointment mentally ready to go!

**Recommendation 7: Consider Hygiene**

When pair programming, you are in close proximity to your partner for an extended period of time. Remember to shower, use deodorant, and brush your teeth! Bring gum or mints to share with your partner (as a proactive measure in case your partner forgot to be as considerate).

**Recommendation 8: Don't Suffer in Silence**

Finally, if you are having problem with your partner, don't suffer in silence – tell you teacher or your teaching assistant. The teacher can tactfully handle the situation. It can take some students awhile to use to working in pairs – and your partner may be one of these. And, as we all know, some students may not care as much as you do. Your teacher can help out with making that kind of situation as fair as possible to you.

# 6. Summary

A main goal of software reviews and pair programming is to remove defects in software products. As has been discussed, both of these techniques also provide excellent learning environments for team members. Additionally, pair programming also prevents defects from being injected in the product in the first place. These ideas are summarized in Table 1.

Table 1: Key Ideas for Software Reviews and Inspection

| | |
|---|---|
| 🔑 | The sooner a defect is found and fixed in a product, the less expensive it is for the product – and the less frustrating it is for the software engineer. |
| 🔑 | Sometimes programmers avoid software reviews because they think they take too much time or because they don't want to publicly expose their defects. However, software reviews have been shown to be very beneficial for removing defects and for educating the team. |
| 🔑 | Software engineers should review their code via a personal review to remove as many defects as possible before others get involved with helping them remove their defects. |
| 🔑 | Walkthroughs are fairly informal, small group reviews of software artifacts, often involving two or three people. |
| 🔑 | Inspections are more formal reviews of software artifacts that involve three to six people. |
| 🔑 | Pair programming also helps with removing defects, efficiently as the code is being produced. Many people thing this higher quality will cost twice as much, but this has not been shown to be the case. |
| 🔑 | Not quality assurance filter (such as reviews, pair programming, and testing) removes all the defects in a product. |
| 🔑 | Quality assurance filters are economically beneficial for removing defects before they are delivered to a customer. Once a customer gets a product with a defect, the defects make the customer less delighted with the product, the defects are much more costly to find and fix. |

**Glossary of Chapter Terms**

| Word | Definition | Source |
|---|---|---|
| inspection | A static analysis technique that relies on visual examination of development products to detect errors, violations of development standards, and other problems. | [20] |
| pair programming | a style of programming in which *two* programmers work side-by-side at *one* computer, continuously collaborating on the same design, algorithm, code, or test. | [29] |

| review | A process or meeting during which a work product, or set of work products, is presented to project personnel, managers, users, customers, or other interested parties for comment or approval.  Types include code review, design review, formal qualification review, requirements review, test readiness review. | [20] |
|---|---|---|
| walkthrough | A static analysis technique in which a designer or programmer leads members of the development team and other interested parties through a segment of documentation or code, and the participants ask questions and make comments about possible errors, violations of development standards, and other problems. | [20] |

## References

[1]     P. Baheti, E. Gehringer, and D. Stotts, "Exploring the Efficacy of Distributed Pair Programming," in *Extreme Programming/Agile Universe*, Chicago, IL, 2002, pp. 208-220.

[2]     P. Baheti, L. Williams, E. Gehringer, and D. Stotts, "Exploring Pair Programming in Distributed Object-Oriented Team Projects," in *OOPSLA Educator's Syposium*, Seattle, WA, 2002.

[3]     V. R. Basili and R. Selby, "Comparing the Effectiveness of Software Testing Strategies," *IEEE Transactions on Software Engineering,* no. pp. 1278-1296, December 1987.

[4]     K. Beck, *Extreme Programming Explained:  Embrace Change*. Reading, MA: Addison-Wesley, 2000.

[5]     A. Belshee, "Promiscuous pairing and beginner's mind: embrace inexperience," in *Agile Conference 2005*, Denver, CO, 2005, pp. 125 - 131

[6]     B. W. Boehm, *Software Engineering Economics*. Englewood Cliffs, NJ: Prentice-Hall, Inc., 1981.

[7]     F. P. Brooks, *The Mythical Man-Month, Anniversary Edition*: Addison-Wesley Publishing Company, 1995.

[8]     J. Chong and T. Hurlbutt, "The Social Dynamics of Pair Programming," in *International Conference on Software Engineering (ICSE) 2007*, Minneapolis, MN, 2007, pp. 354-363

[9]     J. Chong and R. Siino, "Interruptions on Software Teams:  A Comparison of Paired and Solo Programmers," in *Computer Supported Collaborative Work (CSCW) 2006*, Banff, Alberta, Canada, 2006, pp. 29-38.

[10]    A. Cockburn and L. Williams, "The Costs and Benefits of Pair Programming," in *Extreme Programming and Flexible Processes in Software Engineering (XP2000)*, Cagliari, Sardinia, Italy, 2000.

[11]    A. Cockburn and L. Williams, "The Costs and Benefits of Pair Programming," in *Extreme Programming Examined*, G. Succi and M. Marchesi, Eds. Boston, MA: Addison Wesley, 2001, pp. 223-248.

[12]    M. E. Fagan, "Advances in Software Inspection," *IEEE Transactions on Software Engineering*, vol. 12, no. 7, July 1986 1986.

[13]    M. E. Fagan, "Advances in software inspections to reduce errors in program development," *IBM Systems Journal*, vol. 15, no. pp. 182-211, 1976.

[14]    N. Flor, "Globally Distributed Software Development and Pair Programming," *Communications of the ACM*, vol. 49, no. 10, pp. 57-58, October 2006.

[15]    T. Gilb and D. Graham, *Software Inspection*: Addison Wesley, 1993.

[16]    D. Hamlet and J. Maybee, *The Engineering of Software*. Boston: Addison Wesley, 2001.

[17]    C.-w. Ho, S. Raha, E. Gehringer, and L. Williams, "Sangam: A Distributed Pair Programming Plug-in for Eclipse," in *Eclipse Technology Exchange at Object-Oriented Programming, Systems, Languages, and Applications (OOPSLA) 2004.*, Vancouver, BC, 2004.

[18]    W. S. Humphrey, *A Discipline for Software Engineering*. Reading, Mass.: Addison Wesley Longman, 1995.

[19]    IEEE, "IEEE 1028-1988: IEEE Standard for Software Reviews and Audits," no. 1988.

[20]    IEEE, "IEEE Standard 610.12-1990, IEEE Standard Glossary of Software Engineering Terminology," 1990.

[21]    B. W. Kernighan and R. Pike, *The Practice of Programming*. Reading, Massachusetts: Addison-Wesley, 1999.

[22]    M. Lacey, "Adventures in Promiscuous Pairing: Seeking Beginner's Mind," in *Agile 2006*, Minneapolis, 2006, pp. 263 - 269.

[23]    N. Nagappan, L. Williams, M. Ferzli, K. Yang, E. Wiebe, C. Miller, and S. Balik, "Improving the CS1 Experience with Pair Programming," in *ACM Special Interest Group Computer Science Education (SIGCSE) 2003*, Reno, 2003, pp. 359 - 362.

[24]    H. Natsu, J. Favela, A. Morán, D. Decouchant, and A. Martinez-Enriquez, "Distributed Pair Programming on the Web," in *Mexican International Conference on Computer Science (ENC) 2003*, Ciencias de la Computacion, CICESE, Mexico, 2003, pp. 81-88.

[25]    K. Navoraphan, E. F. Gehringer, J. Culp, K. Gyllstrom, and D. Stotts, "Next-generation DPP with Sangam and Facetop," in *OOPSLA workshop on eclipse technology eXchange*, Portland, Oregon, 2006, pp. 6-10.

[26]    W. C. Wake, *Extreme Programming Explored*. Boston: Addison Wesley, 2001.

[27]    G. M. Weinberg, "Egoless Programming," in *IEEE Software*. vol. January/February, 1999, pp. 118-120.

[28]    G. M. Weinberg, *The Psychology of Computer Programming Silver Anniversary Edition*. New York: Dorset House Publishing, 1998.

[29]    L. Williams and R. Kessler, *Pair Programming Illuminated*. Reading, Massachusetts: Addison Wesley, 2003.

[30]    L. Williams, R. Kessler, W. Cunningham, and R. Jeffries, "Strengthening the Case for Pair-Programming," *IEEE Software*, vol. 17, no. 4, pp. 19-25, July/August 2000 2000.

[31]    L. Williams, A. Shukla, and A. Antón, "An Initial Exploration of the Relationship

Between Pair Programming and Brook's Law," in *Agile Development Conference 2004*, Salt Lake City, 2004, pp. 11-20.

[32]   L. Williams, E. Wiebe, K. Yang, M. Ferzli, and C. Miller, "In Support of Pair Programming in the Introductory Computer Science Course," *Computer Science Education,* vol. 12, no. 3, pp. 197-212, 2002.

[33]   L. Williams, K. Yang, E. Wiebe, M. Ferzli, and C. Miller, "Pair Programming in an Introductory Computer Science Course:  Initial Results and Recommendations," in *OOPSLA Educator's Symposium*, Seattle, WA, 2002, pp. 20-26.

[34]   L. A. Williams, "The Collaborative Software Process," in *Department of Computer Science* Salt Lake City, UT: University of Utah, 2000.

# Testing Overview and Black-Box Testing Techniques

Software testing is an important technique for assessing the quality of a software product. In this chapter, we will explain the following:

> the basics of software testing, a verification and validation practice, throughout the entire software development lifecycle
>
> the two basic techniques of software testing, black-box testing and white-box testing
>
> six types of testing that involve both black- and white-box techniques.
>
> strategies for writing fewer test cases and still finding as many faults as possible
>
> using a template for writing repeatable, defined test cases

## 1   Introduction to Testing

*Software testing* is the *process of analyzing a software item to detect the differences between existing and required conditions (that is, bugs) and to evaluate the features of the software item* [9, 12]. Software testing is an activity that should be done throughout the whole development process [3].

Software testing is one of the "verification and validation," or V&V, software practices. Some other V&V practices, such as inspections and pair programming, will be discussed throughout this book. *Verification* (the first V) is *the process of evaluating a system or component to determine whether the products of a given development phase satisfy the conditions imposed at the start of that phase* [11]. Verification activities include testing and reviews. For example, in the software for the Monopoly game, we can verify that two players cannot own the same house. *Validation* is the *process of evaluating a system or component during or at the end of the development process to determine whether it satisfies specified requirements* [11]. At the end of development validation (the second V) activities are used to evaluate whether the features that have been built into the software satisfy the customer requirements and are traceable to customer requirements. For example, we validate that when a player lands on "Free Parking," they get all the money that was collected. Boehm [4] has informally defined verification and validation as follows:

**Verification:  Are we building the product <u>right</u>?**
Through verification, we make sure the product behaves the way we want it to. For example, on the left in Figure 1, there was a problem because the specification said that players should collect $200 if they land on <u>or</u> pass Go. Apparently a programmer implemented this requirement as if the player had to <u>pass</u> Go to collect. A test case in which the player landed on Go revealed this error.

**Validation:  Are we building the <u>right</u> product?**
Through validation, we check to make sure that somewhere in the process a mistake hasn't been made such that the product build is not what the customer asked for; validation always involves

comparison against <u>requirements</u>. For example, on the right in Figure 1, the customer specified requirements for the Monopoly game – but the programmer delivered the game of Life. Maybe the programmer thought he or she "knew better" than the customer that the game of Life was more fun than Monopoly and wanted to "delight" the customer with something more fun than the specifications stated. This example may seem exaggerated – but as programmers we can miss the mark by that much if we don't listen well enough or don't pay attention to details – or if we second guess what the customer says and think we know better how to solve the customer's problems.

| **Verification** | **Validation** |
|---|---|
| Are we building the product **<u>right</u>**? | Are we building the **<u>right</u>** product? |

"I landed on "Go" but didn't get my $200!"

"I know this game has money and players and "Go" – but this is not the game I wanted."

**Figure 1: Verification vs. Validation**

Both of Boehm's informal definitions use the term "right." But what is "right"? In software we need to have some kind of standard or specification to measure against so that we can identify correct results from incorrect results. Let's think about how the incorrect results might originate. The following terms with their associated definitions [11] are helpful for understanding these concepts:

- o **Mistake** – a human action that produces an incorrect result.
- o **Fault [or Defect]** – an incorrect step, process, or data definition in a program.
- o **Failure** – the inability of a system or component to perform its required function within the specified performance requirement.
- o **Error** – the difference between a computed, observed, or measured value or condition

and the true, specified, or theoretically correct value or condition.
- o **Specification** – a document that specifies in a complete, precise, verifiable manner, the requirements, design, behavior, or other characteristic of a system or component, and often the procedures for determining whether these provisions have been satisfied.

A *mistake* committed by a person becomes a *fault* (or defect) in a software artifact, such as the specification, design, or code. This fault, unless caught, propagates as a defect in the executable code. When a defective piece of code is executed, the fault may become a visible anomaly (a variance from the specification or desired behavior) and a *failure* is observed. Otherwise, the fault remains latent. Testing can reveal failures, but it is the faults that must be found and removed [3]; finding a fault (the cause of a failure) can be time consuming and unpredictable. *Error* is a measure of just how incorrect the results are.

The progression of a software failure is demonstrated in Figure 2. A purpose of testing is to <u>cause failures</u> in order to make faults visible [10] so that the faults can be fixed and not be delivered in the code that goes to customers. Another purpose of testing is to assess the overall quality level of the code. For example, a test team may determine a project with too many high-severity defects should be sent back to development for additional work to improve the quality before the testing effort should continue. Or, the management may have a policy that no product can ship if testing is continuing to reveal high-severity defects.

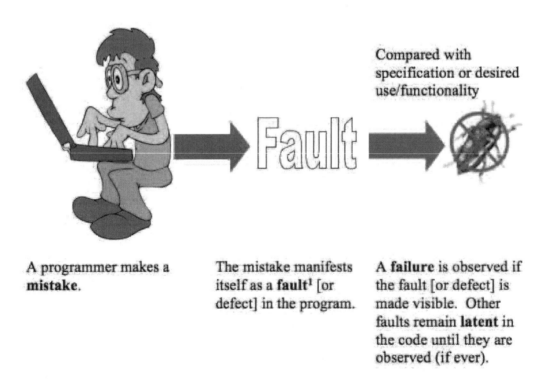

| A programmer makes a **mistake**. | The mistake manifests itself as a **fault**[1] [or defect] in the program. | A **failure** is observed if the fault [or defect] is made visible. Other faults remain **latent** in the code until they are observed (if ever). |

**Figure 2: The progression of a software failure. A purpose of testing is to expose as many failures as possible before delivering the code to customers.**

## 1.1 The Economics of Software Testing

In software development, there are costs associated with testing our programs. We need to write out test plan and our test cases, we need to set up the proper equipment, we need to systematically execute the test cases, we need to follow up on problems that are identified, and we need to remove most of the faults we find. Actually, sometimes we can find low-priority faults in our code and decide that it is too expensive to fix the fault because of the need to redesign, recode, or otherwise remove the fault. These faults can remain latent in the product through a follow-on release or perhaps forever.

For faults that are not discovered and removed before the software has been shipped, there are costs. Some of these costs are monetary, and some could be significant in less tangible ways. Customers can lose faith in our business and can get very angry. They can also lose a great deal of money if their system goes down because of our defects. (Think of the effect on a grocery store that can't check out the shoppers because of its "down" point-of-sale system.) And, software development organizations have to spend a great deal of money to obtain specific information about customer problems and to find and fix the cause of their failures. Sometimes, programmers have to travel to customer locations to work directly on the problem. These trips are costly to the development organization, and the customers might not be overly cheerful to work with when the programmer arrives. When we think about how expensive it is to test, we must also consider how expensive it is to not test – including these intangible costs as well as the more obvious direct costs.

We also need to consider the relative risk associated with a failure depending upon the type of project we work on. Quality is much more important for safety- or mission-critical software, like aviation software, than it is for video games. Therefore, when we balance the cost of testing versus the cost of software failures, we will test aviation software more than we will test video games. As a matter of fact, safety-critical software can spend as much as three to five times as much on testing as all other software engineering steps combined [17]!

To minimize the costs associated with testing and with software failures, a goal of testing must be to uncover as many defects as possible with as little testing as possible. In other words, we want to write test cases that have a high likelihood of uncovering the faults that are the most likely to be observed as a failure in normal use. It is simply impossible to test every possible input-output combination of the system; there are simply too many permutations and combinations. As testers, we need to consider the economics of testing and strive to write test cases that will uncover as many faults in as few test cases as possible. In this chapter, we provide you with disciplined strategies for creating efficient sets of test cases – those that will find more faults with less effort and time.

## 1.2 The Basics of Software Testing

There are two basic classes of software testing, black box testing and white box testing. For now, you just need to understand the very basic difference between the two classes, clarified by the definitions below [11]:

> o *Black box testing* (also called functional testing) is *testing that ignores the internal mechanism of a system or component and focuses solely on the outputs generated in response to selected inputs and execution conditions.*
> o *White box testing* (also called structural testing and glass box testing) is *testing that takes into account the internal mechanism of a system or component.*

The classes of testing are denoted by colors to depict the opacity of the testers of the code. With *black box testing*, the software tester does not (or should not) have access to the source code itself. The code is considered to be a "big black box" to the tester who can't see inside the box. The tester knows only that information can be input into to the black box, and the black box will send something back out. Based on the requirements knowledge, the tester knows what to <u>expect</u> the black box to send out and tests to make sure the black box sends out what it's supposed to send out. Alternatively, *white box testing* focuses on the internal structure of the software code. The white box tester (most often the developer of the code) knows what the code looks like and writes test cases by executing methods with certain parameters. In the language of V&V, black box testing is often used for validation (are we building the right software?) and white box testing is often used for verification (are we building the software right?). This chapter focuses on black box testing.

All software testing is done with executable code. To do so, it might be necessary to create scaffolding code. *Scaffolding* is defined *as computer programs and data files built to support software development and testing but not intended to be included in the final product* [11]. Scaffolding code is code that simulates the functions of components that don't exist yet and allow the program to execute [16]. Scaffolding code involves the creation of stubs and test drivers. *Stubs* are modules that simulate components that aren't written yet, formally defined as a *computer program statement substituting for the body of a software module that is or will be defined elsewhere* [11]. For example, you might write a skeleton of a method with just the method signature and a hard-coded but valid return value. *Test drivers* are defined as a *software module used to involve a module under test and often, provide test inputs, controls, and monitor execution and report test results* [11]. Test drivers simulate the calling components (e.g. hard-coded method calls) and perhaps the entire environment under which the component is to be tested [1]. Another concept is mock objects. *Mock objects* are temporary substitutes for domain code that emulates the real code. For example, if the program is to interface with a database, you might not want to wait for the database to be fully designed and created before you write and test a partial program. You can create a mock object of the database that the program can use temporarily. The interface of the mock object and the real object would be the same. The implementation of the object would mature from a dummy implementation to an actual database.

## *1.4 Six Types of Testing*

There are several types of testing that should be done on a large software system. Each type of test has a "specification" that defines the correct behavior the test is examining so that incorrect behavior (an observed failure) can be identified. The six types and the origin of specification (what you look at to develop your tests) involved in the test type are now discussed. There are two issues to think about in these types of testing – one is the **opacity** of the tester's view of the code (is it white or black box testing). The other issue is **scale** (is the tester examining a small bit of code or the whole system and its environment).

1. Unit Testing
   Opacity:  White box testing
   Specification:  Low-level design and/or code structure

*Unit testing* is the *testing of individual hardware or software units or groups of related units* [11]. Using white box testing techniques, testers (usually the developers creating the code implementation) verify that the code does what it is intended to do at a very low structural level. For example, the tester will write some test code that will call a method with certain parameters and will ensure that the return value of this method is as expected. Looking at the code itself, the tester might notice that there is a branch (an `if-then`) and might write a second test case to go down the path not executed by the first test case. When available, the tester will examine the low-level design of the code; otherwise, the tester will examine the structure of the code by looking at the code itself. Unit testing is generally done within a class or a component.

2. Integration testing
   Opacity:  Black- and white-box testing
   Specification:  Low- and high-level design

*Integration test* is *testing in which software components, hardware components, or both are combined and tested to evaluate the interaction between them* [11]. Using both black and white box testing techniques, the tester (still usually the software developer) verifies that units work together when they are integrated into a larger code base. Just because the components work individually, that doesn't mean that they all work together when assembled or integrated. For example, data might get lost across an interface, messages might not get passed properly, or interfaces might not be implemented as specified. To plan these integration test cases, testers look at high- and low-level design documents.

3. Functional and system testing
   Opacity:  Black-box testing
   Specification:  high-level design, requirements specification

Using black box testing techniques, testers examine the high-level design and the customer requirements specification to plan the test cases to ensure the code does what it is intended to do. *Functional testing* involves ensuring that the functionality specified in the requirement specification works. System testing involves putting the new program in many different environments to ensure the program works in typical customer environments with various versions and types of operating systems and/or applications. *System testing* is *testing conducted on a complete, integrated system to evaluate the system compliance with its specified requirements* [11]. Because system test is done with a full system implementation and environment, several classes of testing can be done that can examine non-functional properties of the system. It is best when function and system testing is done by an unbiased, independent perspective (e.g. not the programmer) [3].

Stress testing, performance testing, and usability testing are three specific types of system testing.

- o *Stress testing – testing conducted to evaluate a system or component at or beyond the limits of its specification or requirement* [11]. For example, if the team is developing software to run cash registers, a non-functional requirement might state that the server can handle up to 30 cash registers looking up prices simultaneously. Stress testing might occur in a room of 30 actual cash registers running automated test transactions repeatedly for 12 hours. There also might be a few more cash registers in the test lab to see if the system can exceed its stated requirements.
- o *Performance testing – testing conducted to evaluate the compliance of a system or component with specified performance requirements* [11]. To continue the above example, a performance requirement might state that the price lookup must complete in less than 1 second. Performance testing evaluates whether the system can look up prices in less than 1 second (even if there are 30 cash registers running simultaneously).
- o *Usability testing – testing conducted to evaluate the extent to which a user can learn to operate, prepare inputs for, and interpret outputs of a system or component.* While stress and usability testing can be and is often automated, usability testing is done by human-computer interaction specialists that observe humans interacting with the system.

4. Acceptance testing
   Opacity: Black-box testing
   Specification: requirements specification

After functional and system testing, the product is delivered to a customer and the customer runs black box acceptance tests based on their expectations of the functionality. *Acceptance testing is formal testing conducted to determine whether or not a system satisfies its acceptance criteria (the criteria the system must satisfy to be accepted by a customer) and to enable the customer to determine whether or not to accept the system* [11]. These tests are often pre-specified by the customer and given to the test team to run before attempting to deliver the product. The customer reserves the right to refuse delivery of the software if the acceptance test cases do not pass. However, customers are not trained software testers. Customers generally do not specify a "complete" set of acceptance test cases. Their test cases are no substitute for creating your own set of functional/system test cases. The customer is probably very good at specifying at most one good test case for each requirement. As you will learn below, many more tests are needed. Whenever possible, we should run customer acceptance test cases ourselves so that we can increase our confidence that they will work at the customer location.

5. Regression testing
   Opacity: Black- and white-box testing
   Specification: Any changed documentation, high-level design

Throughout all testing cycles, *regression* test cases are run. *Regression testing is selective retesting of a system or component to verify that modifications have not caused unintended effects and that the system or component still complies with its specified requirements* [11]. Regression tests are a subset of the original set of test cases. These test cases are re-run often, after any significant changes (bug fixes or enhancements) are made to the code. The purpose of running the regression test case is to make a "spot check" to examine whether the new code works properly and has not damaged any previously-working functionality by propagating unintended side effects. Most often, it is impractical to re-run all the test cases when changes are made. Since regression tests are run throughout the development cycle, there can be white box regression tests at the unit and integration levels and black box tests at the integration, function, system, and acceptance test levels.

The following guidelines should be used when choosing a set of regression tests (also referred to as the regression test *suite*):

> Choose a representative sample of tests that exercise all the existing software functions;
> Choose tests that focus on the software components/functions that have been changed; and
> Choose additional test cases that focus on the software functions that are most likely to be affected by the change.

A subset of the regression test cases can be set aside as smoke tests. A *smoke test* is a *group of test cases that establish that the system is stable and all major functionality is present and works under "normal" conditions* [6]. Smoke tests are often automated, and the selection of the test cases are broad in scope. The smoke tests might be run before deciding to proceed with further testing (why dedicate resources to testing if the system is very unstable). The purpose of smoke tests is to demonstrate stability, not to find bugs with the system.

6.  Beta testing
    Opacity: Black-box testing
    Specification: None.

When an advanced partial or full version of a software package is available, the development organization can offer it free to one or more (and sometimes thousands) potential users or *beta testers*. These users install the software and use it as they wish, with the understanding that they will report any errors revealed during usage back to the development organization. These users are usually chosen because they are experienced users of prior versions or competitive products. The advantages of running beta tests are as follows [8]:

> *Identification of unexpected errors* because the beta testers use the software in unexpected ways.
> *A wider population search for errors* in a variety of environments (different operating systems with a variety of service releases and with a multitude of other applications running).
> *Low costs* because the beta testers generally get free software but are not compensated.

The disadvantages of beta testing are as follows [8]:

*Lack of systematic testing* because each user uses the product in any manner they choose.
*Low quality error reports* because the users may not actually report errors or may report errors without enough detail.
*Much effort is necessary to examine error reports* particularly when there are many beta testers.

Throughout all testing cycles, *regression* test cases are run. *Regression testing is selective retesting of a system or component to verify that modifications have not caused unintended effects and that the system or component still complies with its specified requirements.*

These six levels of testing are summarized in Table 1.

| Testing Type | Specification | General Scope | Opacity | Who generally does it? |
|---|---|---|---|---|
| Unit | Low-Level Design Actual Code Structure | Small unit of code no larger than a class | White Box | Programmer who wrote code |
| Integration | Low-Level Design High-Level Design | Multiple classes | White Box Black Box | Programmers who wrote code |
| Functional | High Level Design | Whole product | Black Box | Independent tester |
| System | Requirements Analysis | Whole product in representative environments | Black Box | Independent tester |
| Acceptance | Requirements Analysis | Whole product in customer's environment | Black Box | Customer |
| Beta | Ad hoc | Whole product in customer's environment | Black box | Customer |
| Regression | Changed Documentation High-Level Design | Any of the above | Black Box White Box | Programmer(s) or independent testers |

**Table 1: Levels of Software Testing**

It is best to find a fault as early in the development process as possible. When a test case fails, you have now seen a symptom of the failure [13] and still need to find the fault that caused the failure. The further you go into the development process the harder it is to track down the cause of the failure. If you unit test often, a new failure is likely to be in the code you just wrote/tested and should be reasonably easy to find. If you wait until system or acceptance testing, a failure could be anywhere in the system – you will have to be an astute detective to find the fault now.

## 1.5 Test Planning

Test planning should be done throughout the development cycle, especially early in the development cycle. A *test plan* is a *document describing the scope, approach, resources, and schedule of intended test activities. It identifies test items, the features to be tested, the testing tasks, who will do each task, and any risks requiring contingency plans* [11]. An important component of the test plan is the individual test cases. A *test case* is a *set of test inputs, execution conditions, and expected results developed for a particular objective, such as to exercise a particular program path or to verify compliance with a specific requirement* [11].

Write the test plan early in the development cycle when things are generally still going pretty smoothly and calmly. This allows you to think through a thorough set of test cases. If you wait until the end of the cycle to write <u>and</u> execute test cases, you might be in a very chaotic, hurried time period. Often good test cases are not written in this hurried environment, and ad hoc testing takes place. With ad hoc testing, people just start trying anything they can think of without any rational roadmap through the customer requirements. The tests done in this manner are not repeatable.

## 1.6 *Testing as Part of the Development Process*

It is essential in testing to start planning as soon as the necessary artifact is available. For example, as soon as customer requirements analysis has completed, the test team should start writing black box test cases against that requirements document. By doing so this early, the testers might realize the requirements are not complete. The team may ask questions of the customer to clarify the requirements so a specific test case can be written. The answer to the question is helpful to the code developer as well. Additionally, the tester may request (of the programmer) that the code is designed and developed to allow some automated test execution to be done. To summarize, the earlier testing is planned at all levels, the better.

It is also very important to consider test planning and test execution as iterative processes. As soon as requirements documentation is available, it is best to begin to write functional and system test cases. When requirements change, revise the test cases. As soon as some code is available, execute test cases. When code changes, run the test cases again. By knowing how many and which test cases actually run you can accurately track the progress of the project. All in all, testing should be considered an iterative and essential part of the entire development process.

## 2 Performing Black Box Testing

Black box testing, also called *functional testing and behavioral testing*, focuses on determining whether or not a program does what it is supposed to do based on its functional requirements.

Black box testing attempts to find errors in the external behavior of the code in the following categories [17]: (1) incorrect or missing functionality; (2) interface errors; (3) errors in data structures used by interfaces; (4) behavior or performance errors; and (5) initialization and termination errors. Through this testing, we can determine if the functions appear to work according to specifications. However, it is important to note that no amount of testing can unequivocally demonstrate the absence of errors and defects in your code.

It is best if the person who plans and executes black box tests is *not* the programmer of the code and does not know anything about the structure of the code. The programmers of the code are innately biased and are likely to test that the program does *what they programmed it to do*. What are needed are tests to make sure that the program does *what the customer wants it to do*. As a result, most organizations have independent testing groups to perform black box testing. These testers are not the developers and are often referred to as *third-party* testers. Testers should just be able to understand and specify what the desired output should be for a given input into the program, as shown in Figure 3.

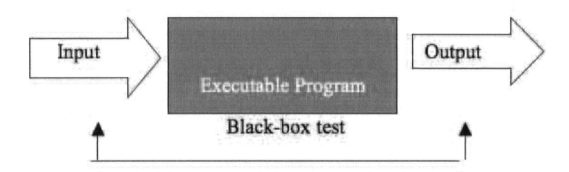

**Figure 3: Black Box Testing. A black-box test takes into account only the input and output of the software without regard to the internal code of the program.**

## 2.1 The Anatomy of a Test Case

The format of your test case design is very important. We will use a particular format for our test cases, as shown in Table 2. We recommend you use this template in your test planning.

| Test ID | Description | Expected Results | Actual Results |
|---|---|---|---|
| | | | |
| | | | |
| | | | |

**Table 2:  Test Case Planning Template**

First, you give each test case a unique identifier.  When you are tracking large projects, you might need to itemize those test cases that have not yet passed.  This identifier is recorded in the first column.  For example, you might need to say something like, "All my test cases are running except playerMovement1.  I'm working on that one today."  Next in the second column of the table, you specifically describe the set of steps and/or input for the particular condition you want to test (including what needs to be done to prepare for the test case to be run which are listed as *preconditions*).  The third column is the expected results for an input/output oracle – what is expected to come out of the "black box" based upon the input (as described in the "description").  An *oracle* is *any program, process, or body of data that specified the expected outcome of a set of tests as applied to a tested object* [1]; and *input/output oracle* is an *oracle that specifies the expected output for a specified input* [1].  In the last column, the actual results are recorded after the tests are run including the name of the tester who ran the test and the date the test was run.  If a test passes, the actual results will indicate "Pass."  If a test fails, it is helpful to record "Fail", a description of the failure ("what came out") in the actual results column.

Software engineering is not only about systems, but also about people. Including the name of the tester facilitates communication in the event that the test results are not clear. If, for example, you suspect that the tester did not look at the right part of the screen, it is extremely helpful to know that Bob did the actual test. Thus, you can go check with him. If the error exposed is a validation issue as opposed to a verification issue, this is even more helpful. If you utilize paper test scripts as opposed to digital test scripts (as is often the case), it can also be helpful to leave room for additional comments and notes the tester may wish to make.

Also note the preconditions. All test cases require that the system be in a certain state. This state may be as simple as "fresh install" or as complex as the system being connected to twenty specific databases with one hundred configuration options set to certain values. A common mistake programmers make when writing tests scripts is assuming the state of the system will be the same as the version they used when writing the test case. This simply isn't the case. Those executing the tests are often engaged in executing many tests constantly. If, for example, the tester has just completed a stress test, the system may be filled with data that makes your script impossible to run.

## *2.2  Clear Descriptions*

It is of prime importance that the test case description be very clear and specific so that the test case execution is repeatable.  Even if you will always be the person executing the test cases, pretend you are passing the test planning document to someone else to perform the tests.  You need your directions to clear enough for that other person to be able to follow the directions explicitly so that the exact same test is executed every time.  For example, consider a basic test case to ensure that players can move on a Monopoly board.  Example of poorly specified test case is shown in Table 3:

47

| Test ID | Description | Expected Results | Actual Results |
|---------|-------------|------------------|----------------|
| 1 | Player 1 rolls dice and moves. | Player 1 moves on board. | |
| 2 | Player 2 rolls dice and moves. | Player 2 moves on board. | |

**Table 3: Poor Specification of a Test Case**

The problem is that the description does not give exact values of how many spaces the players moved. This is an overly simplistic problem – but maybe the program crashes for some reason when Player 1 and Player 2 land on the same spot. If you don't remember what was actually rolled (you let the rolls be determined randomly and don't record them), you might never be able to cause the problem to happen again because you don't remember the circumstances leading up to the problem. *Recreating the problem* is essentially important in testing so that problems that are identified can be repeated and corrected. Instead write specific descriptions, such as shown in Table 4.

| Test ID | Description | Expected Results | Actual Results |
|---------|-------------|------------------|----------------|
| 3 | Precondition: Game is in test mode, SimpleGameBoard is loaded, and game begins. Number of players: 2 Money for player 1: $1200 Money for player 2: $1200 Player 1 dice roll: 3 | Player 1 is located at Blue 3. | |
| 4 | Precondition: Test case 3 has successfully completed Player 2 dice roll: 3 | Player 1 is located on Blue 3. Player 2 is located on Blue 3. | |

**Table 4: Preferred Specification of a Test Case**

There a few things to notice about the test cases in Table 4. First, notice the Precondition in the Description field. The precondition defines what has to happen before the test case can run properly. There may be an order of execution [5] whereby a test case may depend upon another test case running successfully and leaving the system in a state such that the second test case can successfully be executed. For example, maybe one test case (call it Test 11) tests whether a new user can create an ID in a system. Another test case (call it Test 22) may depend upon this new user logging in. Therefore Test 11 must run before Test 22 can run. Additionally, if Test 11 fails, than Test 22 cannot be run yet. Alternately, perhaps Test 11 passes but Test 22 fails. Later when the functionality is fixed, Test 11 must be re-run before the testers try to re-run Test 22. Or, maybe a database or the system needs to be re-initialized before a test case can run.

There's also something else important to notice in the Preconditions for test case 3 in Table 4.

How can the test case ensure the player rolled a 3 when the value the dice rolls needs to be random in the real game? Sometimes we have to add a bit of extra functionality to put a program in "test mode" so we can run our test cases in a repeatable manner and so we can easily force a condition happen. For example, we may want to test what happens when a player lands on "Go" or on "Go to Jail" and want to force this situation to occur. The Monopoly programmers needed to create a test mode in which (1) the dice rolls could be input manually and (2) the amount of money each player starts with is input manually. It is also important to run some non-repeatable test cases in the regular game mode to test whether random dice input does not appear to change expected behavior.

The expected results must also be written in a very specific way, as in Table 4. You need to record what the output of the program should be, given a particular input/set of steps. Otherwise, how will you know if the answer is correct (every time you run it) if you don't know what the answer is supposed to be? Perhaps your program performs mathematical calculations. You need to take out your calculator, perform some calculations by hand, and put the answer in the expected result field. You need to pre-determine what your program is supposed to do ahead of time, so you'll know right away if your program responds properly or not.

## 3   Strategies for Black Box Testing

Ideally, we'd like to test every possible thing that can be done with our program. But, as we said, writing and executing test cases is expensive. We want to make sure that we definitely write test cases for the kinds of things that the customer will do most often or even fairly often. Our objective is to find as many defects as possible in as few test cases as possible. To accomplish this objective, we use some strategies that will be discussed in this subsection. We want to avoid writing redundant test cases that won't tell us anything new (because they have similar conditions to other test cases we already wrote). Each test case should probe a different mode of failure. We also want to design the simplest test cases that could possibly reveal this mode of failure – test cases themselves can be error-prone if we don't keep this in mind.

### 3.1   Tests of Customer Requirements

Black box test cases are based on customer requirements. We begin by looking at each customer requirement. To start, we want to make sure that every single customer requirement has been tested at least once. As a result, we can trace every requirement to its test case(s) and every test case back to its stated customer requirement. The first test case we'd write for any given requirement is the most-used *success path* for that requirement. By success path, we mean that we want to execute *some desirable functionality (something the customer wants to work) without any error conditions.* We proceed by planning more success path test cases, based on other ways the customer wants to use the functionality and some test cases that execute *failure paths*. Intuitively, failure paths *intentionally have some kind of errors in them, such as errors that users can accidentally input.* We must make sure that the program behaves predictably and gracefully in the face of these errors. Finally, we should plan the execution of our tests out so that the most troublesome, risky requirements are tested first. This would allow more time for fixing problems before delivering the product to the customer. It would be devastating to find a critical flaw right before the product is due to be delivered.

We'll start with one basic requirement. We can write many test cases based on this one requirement, which follows below. As we've said before, it is impossible to test every single possible combination of input. We'll outline an incomplete sampling of test cases and reason about them in this section.

*Requirement: When a user lands on the "Go to Jail" cell, the player goes directly to jail, does not pass go, does not collect $200. On the next turn, the player must pay $50 to get out of jail and does not roll the dice or advance. If the player does not have enough money, he or she is out of the game.*

There are many things to test in this short requirement above, including:
1. Does the player get sent to jail after landing on "Go to Jail"?
2. Does the player receive $200 if "Go" is between the current space and jail?
3. Is $50 correctly decremented if the player has more than $50?
4. Is the player out of the game if he or she has less than $50?

At first it is good to start out by testing some input that you know should definitely pass or definitely fail. If these kinds of tests don't work properly, you know you should just quit testing and put the code back into development. We can start with a two obvious passing test case, as shown in Table 5.

| Test ID | Description | Expected Results | Actual Results |
|---|---|---|---|
| 5 | Precondition: Game is in test mode. Number of players: 1 Money for player 1: $1200 Player 1 dice roll: 3 | | |
| | Player 1 clicks "End Turn" button. | | |
| | | Player 1 is sent to jail Only "Get Out of Jail" button is enabled for Player 1. | |

| | | | |
|---|---|---|---|
| | Player 1 clicks "Get Out of Jail" button. | | |
| | | Money for Player 1: $1150 | |
| 6 | Precondition: Game is in test mode.<br>Number of players:  2<br>Money for player 1:  $1200 | | |
| | Money for player 2: $1200<br>Player 1 dice roll:  3<br>Player 1 clicks "End Turn" button. | | |
| | | Player 1 is sent to jail | |

| | | | |
|---|---|---|---|
| | Player 2 dice roll: 2<br>Player 2 clicks "End Turn" button. | | |
| | | Only "Get Out of Jail" button is enabled for Player 1. | |
| | Player 1 clicks "Get out of Jail" button. | | |
| | | Money for Player 1: $1150 | |

**Table 5: Test Plan #1 for the Jail Requirement**

You will also note that we should *test the simplest possible means to force the condition we are trying to achieve*. For example, in Test Case 5, we only have one player so we temporarily didn't have to spend our time with Player 2. We add Player 2 in Test Case 6 so we can observe that the loss of $50 and dice roll occurs on the next turn (after Player 2 goes). We could go on and test many more aspects of the above requirement. We will now discuss some strategies to consider in creating more test cases.

## 3.2 Equivalence Partitioning

To keep down our testing costs, we don't want to write several test cases that test the same aspect of our program. A good test case uncovers a different class of errors (e.g., incorrect processing of all character data) than has been uncovered by prior test cases. [17] Equivalence partitioning is a strategy that can be used to reduce the number of test cases that need to be developed. Equivalence partitioning divides the input domain of a program into classes. For each of these equivalence classes, the set of data should be treated the same by the module under test and should produce the same answer. Test cases should be designed so the inputs lie within these equivalence classes. [2] For example, for tests of "Go to Jail" the most important thing is whether the player has enough money to pay the $50 fine. Therefore, the two equivalence classes can be partitioned, as shown in Figure 4.

| Less than $50 | $50 or more |

**Figure 4: Equivalence Classes for Player Money**

Once you have identified these partitions, you choose test cases from each partition. To start, choose *a typical value somewhere in the middle of (or well into) each of these two ranges*. See Table 6 for test cases written to test the equivalent classes of money. However, you will note that Test Cases 6 (Player 1 has $1200) and 7 (Player 1 has $100) are both in the same equivalence class. Therefore, Test Case 7 is unlikely to discover any defect not found in Test Case 6.

| Test ID | Description | Expected Results | Actual Results |
|---|---|---|---|
| 7 | Precondition: Game is in test mode.<br>Number of players: 2<br>Money for player 1: $100<br>Money for player 2: $100<br>Player 1 dice roll: 3<br>Player 1 clicks "End Turn" | | |
| | | Player 1 is sent to jail | |
| | Player 2 dice roll: 2<br>Player 2 clicks "End Turn" | | |
| | | Only "Get Out of Jail" is enabled for Player 1. | |
| | Player 1 clicks "Get Out of Jail" | | |
| | | Money for Player 1: $50 | |
| 8 | Precondition: Game is in test mode.<br>Number of players: 2<br>Money for player 1: $25<br>Money for player 2: $25<br>Player 1 dice roll: 3<br>Player 1 clicks "End Turn" | | |
| | | Player 1 is sent to jail | |
| | Player 2 dice roll: 2<br>Player 2 clicks "End Turn" | | |
| | | Only "Get Out of Jail" is enabled for Player 1. | |
| | Player 1 clicks "Get out of Jail" | | |
| | | Player 1 is out of game | |

**Table 6: Test Plan #2 for the Jail Requirement**

For each equivalent class, the test cases can be defined using the following guidelines [17]:

1. If input conditions specify a *range of values*, create one valid and one or two invalid equivalence classes. In the above example, this is (1) less than 50/invalid; (2) 50 or more/valid.

2. If input conditions require a certain value (for example R and L for the side in our train example), create an equivalence class of the valid values (R and L) and one of invalid values (all other letters other than R and L). In this case, you need to test all valid values individually and several invalid values.

3. If input conditions specify a member of a set, create one valid and one invalid

equivalence class.
4. If an input condition is a Boolean, define one valid and one invalid class.

Equivalence class partitioning is just the start, though. An important partner to this partitioning is boundary value analysis.

## 3.3  Boundary Value Analysis

Boris Beizer, well-known author of testing book advises, "Bugs lurk in corners and congregate at boundaries." [1]  Programmers often make mistakes on the boundaries of the equivalence classes/input domain. As a result, we need to focus testing at these boundaries. This type of testing is called Boundary Value Analysis (BVA) and guides you to create test cases at the "edge" of the equivalence classes. *Boundary value* is defined as a *data value that corresponds to a minimum or maximum input, internal, or output value specified for a system or component* [11]. In our above example, the boundary of the class is at 50, as shown in Figure 5. We should create test cases for the Player 1 having $49, $50, and $51. These test cases will help to find common off-by-one errors, caused by errors like using >= when you mean to use >.

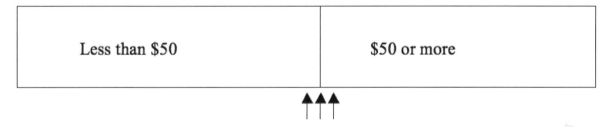

**Figure 5:  Boundary Value Analysis. Test cases should be created for the boundaries (arrows) between equivalence classes.**

When creating BVA test cases, consider the following [17]:
1. If input conditions have a range from **a** to **b** (such as a=100 to b=300), create test cases:
   immediately below **a** (99)
   at **a** (100)
   immediately above **a** (101)
   immediately below **b** (299)
   at **b** (300)
   immediately above **b** (301)
2. If input conditions specify a *number* of values that are allowed, test these limits. For example, input conditions specify that only one train is allowed to start in each direction on each station. In testing, try to add a second train to the same station/same direction. If (somehow) three trains could start on one station/direction, try to add two trains (pass), three trains (pass), and four trains (fail).

## 3.4  Decision Table Testing

Decision tables are used to record complex business rules that must be implemented in the program, and therefore tested. A sample decision table is found in Table 7. In the table, the conditions represent possible input conditions. The actions are the events that should trigger, depending upon the makeup of the input conditions. Each column in the table is a unique combination of input conditions (and is called a rule) that result in triggering the action(s) associated with the rule. Each rule (or column) should become a test case.

*If a Player (A) lands on property owned by another player (B), A must pay rent to B. If A does not have enough money to pay B, A is out of the game.*

**Table 7: Decision table**

|  | Rule 1 | Rule 2 | Rule 3 |
|---|---|---|---|
| **Conditions** | | | |
| A lands on B's property | Yes | Yes | No |
| A has enough money to pay rent | Yes | No | -- |
| **Actions** | | | |
| A stays in game | Yes | No | Yes |

## 3.5 Failure ("Dirty") Test Cases

Donald Knuth is many times referred to as one of the fathers of computer science. He is also known as a stickler when it comes to bugs in his code (and in his books. He sends checks to readers who find errors in his books!). Anticipating the unexpected is one of his techniques. Think the way Knuth does when you write your test cases. Be mean and nasty!

*My test programs are intended to break the system, to push it to its extreme limits, to pile complication on complication, in ways that the system programmer never consciously anticipated. To prepare such test data, I get into the meanest, nastiest frame of mind that I can manage, and I write the cruelest code I can think of; then I turn around and embed that in even nastier constructions that are almost obscene.* [14]

Think diabolically! Think of every possible thing a user could possibly do with your system to demolish the software. You need to make sure your program is robust – in that it can properly respond in the face of erroneous user input. This type of testing is called *robustness testing*, whereby test cases are chosen outside the domain to test robustness to unexpected, erroneous input [3], and is included in *defensive testing* which includes *tests under both normal and abnormal conditions* [5]. Look at every input. Does the program respond "gracefully" to these error conditions?

1. Can any form of input to the program cause division by zero?  Get creative!
2. What if the input type is wrong? (You're expecting an integer, they input a float.  You're expecting a character, you get an integer.)
3. What if the customer takes an illogical path through your functionality?
4. What if mandatory fields are not entered?
5. What if the program is aborted abruptly or input or output devices are unplugged?

## 3.5 Test Early and Often

As was said in the beginning of the chapter, executing your test cases as soon as possible is an excellent way of getting concrete feedback about your program.  In order to run test cases early, programmers need to integrate the pieces of their code into the code base often.  Programmers could be tempted to work on their own computer until the finish implementing a "whole" requirement.  In industry, this could quite feasibly mean they keep their code to themselves for several months.  However, this is a dangerous practice – and can lead to what is known in industry as *integration hell*.  Just because a component works on a programmer's own computer, this doesn't mean it will work when it is assembled with the code other programmers are working on.  The earlier it is known that there are some interface problems or some data that's not getting passed properly the better.  This knowledge can only be gained by integrating code and testing early and often.   Then, integration problems can be more easily localized in the work that was just integrated.  By localizing the code that contains a new defect, the programmer can efficiently identify and remove defects.

## 4   Acceptance Testing

 Acceptance test cases are written by the customer.  In custom software development, often contracts between the customer and the development organization state that the customer can refuse to take delivery of the product if their acceptance test cases do not run properly in the customer's own (software and hardware) environment.  Sometime the customer shares the acceptance test cases with the team, which gives them a shared specific goal.  Other times, the customer hides the acceptance test cases from the developers and runs them after receiving the code (in the same way as a teacher often doesn't tell the students the test cases they will run to grade their class projects).  We believe it is much more productive for the customer and the development team to work openly and collaboratively on the creation of the acceptance test cases.  Then, together the customer and the development team have a similar vision of what the software has to look like for the customer to be happy.  In our experience, the collaborative acceptance test case creation serves as an excellent means of clarifying requirements by making requirements specified in a way that is quantifiable, measurable, and unambiguous long before testing commences.  Likewise, they can together track the progress of system development as the team can tell the customer which acceptance test cases are passing.

## 5   Black Box Test Case Automation

By their nature, black box test cases are designed and run by people who do not see the inner workings of the code.  Ultimately, system and acceptance cases are intended to be run through the product user interface (UI) to show that the whole product really works. Test automation can be difficult because the developer has no knowledge of the inner workings of the software and because system and acceptance cases must be run through the UI. However, the more automated testing can be, the easier it is to run the test cases and to re-run them again and again. The simpler it is to run a suite of tests, the more often those tests will be run. The more the tests are run, the faster any deviation from those tests will be found. [15]

If your role on the team is as a software developer, it is always good to consider the types of black box test cases (functional, system, and acceptance) that will ultimately be run on your code and to automate test cases to test the logic (separate from the UI logic) behind these black box test cases. Automated test cases can be run often with minimal time investment once they are written. By automating the testing of the logic behind the black box test cases, (1) you are ensuring that the logic "behind the scenes" is working properly so that the inevitable black box test cases can run smoothly through the UI by the testers and the customers; and (2) you are more motivated to decouple program/business logic separate from the UI logic (which is always a good design technique).

When test cases are automated, they can then become compile-able and executable documentation.

## 6 Summary

Several practical tips for black box testing were presented throughout this chapter. The keys for successful black box testing are summarized in Table 8.

| | |
|---|---|
| | You need to test for what the customer wants the program to do, not what the programmer programmed it to do. The programmer is biased (through no fault of her/her own) by knowing the intimate details of what the program does. Black box testing is best done by someone with a fresh, objective perspective of the customer requirements. |
| | Use the four-item test case template (ID, Description, Expected Results, Actual Results) when planning your test cases. |

| | |
|---|---|
| 🔑 | In the test case, specify exactly what the tester has to do to create the desired input conditions and exactly how the program should respond (the output). Be explicit in this documentation so that multiple testers (other than yourself) would be able to run the exact same test case using the directions in the test case. These directions will be especially important if a failure need to be re-created for the programmer to a failure. |
| 🔑 | Test early and often. |
| 🔑 | Write the simplest test cases that could possibly reveal a mode of failure. (Test cases can also be error-prone.) |
| 🔑 | Use *equivalence class partitioning* to manage the number of test cases run. Test cases in the same equivalence class will all reveal the same fault. |
| 🔑 | Use *boundary value analysis* to find the very-common bugs that lurk in corners and congregate at boundaries. |
| 🔑 | Use *decision tables* to record complex business rules that the system must implement and that must be tested. |
| 🔑 | Run the equivalence class test cases first. If the program doesn't work for the simplest case (smack in the middle of an equivalence class), it probably won't work for the boundaries either. If you run a boundary test ~~first, you'll probably go run the general case~~ (equivalence class test) before investigating the problem. So, instead just run the simple case first. |

| | |
|---|---|
| 🔑 | Avoid having test cases dependant upon each other (i.e. having preconditions of another test case passing). Consider that you have 17 test cases, each having a precondition of the prior test case passing – and you pass the first 16 test cases but fail the $17^{th}$ test case. It take you some time (until the next day) to debug your program. Now, in order to re-run the $17^{th}$ test case to see if it now passes, you have to re-run the 16 you know pass. This can be time consuming ☹ |
| 🔑 | Write each test case so that it can reveal one type of fault. Consider a test case that has three different forms of invalid input. If the test case fails, you might not know which of the three inputs make it the test case fail, and you will have to run different, smaller test cases to see which of the inputs caused problems. |
| 🔑 | Think diabolically! What are the worst things someone could try to do to your program? Write test for these. |
| 🔑 | Encourage a collaborative approach to acceptance testing with the customer. |
| 🔑 | When black box test cases surface failures, they only reveal the symptoms of faults. You need to use your detective skills to find the fault in the code that caused the failure to occur. |

**Table 8:  Key Ideas for Black Box Testing**

Reminds Dijkstra, "Program testing can be used to show the *presence* of bugs, but never to show their absence!" [7]  Mostly, testing can be used to check how well defect-prevention activities worked.  As a beneficial side effect, testing can also be used to identify anomalies in code via dynamic execution of the code.

In this chapter, we learned that complete, exhaustive testing is impractical.  However, there are good software engineering strategies, such as equivalence class partitioning and boundary value analysis, for writing test cases that will maximize your chance of uncovering as many defects as possible with a reasonable amount of testing.  It is most prudent to plan your test cases as early in the development cycle as possible, as a beneficial extension of the requirements gathering process. Likewise, it is beneficial to integrate code as often as possible and to test the integrated code. In this manner, we can isolate defects in the new code – and find and fix them as efficiently as possible. Lastly, we learned the benefits of partnering with a customer to write the acceptance test cases and to automate the execution of these (and other test cases) to form compile-able and executable documentation of the system.

**Glossary of Chapter Terms**

| Term | Definition | Source |
|---|---|---|
| Acceptance testing | formal testing conducted to determine whether or not a system satisfies its acceptance criteria (the criteria the system must satisfy to be accepted by a customer) and to enable the customer to determine whether or not to accept the system | [11] |
| Black box testing (also called functional testing or behavioral testing) | testing that ignores the internal mechanism of a system or component and focuses solely on the outputs generated in response to selected inputs and execution conditions | [11] |
| Boundary value | data value that corresponds to a minimum or maximum input, internal, or output value specified for a system or component | [11] |
| Defect | See fault | |
| Defensive testing | Testing which includes tests under both normal and abnormal conditions | [5] |
| Error | the difference between a computed, observed, or measured value or condition and the true, specified, or theoretically correct value or condition | [11] |

| Failure | the inability of a system or component to perform its required function within the specified performance requirement | [11] |
|---|---|---|
| Failure path | a test case that intentionally forces an error condition to occur | |
| Fault | an incorrect step, process, or data definition in a program | [11] |
| Integration testing | testing in which software components, hardware components, or both are combined and tested to evaluate the interaction between them | [11] |
| Input/output oracle | an oracle that specifies the expected output for a specified input | [1] |
| Mistake | human action that produces an incorrect result | [11] |
| oracle | any program, process, or body of data that specified the expected outcome of a set of tests as applied to a tested object | [1] |
| Performance testing | testing conducted to evaluate the compliance of a system or component with specified performance requirements | [11] |
| Regression testing | selective retesting of a system or component to verify that modifications have not caused unintended effects and that the system or component still complies with its specified requirements | [11] |
| Robustness testing | Testing whereby test cases are chosen outside the domain to test robustness to unexpected, erroneous input | [3] |

| Scaffolding code | computer programs and data files built to support software development and testing but not intended to be included in the final product | [11] |
|---|---|---|
| Smoke tests | group of test cases that establish that the system is stable and all major functionality is present and works under "normal" | [6] |
| | conditions | |
| Specification | a document that specifies in a complete, precise, verifiable manner, the requirements, design, behavior, or other characteristic of a system or component, and often the procedures for determining whether these provisions have been satisfied | [11] |
| Stress testing | testing conducted to evaluate a system or component at or beyond the limits of its specification or requirement | [11] |
| Stubs | computer program statement substituting for the body of a software module that is or will be defined elsewhere | [11] |
| Success path | a test case that execute some desirable functionality (something the customer wants to work) without any error conditions | |
| System testing | testing conducted on a complete, integrated system to evaluate the system compliance with its specified requirements | [11] |

| Test case | set of test inputs, execution conditions, and expected results developed for a particular objective, such as to exercise a particular program path or to verify compliance with a specific requirement | [11] |
|---|---|---|
| Test driver | software module used to involve a module under test and often, provide test inputs, controls, and monitor execution and report test results | [11] |
| Test plan | document describing the scope, approach, resources, and schedule of intended test activities.  It identifies test items, the features to be tested, the testing tasks, who will do each task, and any risks requiring contingency plans | [11] |
| Unit testing | testing of individual hardware or software units or groups of related units | [11] |
| Usability testing | testing conducted to evaluate the extent to which a user can learn to operate, prepare inputs for, and interpret outputs of a system or component | [11] |
| Validation | the process of evaluating a system or component during or at the end of the development process to determine whether it satisfies specified requirements | [11] |

| Verification | the process of evaluating a system or component to determine whether the products of a given development phase satisfy the conditions imposed at the start of that phase | [11] |
| --- | --- | --- |
| White box testing | testing that takes into account the internal mechanism of a system or component | [11] |

## References:

[1]    B. Beizer, *Software Testing Techniques*. London: International Thompson Computer Press, 1990.

[2]    B. Beizer, *Black Box Testing*. New York: John Wiley & Sons, Inc., 1995.

[3]    A. Bertolino, "Chapter 5: Software Testing," in *IEEE SWEBOK Trial Version 1.00*, May 2001.

[4]    B. W. Boehm, *Software Engineering Economics*. Englewood Cliffs, NJ: Prentice-Hall, Inc., 1981.

[5]    L. Copeland, *A Practitioner's Guide to Software Test Design*. Boston: Artech House Publishers, 2004.

[6]    R. D. Craig and S. P. Jaskiel, *Systematic Software Testing*. Norwood, MA: Artech House Publishers, 2002.

[7]    E. W. Dijkstra, "Notes on Structured Programming," Technological University Eindhoven T.H. Report 70-WSK-03, Second edition, April 1970.

[8]    D. Galin, *Software Quality Assurance*. Harlow, England: Pearson, Addison Wesley, 2004.

[9]    IEEE, "ANSI/IEEE Standard 1008-1987, IEEE Standard for Software Unit Testing," no., 1986.

[10]   IEEE, "ANSI/IEEE Standard 1008-1987, IEEE Standard for Software Unit Testing," no., 1987.

[11]   IEEE, "IEEE Standard 610.12-1990, IEEE Standard Glossary of Software Engineering Terminology," 1990.

[12]   IEEE, "IEEE Standards Collection: Glossary of Software Engineering Terminology," IEEE Standard 610.12-1990, 1990.

[13]   C. Kaner, J. Bach, and B. Pettichord, *Lessons Learned in Software Testing*: John Wiley & Sons, 2002.

[14]   D. E. Knuth, "The errors of TeX. Software--Practice and Experience," in *Literate Programming; CSLI Lecture Notes, no. 27*, vol. 19: CSLI, 1992, pp. 607--681.

[15]   R. C. Martin, *Agile Software Development: Principles, Patterns, and Practices*. Upper Saddle River: Prentice Hall, 2003.

[16]   G. J. Myers, *The Art of Software Testing*. New York: John Wiley, 979.

[17]   R. Pressman, *Software Engineering:   A Practitioner's Approach*. Boston: McGraw Hill, 2001.

# Chapter Questions

1.  What is the difference between black-box and white-box testing? During the software development, how can we derive black-box tests? How about white-box tests?

2.  Dharma City is installing the AutoCop Traffic Law Enforcement System. AucoCop is a sensor-camera combo installed near a traffic light. When the sensor detects a speeding (faster than 40miles/hour) car passing by or a car running through the red light, AutoCop will activate the camera and take a picture of the plate. Use the equivalence partitioning and boundary value analysis methods to derive the test cases to test the camera activation logic.

3.  From the perspective of automating software testing, what is the problem if the user interface and the business logic are heavily coupled?

4.  Describe in your own words the difference between validation and verification.

5.  In XP, the customer and developers work cooperatively to specify the acceptance tests. What are to pros and cons if the customer and developers work together on acceptance tests?

6.  What's the advantage if acceptance tests can be automated?

7.  Suppose you are writing a program that counts the number of alphanumeric characters in a string. May we apply equivalence partitioning for this program? What about boundary value analysis? Do we need more test cases to validate the program?

8.  Suppose we are developing a program which decides, in a two-dimensional coordinate system, whether a point P falls in a circle C or on its edge. The program reads five real numbers. The first two numbers are the x- and y-coordinate of the center of C, the third number is the radius of C, and the fourth and fifth numbers represent the coordinate of P. Develop the test cases that you feel are adequate for this program.

9.  Some organizations have independent testing groups. What tests are best designed by the testing group? What tests are best designed by the developers? And what tests are best designed by the customer? Justify your answer.

10. You are testing an automatic auction system. Suppose there is an auction of which the bids can only be placed between 1/1/2008 and 1/7/2008. The starting bid price of this auction must be at least $20.00, and a minimum incremental bid of $5.00 is required. Using the equivalence partitioning and boundary value analysis methods to derive a set of test cases for the bid placement. Also give some "dirty" test cases.

11. Suppose you are writing a simple calculator program. This program can handle positive integer calculation, including addition, subtraction, multiplication, and division. The input is a string composed of digits (0, 1, 2, …, 9) and operators (+, -, *, /). No space is allowed. The input string can be at most 100 characters long, and each number can compose of at most 10 digits. Division of two integers produces one integer by truncation. If the answer contains more than 10 digits, this program simply outputs an overflow error message. Using the equivalence partitioning and boundary value analysis methods, derive a set of test cases for

the program. Also give some dirty test cases.

12. Acceptance tests are specified by the customer with the help of developers. Usually the customer has better knowledge in their business than in programming. Therefore, it is next to impossible for the customer to write or understand the tests using the programming language. What do you think is a feasible form of acceptance tests? (Remember that we'd like the acceptance tests executable.)

# White-Box Testing

White-box testing is a verification technique software engineers can use to examine if their code works as expected.  In this chapter, we will explain the following:
>a method for writing a set of white-box test cases that exercise the paths in the code
>the use of equivalence partitioning and boundary value analysis to manage the number of test cases that need to be written and to examine error-prone/extreme "corner" test cases
>how to measure how thoroughly the test cases exercise the code

*White-box testing* is *testing that takes into account the internal mechanism of a system or component* (IEEE, 1990).  White-box testing is also known as *structural testing*, *clear box testing,* and *glass box testing* (Beizer, 1995).  The connotations of "clear box" and "glass box" appropriately indicate that you have full visibility of the internal workings of the software product, specifically, the logic and the structure of the code.

Using the  white-box testing techniques outlined in this chapter, a software engineer can design test cases that (1) exercise independent paths within a module or unit; (2) exercise logical decisions on both their true and false side; (3) execute loops at their boundaries and within their operational bounds; and (4) exercise internal data structures to ensure their validity (Pressman, 2001).

There are six basic types of testing:  unit, integration, function/system, acceptance, regression, and beta.   White-box testing is used for three of these six types:
>*Unit testing,* which is *testing of individual hardware or software units or groups of related units* (IEEE, 1990).   A *unit* is *a software component that cannot be subdivided into other components* (IEEE, 1990).  Software engineers write white-box test cases to examine whether the unit is coded correctly.  Unit testing is important for ensuring the code is solid before it is integrated with other code.  Once the code is integrated into the code base, the cause of an observed failure is more difficult to find.  Also, since the software engineer writes and runs unit tests him or herself, companies often do not track the unit test failures that are observed– making these types of defects the most "private" to the software engineer.  We all prefer to find our own mistakes and to have the opportunity to fix them without others knowing.  Approximately 65% of all bugs can be caught in unit testing (Beizer, 1990).
>*Integration testing,* which is *testing in which software components, hardware components, or both are combined and tested to evaluate the interaction between them* (IEEE, 1990).  Test cases are written which explicitly examine the interfaces between the various units.  These test cases can be black box test cases, whereby the tester understands that a test case requires multiple program units to interact.  Alternatively, white-box test cases are written which explicitly exercise the interfaces that are known to the tester.
>*Regression testing,* which is *selective retesting of a system or component to verify that modifications have not caused unintended effects and that the system or component still*

*complies with its specified requirements* (IEEE, 1990). As with integration testing, regression testing can be done via black-box test cases, white-box test cases, or a combination of the two. White-box unit and integration test cases can be saved and re-run as part of regression testing.

## 1   White-Box Testing by Stubs and Drivers

With white-box testing, you must run the code with predetermined input and check to make sure that the code produces predetermined outputs. Often programmers write stubs and drivers for white-box testing. A *driver* is *a software module used to invoke a module under test and, often, provide test inputs, control and monitor execution, and report test results* (IEEE, 1990) or most simplistically a *line of code that calls a method and passes that method a value*. For example, if you wanted to move a Player instance, Player1, two spaces on the board, the driver code would be

```
movePlayer(Player1, 2);
```

This driver code would likely be called from the main method. A white-box test case would execute this driver line of code and check `Player.getPosition()` to make sure the player is now on the expected cell on the board.

A *stub* is a *computer program statement substituting for the body of a software module that is or will be defined elsewhere* (IEEE, 1990) or a *dummy component or object used to simulate the behavior of a real component* (Beizer, 1990) until that component has been developed. For example, if the movePlayer method has not been written yet, a stub such as the one below might be used temporarily – which moves any player to position 1.

```
public void movePlayer(Player player, int diceValue) {
        player.setPosition(1);
}
```

Ultimately, the dummy method would be completed with the proper program logic. However, developing the stub allows the programmer to call a method in the code being developed, even if the method does not yet have the desired behavior.

Stubs and drivers are often viewed as throwaway code (Kaner, Falk et al., 1999). However, they do not have to be thrown away: Stubs can be "filled in" to form the actual method. Drivers can become automated test cases.

## 2   Deriving Test Cases

In the following sections, we will discuss various methods for devising a thorough set of white-box test cases. We will refer to the Monopoly example to illustrate the methods under discussion. These methods can serve as guidelines for you as you design test cases. Even though it may seem like a lot of work to use these methods, statistics show [1] that the act of careful, complete, systematic test **design** will catch as many bugs as the act of testing. The test design process, at all levels, is at least as effective at catching bugs as is running the test case designed by that process.

Each time you write a code module, you should write test cases for it based on the guidelines. A possible exception to this recommendation is the accessor methods (i.e., getters and setters) of your projects. You should concentrate your testing effort on code that could easily be broken. Generally, accessor methods will be written error-free.

## 2.1 Basis Path Testing

*Basis path testing* (McCabe, 1976) is a means for ensuring that all independent paths through a code module have been tested. An *independent path* is any path through the code that introduces at least one new set of processing statements or a new condition. (Pressman, 2001) Basis path testing provides a minimum, lower-bound on the number of test cases that need to be written.

To introduce the basis path method, we will draw a flowgraph of a code segment. Once you understand basis path testing, it may not be necessary to draw the flowgraph – though you may always find a quick sketch helpful. If you test incrementally and the modules you test are small enough, you can consider having a mental picture of the flow graph. As you will see, the main objective is to identify the number of decision points in the module and you may be able to identify them without a written representation.

A flowgraph of purchasing property appears in Figure 1. The flowgraph is intended to depict the following requirement.

> *If a player lands on a property owned by other players, he or she needs to pay the rent. If the player does not have enough money, he or she is out of the game. If the property is not owned by any players, and the player has enough money buying the property, he or she may buy the property with the price associated with the property.*

In the simple flowgraph in Figure 2, a rectangle shows a sequence of processing steps that are executed unconditionally. A diamond represents a *logic conditional* or *predicate*. Some examples of logical conditionals are if-then, if-then-else, selection, or loops. The head of the arrow indicates the flow of control. For a rectangle, there will be one arrow heading out. For a predicate, there will be two arrows heading out – one for a true/positive result and the other for a false/negative result.

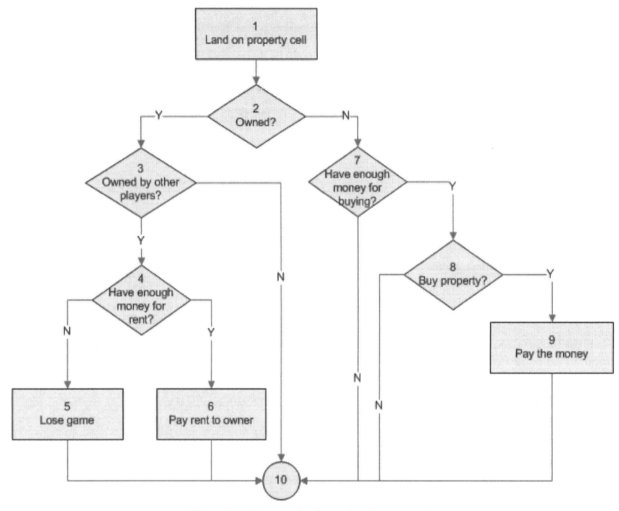

**Figure 1: Flowgraph of purchasing property**

Using this flow graph, we can compute the number of independent paths through the code. We do this using a metric called the *cyclomatic number* (McCabe, 1976), which is based on graph theory.

You can compute the cyclomatic number via the formula:

Edge – Nodes + 2

In our example above, 14 edges and 10 nodes. Therefore, our cyclomatic number is 6, and we have six independent paths through the code. We can now enumerate them:

1.  1-2-3-4-5-10          (property owned by others, no money for rent)
2.  1-2-3-4-6-10          (property owned by others, pay rent)
3.  1-2-3-10              (property owned by the player)
4.  1-2-7-10              (property available, don't have enough money)
5.  1-2-7-8-10            (property available, have money, don't want to buy it)
6.  1-2-7-8-9-10          (property available, have money, and buy it)

We would want to write a test case to ensure that each of these paths is tested at least once. As said above, the cyclomatic number is the lower bound on the number of test cases we will write. The test cases that are determined this way are the ones we use in basis path testing. There are other things to consider, as we now discuss.

## 2.2   Equivalence Partitioning/Boundary Value Analysis

Equivalence partitioning (EP) and boundary value analysis (BVA) provide a strategy for writing white-box test cases. Undoubtedly, whenever you encounter any kind of number or limit in a requirement, you should be alert for EP/BVA issues. For example, a person might want to buy a house, but may or may not have enough money. Considering EP/BVA, we would want to ensure our test cases include the following:

1. property costs $100, have $200 (equivalence class "have enough money")
2. property costs $100, have $50 (equivalence class, "don't have enough money")
3. property costs $100, have $100  (boundary value)
4. property costs $100, have $99  (boundary value)
5. property costs $100, have $101 (boundary value)

With programming loops (such as while loops), consider EP and execute the loops in the middle of their operational bound. For BVA, you will want to ensure that you execute loops right below, right at, and right above their boundary conditions.

## 3   Control-flow/Coverage Testing

Another way to devise a good set of white-box test cases is to consider the control flow of the program. The *control flow* of the program is represented in a flow graph, as shown in Figure 1. We consider various aspects of this flowgraph in order to ensure that we have an adequate set of test cases. The adequacy of the test cases is often measured with a metric called coverage. *Coverage* is a measure of the completeness of the set of test cases. To demonstrate the various kinds of coverage, we will use the simple code example shown in Figure 2 as a basis of discussion as we take up the next five topics.

```
1     int foo (int a, int b, int c, int d, float e)  {
2          float e;
3          if (a == 0)  {
4              return 0;
5          }
6          int x = 0;
7          if ((a==b) OR ((c == d) AND bug(a) )) {
8              x=1;
9          }
10          e = 1/x;
```

```
11      return e;
12      }
```

**Figure 2:  Sample Code for Coverage Analysis**

Keeping with a proper testing technique, we write methods to ensure they are testable – most simply by having the method return a value.  Additionally, we predetermine the "answer" that is returned when the method is called with certain parameters so that our testing returns that predetermined value.  Another good testing technique is to use the simplest set of input that could possibly test your situation – it's better not to input values that cause complex, error-prone calculations when you are predetermining the values.  We'll illustrate this principle as we go through the next items.

## 3.1    Method Coverage

*Method coverage* is *a measure of the percentage of methods that have been executed by test cases.*  Undoubtedly, your tests should call 100% of your methods.  It seems irresponsible to deliver methods in your product when your testing never used these methods.  As a result, you need to ensure you have 100% method coverage.

In the code shown in Figure 3, we attain 100% method coverage by calling the foo method. Consider Test Case 1:  the method call **foo(0, 0, 0, 0, 0.)**, expected return value of 0.  If you look at the code, you see that if a has a value of 0, it doesn't matter what the values of the other parameters are – so we'll make it really easy and make them all 0.  Through this one call we attain 100% method coverage.

## 3.2    Statement Coverage

*Statement coverage* is *a measure of the percentage of statements that have been executed by test cases.*  Your objective should be to achieve 100% statement coverage through your testing. Identifying your cyclomatic number and executing this minimum set of test cases will make this statement coverage achievable.

In Test Case 1, we executed the program statements on lines 1-5 out of 12 lines of code.  As a result, we had 42% (5/12) statement coverage from Test Case 1.  We can attain 100% statement coverage by one additional test case, Test Case 2:  the method call **foo(1, 1, 1, 1, 1.)**, expected return value of 1.  With this method call, we have achieved 100% statement coverage because we have now executed the program statements on lines 6-12.

## 3.3    Branch Coverage

*Branch coverage* is *a measure of the percentage of the decision points (Boolean expressions) of the program have been evaluated as both true and false in test cases.*  The small program in

Figure 3 has two decision points – one on line 3 and the other on line 7.

```
3               if (a == 0)  {
7               if ((a==b) OR ((c == d) AND bug(a) )) {
```

For decision/branch coverage, we evaluate an entire Boolean expression as one true-or-false predicate even if it contains multiple logical-and or logical-or operators – as in line 7. We need to ensure that each of these predicates (compound or single) is tested as both true and false. Table 1 shows our progress so far:

**Table 1:  Decision Coverage**

| Line # | Predicate | True | False |
|--------|-----------|------|-------|
| 3 | (a == 0) | Test Case 1 **foo(0, 0, 0, 0, 0) return 0** | Test Case 2 **foo(1, 1, 1, 1, 1) return 1** |
| 7 | ((a==b) OR ((c == d) AND bug(a) )) | Test Case 2 **foo(1, 1, 1, 1, 1) return 1** | |

Therefore, we currently have executed  three of the  four necessary conditions; we have achieved 75% branch coverage thus far.  We add Test Case 3 to bring us to 100% branch coverage: **foo(1, 2, 1, 2, 1)**.  When we look at the code to calculate an expected return value, we realize that this test case uncovers a previously undetected division-by-zero problem on line 10!  We can then immediately go to the code and protect from such an error . This illustrates the value of test planning.  Through the test case, we achieve 100% branch coverage.

In many cases, the objective is to achieve 100% branch coverage in your testing, though in large systems only 75%-85% is practical.  Only 50% branch coverage is practical in very large systems of 10 million source lines of code or more (Beizer, 1990).

## 3.4   Condition Coverage

We will go one step deeper and examine condition coverage.  *Condition coverage is a measure of percentage of Boolean sub-expressions of the program that have been evaluated as both true or false outcome [applies to compound predicate] in test cases.*  Notice that in line 7 there are three sub-Boolean expressions to the larger statement (a==b), (c==d), and bug(a).  Condition coverage measures the outcome of each of these sub-expressions independently of each other. With condition coverage, you ensure that each of these sub-expressions has independently been tested as both true and false.  We consider our progress thus far in Table 2.

**Table 2: Condition coverage**

| Predicate | True | False |
|---|---|---|
| (a==b) | Test Case 2<br>**foo(1, 1, x, x, 1)**<br>**return value 0** | Test Case 3<br>**foo(1, 2, 1, 2, 1)**<br>**division by zero!** |
| (c==d) | | Test Case 3<br>**foo(1, 2, 1, 2, 1)**<br>**division by zero!** |
| bug(a) | | |

At this point, our condition coverage is only 50%. The true condition (c==d) has never been tested. Additionally, short-circuit Boolean has prevented the method bug(int) from ever being executed. We examine our available information on the bug method and determine that is <u>should</u> return a value of true when passed a value of a=1. We write Test Case 4 to address test (c==d) as true: **foo(1, 2, 1, 1, 1)**, expected return value 1. However, when we actually run the test case, the function bug(a) actually returns false, which causes our actual return value (division by zero) to not match our expected return value. This allows us to detect an error in the bug method. Without the addition of condition coverage, this error would not have been revealed.

To finalize our condition coverage, we must force bug(a) to be false. We again examine our bug() information, which informs us that the bug method should return a false value if fed any integer greater than 1. So we create Test Case 5, **foo(3, 2, 1, 1, 1)**, expected return value "division by error". The condition coverage thus far is shown in Table 15.3.

**Table 3: Condition Coverage Continued**

| Predicate | True | False |
|---|---|---|
| (a==b) | Test Case 2<br>**foo(1, 1, 1, 1, 1)**<br>**return value 0** | Test Case 3<br>**foo(1, 2, 1, 2, 1)**<br>**division by zero!** |
| (c==d) | Test Case 4<br>**foo(1, 2, 1, 1, 1)**<br>return value 1 | Test Case 3<br>**foo(1, 2, 1, 2, 1)**<br>**division by zero!** |
| bug(a) | Test Case 4<br>**foo(1, 2, 1, 1, 1)**<br>return value 1 | Test Case 5<br>**foo(3, 2, 1, 1, 1)**<br>**division by zero!** |

There are no industry standard objectives for condition coverage, but we suggest that you keep condition coverage in mind as you develop your test cases. You have seen that our condition coverage revealed that some additional test cases were needed.

There are commercial tools available, called *coverage monitors*, that can report the coverage metrics for your test case execution. Often these tools only report method and statement coverage. Some tools report decision/branch and/or condition coverage. These tools often also will color code the lines of code that have not been executed during your test efforts. It is recommended that coverage analysis is automated using such a tool because manual coverage analysis is unreliable and uneconomical (IEEE, 1987).

## 4  Data Flow Testing

In data flow-based testing, the control flowgraph is annotated with information about how the program variables are defined and used. Different criteria exercise with varying degrees of precision how a value assigned to a variable is used along different control flow paths. A reference notation is a definition-use pair, which is a triple of (d, u, V) such that V is a variable, d is a note in which V is defined, and us is a node in which V is used. There exists a path between d and u in which the definition of V in d is used in u.

## 5  Failure ("Dirty") Test Cases

As with black-box test cases, you must think diabolically about the kinds of things users might do with your program. Look at the structure of your code and think about every possible way a user might break it. These devious ways may not be uncovered by the previously mentioned methods for forming test cases. You need to be smart enough to think of your particular code and how people might outsmart it (accidentally or intentionally). Augment your test cases to handle these cases. Some suggestions follow:

> Look at every input into the code you are testing. Do you handle each input if it is incorrect, the wrong font, or too large (or too small)?
> Look at code from a security point of view. Can a user overflow a buffer, causing a security problem?
> Look at every calculation. Could it possible create an overflow? Have you protected from possible division by zero?

## 6  Flow Graphs Revisited

The flowgraph of Figure 1 was fairly straightforward because there were no compound Boolean predicates. Let's go back and look at what a flowgraph of the code in Figure 2 would look like. When you encounter a compound predicate, such as in line 7, you must break the expression up so that each Boolean sub-expression is evaluated on its own, as shown below in Figure 3.

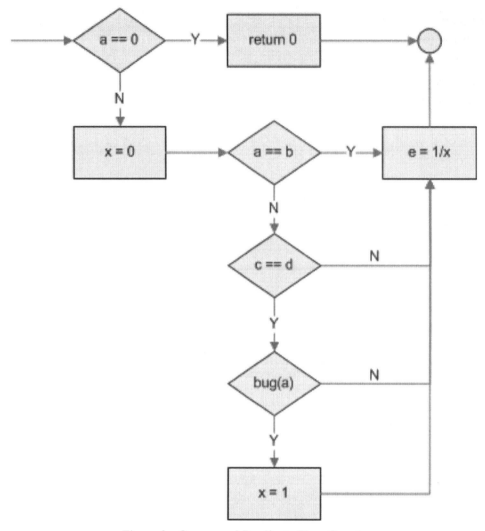

**Figure 3: Compound Predicate Flow Graph**

If you look back at the previous section on deriving test cases, you see that as we strove to get 100% method, statement, decision/branch and condition coverage, we wrote five test cases. Examining Figure 3, you can see we have four predicates (diamonds). Therefore, our cyclomatic number is 4 + 1 = 5 – which is the number of test cases we wrote.

As code becomes larger and more complex, devising the flowgraph and calculating the cyclomatic complexity can become difficult or impossible. However, if you write methods that are not overly long (which is a good practice anyway), the methods we have discussed in this chapter are quite helpful in your quest for high quality.

# 7 Summary

Properly planned with explicit input/output combinations, white-box testing is a controlled V&V technique. You run a test case, you know what lines of code you execute, and you know what the "answer" should be. If you don't get the right answer, the test case reveals a *problem* (a fault). Fortunately, you know which lines of code to look at based upon the test case that fails. Because of this control, removing defects in unit test is more economical than later phases in the development cycle. Later testing phases that involve block-box testing can be more chaotic. In those phases, a test case no longer reveals a problem (and an approximate location of where the problem needs to be fixed). Instead, a failed black-box test case reveals a *symptom of a problem (a failure)*. It can be difficult, time consuming, and take an unpredictable amount of time to find the root cause of the symptom (the fault that caused the failure) so that the software engineer knows what to change in the code. Therefore, unit testing is a more economical defect removal technique when compared with black box testing. Therefore, as much as possible should be tested at the unit level (IEEE, 1987). A comparison between white-box testing and black box testing can be found in Table 5.

**Table 5. A comparison of white-box testing and black-box testing**

| Type of Testing | White-box Testing | Black-box Testing |
|---|---|---|
| Tester visibility | have visibility to the code and write test cases based upon the code | have no visibility to the code and write test cases based on possible inputs and outputs for functionality documented in specifications and/or requirements |
| A failed test case reveals | a problem (fault) | a symptom of a problem (a failure) |

| Controlled? | Yes – the test case helps to identify the specific lines of code involved | No – it can be hard to find the cause of the failure |
|---|---|---|

Both white-box and black-box testing techniques are important and are intended to find different types of faults. Simple unit faults might need to be found in black-box testing if adequate white-box testing is not done adequately). You should strive to remove as many defects as possible using white-box testing techniques when the identification of the faults is more controllable.

Several practical tips for risk management were presented throughout this chapter. The keys for successful risk management are summarized in Table 6.

**Table 6. Key Ideas for White-Box Testing**

| | |
|---|---|
| 🔑 | Use an automated coverage monitor for the analysis of control flow-based unit testing. |
| 🔑 | Compute the cyclomatic complexity to determine the least number of test cases that should be written. This number does not consider equivalence class partitioning or boundary value analysis – which should be done for most decision points. |
| 🔑 | Draw the flowgraph for a code segment – at least until you get more used to computing cyclomatic complexity. |
| 🔑 | At a minimum, write enough white box test cases to cover 100% of your statements. Get as high a coverage as possible with your decision/branch and condition coverage. |

## Glossary of Chapter Terms

| Word | Definition | Source |
|---|---|---|
| branch coverage | a measure of the percentage of the decision points (Boolean expressions) of the program have been evaluated as both true and false in test cases | |
| condition coverage | a measure of the percentage of Boolean sub-expressions of the program that have been evaluated as both true or false outcome [applies to compound predicate] in test cases | |
| driver | software module used to invoke a module under test and, often, provide test inputs, control and monitor execution, and report test results | (IEEE, 1990) |
| integration testing | testing in which software components, hardware components, or both are combined and tested to evaluate the interaction between them | (IEEE, 1990) |
| method coverage | a measure of the percentage of methods that have been executed by test cases. | |
| regression testing | selective retesting of a system or component to verify that modifications have not caused unintended effects and that the system or component still complies with its specified requirements | (IEEE, 1990) |
| statement coverage | a measure of the percentage of statements that have been executed by test cases | |
| stub | computer program statement substituting for the body of a software module that is or will be defined elsewhere | (IEEE, 1990) |
| unit | a separable, testable element specified n the design of a computer software component; a software component that cannot be subdivided into other components | (IEEE, 1990) |
| unit testing | testing of individual hardware or software units or groups of related units | (IEEE, 1990) |
| white-box testing | testing that takes into account the internal mechanism of a system or component | (IEEE, 1990) |

## References

Beizer, B. (1990). Software Testing Techniques. Boston, International Thompson Computer Press.

Beizer, B. (1995). Black Box Testing. New York, John Wiley & Sons, Inc.

IEEE (1987). "ANSI/IEEE Standard 1008-1987, IEEE Standard for Software Unit Testing."

IEEE (1990). IEEE Standard 610.12-1990, IEEE Standard Glossary of Software Engineering Terminology.

Kaner, C., J. Falk, et al. (1999). Testing Comptuer Software. New York, Wiley Computer Publishing.

McCabe, T. (1976). "A Software Complexity Measure." IEEE Transactions on Software Engineering **SE-2**: 308-320.

Pressman, R. (2001). Software Engineering: A Practitioner's Approach. Boston, McGraw Hill.

## Chapter Questions

1.      If we have a program which has 10 *independent* if...then...else... statements, there are totally $2^{10}$ execution paths. Suppose that, on average, each test case needs 50 microseconds to exercise one execution path and the program itself takes 100 microseconds. If we write a test case for each possible execution path, how much time does it take to run all the test cases?

2.      If a program passes all the black box tests, it means that this program should work properly. Then, in addition to black-box testing, why do we need white-box testing?

3.      Consider the following Java code snippet:

```
Class ProductDB{
   :

   /**
    * returns an instance of product database
    */
   public static ProductDB getInstance(){
         :
         :
   }

   /**
    * returns the price of a product.
    * throws Exception if the product is not found
    */
   public float getProductPrice(String productID)
             throws Exception{
         :
         :
   }
}
Class Cashier{
   ProductDB db;

   public Cashier(ProductDB db){
        this.db = db;
   }
   :
   /**
    * Calculate the total of the prices of several products
    * param productIDs a String array that contains all the
    * product IDs.
    * return The total price of the products.
    */
   public float calculateTotal(String[] productIDs)
             throws Exception{
        float total = 0;

        if(productIDs == null)
             return 0;
        for(int x=0; x<productIDs.length; x++){
             float price =
                   db.getProductPrice(productIDs[x]);
             total += price;
```

```
        }
        return total;
    }
}
```

The `getInstance` method of `ProductDB` returns an instance of the product database. Assume that `ProductDB` is a tested component. Suppose we are going to write a unit test to test this `calculateTotal` method. Write suitable test drivers. Make proper assumptions.

4.  Consider the calculateTotal method in question 3 and the following test case:
```
public void testCalculateTotal(){
    Cashier cashier = new Cashier(new MockProductDB());
    String[] products = new String[0];
    assertEquals(0, cashier.calculateTotal(products);
}
```
A.  Compute the statement coverage of the test for the `calculateTotal` method.

B.  Can we say this test achieves 100% branch coverage for the method?

5.  Read the following pseudo code:
```
if (input is in AllowedCharacterSet)
    if (input is a number)
        if (input >= 0)
            put input into positiveNumberList
        else
            put input into negativeNumberList
    else
        if (input is an alphabet)
            put input into alphabetList
        else
            put input into symbolList
else
    exception("Illegal character")
```
A.  Draw a flow diagram that depicts the pseudo code. Label each node in the diagram with a unique alphabet.

B.  What is the cyclomatic number of the program?

C.  Identify each independent execution path in this program.

6.  Following is the code from the information system of Video Buster video rental company. The purpose of the following program is to calculate the fee of the rental.
```
Float calcRentalFee(Tape[] tapes, Customer customer){
    float total = 0;
    for(int I = 0; I < tapes.length; I++){
        total += tapes[I].price;
    }
    if (tapes.length > 10){
        total *= .8;
    } else if(tapes.length > 5){
        total *= .9;
    }
    if(customer.isPremium()){
        total *= .9;
    }
    return total;
}
```
A.  Using EP/BVA techniques, how many test cases are needed?

B.  How many test cases are needed to achieve 100% branch coverage?

7.  Read the program snippet in question 6.

A. Derive the test cases that achieve 100% statement coverage and branch coverage.

B. This program will throw a null pointer exception if we use null as the either of the two arguments. Do any of your test cases catch this bug?

C. From this experience, we can find that it is wise to add test cases to test the null values. This is a good rule for dirty tests. Write this finding in your notebook.

8. From question 7, we know that even if the test cases have 100% test coverage, it is still possible for the program to go wrong. Find some rules that can help software developers discover more test cases (or dirty test cases) that are useful.

9. Discuss the meaning of cyclomatic number, and why it is useful.

10. Consider the following Java code segment:

```java
public Hashtable countAlphabet(String aString){
    Hashtable table = new Hashtable();
    If (aString.length > 4000) return table;
    StringBuffer buffer = new StringBuffer(aString);
    while (buffer.length() > 0){
        String firstChar = buffer.substring(0, 1);
        Integer count = (Integer)table.get(firstChar);
        if (count == null){
            count = new Integer(1);
        } else{
            count = new Integer(count.intValue() + 1);
        }
        table.put(firstChar, count);
        buffer.delete(0, 1);
    }
    return table;
}
```

The program counts the numbers of each alphabet in a string, and put the result in a hashtable. Develop a minimum set of test cases that:

A. Guarantees that all independent execution path is exercised at least once;

B. Guarantees that both the true and false side of all logical decisions are exercised;

C. Executes the loop at the boundary values and within the boundaries.

# Automated Testing including JUnit

By automating test cases, software engineers can easily run their test cases often. In this chapter, we will explain the following:

Guidelines on when to automate test cases, considering the cost of creating the test cases

the XP test-driven development practice and the open-source JUnit tool which is used to create these automated test cases

the automation of acceptance tests, particularly with the open source FIT framework

The test practices discussed in this chapter come from the test-centric XP methodology. XP has two important test practices: test-driven development (TDD) [2] and customer acceptance testing. *Acceptance testing* is *formal testing conducted to determine whether or not a system satisfies its acceptance criteria (the criteria the system must satisfy to be accepted by a customer) and to enable the customer to determine whether or not to accept the system.* [9] In this chapter, we will discuss both of these practices along with the open source tools that are often used to support them. We will also provide an extensive code example of the practices in action. Because agile methods emphasize automating all testing, this chapter provides a good deal of information about automated testing in general.

One overriding emphasis of both TDD and acceptance testing is that the tests should be automated [5]. By automated, we mean that the tests themselves are code. The tests can then be run over and over again with very little effort, at any time, and by anyone [10]. There are three main advantages to automating tests:

Running the tests over and over again gives you *confidence* that the new work just added to the system didn't break or destabilize anything that used to work and that the new code does what it is supposed to do.

Running the tests over and over (particularly acceptance tests) can also help you understand *what portion of the desired functionality has been implemented.*

Together the set of automated tests can form a regression test suite. *Regression testing* is selective retesting of a system or component to verify that modifications have not caused unintended effects and that the system or component still complies with its specified requirements [9]. The purpose of these regression tests is to show that the software's behavior is unchanged unless it is specifically changed due to the latest software or data change [3].

When tests have to be run manually (with someone sitting at the computer typing the input on the keyboard), the execution of the manual tests and the examination of the results can be error-prone and time consuming. When schedule pressures rise, manual testing often gets forgotten. So, automating tests can be very beneficial and is emphasized in agile development.

We do, however, need to be somewhat flexible and sensible in our quest for total test automation. Automating tests can be time consuming and expensive. Writing an automated test can take several orders of magnitude more time (2X – 10X more) than executing the test by hand once [10]. Often, XP projects have at least as much test code as production code [2] and, therefore, are themselves software applications [4]. This test code needs to be maintained just as implementation code does. Debugging and handling customer complaints can also be time consuming and expensive – so there is a tradeoff between spending the time to automate tests and spending time and money on customer complaints. The benefits of automated testing include: (1) production of a reliable system, (2) improvement of the quality of the test effort, (3) reduction of the test effort and (4) minimization of the schedule [6]. We need to prudently trade off the costs and benefits of test automation.

Based on many years of building and maintaining automated unit and acceptance tests, Meszaros et al. [12] created their Test Automation Manifesto. The Manifesto contains lots of good advice to remember as you create your automated tests.

Automated tests should be:

**Concise** – Test should be as simple as possible and no simpler.

**Self Checking** – Test should report its results such that no human interpretation is necessary.

**Repeatable** – Test can be run repeatedly without human intervention.

**Robust** – Test produces same result now and forever. Tests are not affected by changes in the external environment.

**Sufficient** – Tests verify all the requirements of the software being tested.

**Necessary** – Everything in each test contributes to the specification of desired behavior.

**Clear** – Every statement is easy to understand.

**Efficient** – Tests run in a reasonable amount of time.

**Specific** – Each test failure points to a specific piece of broken functionality (e.g. each test case tests one possible point of failure).

**Independent** – Each test can be run by itself or in a suite with an arbitrary set of other tests in any order.

**Maintainable** – Tests should be easy to modify and extend.

**Traceable** – Tests should be traceable to the requirements; requirements should be traceable to the tests.

# 1  Test-Driven Development

TDD is a design and testing practice that is used by software developers as they write code. TDD is depicted in Figure 1.

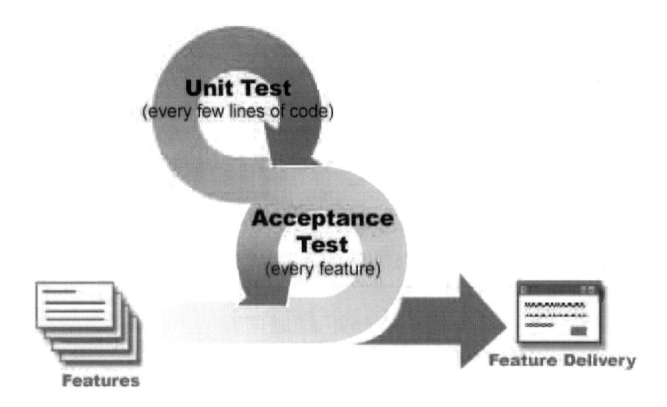

In the upper cycle of Figure 1, software engineers develop production code through rapid iterations (minute-by-minute) of the following steps :

1. Writing a small number of automated unit test cases;
2. Running these unit test cases to ensure they fail (since there is no code to run yet);
3. Implementing code that should allow the unit test cases to pass;
4. Running all the unit test cases to ensure they now pass with the new code; and
5. Restructuring the production and the test code (called refactoring, see Maintenance chapter), as necessary, to make it run better and/or to have better design.

As we said, there are rapid iterations of these five steps. In implementing some code, the programmer will often iterate steps 1 through 4 on a minute-by-minute basis. You might wonder about step 2. Why run the test cases to make sure they fail? There are three reasons why step 2 is done – all involving the unexpected event that the new test cases actually pass even though the new code hasn't been added yet:

1. there's a problem with the test, and it isn't testing what you think it is testing;
2. there's a problem with the code, and it's doing something you didn't expect it to do (it's a good idea to check this area of the code to find out what other unexpected things it's doing); and
3. maybe the code legitimately already performs the functionality correctly – and no more new code is needed (this is a good thing to know).

When programmers thoroughly follow TDD, a good set of automated unit test cases are produced. These test cases can be run over and over again – potentially multiple times each hour or at least once per day. There are three advantages to running these automated unit tests often:

The test results tell us when we inadvertently break some existing functionality [11].

You can add functions to a program or change the structure of the program without fear that you are breaking something important in the process [11]. A good set of tests will probably tell you if you break something.

Automated unit tests prevent backtracking and maintain development momentum [10].

Programmers who use TDD find these automated unit-tests very helpful when maintaining code. When a problem is found in the code (by a software tester or by the customer), the first thing the programmer does is add a unit test case that would have found that error. The programmer runs the test to make sure the code fails in a similar manner to the newly identified defect and then fixes the code until the test case passes. In this way, the programmer also learns more about the kinds of tests that need to be written for a high quality system.

Research has been done to see whether or not TDD is a good practice to follow. Two major research studies found that the TDD practice helps programmers produce higher quality systems [7, 14]. One research study found that TDD did not help to produce a higher quality system [13]. However, in this last study, the programmers involved in the study had to write all their automated unit test cases before writing any production code. Normally, TDD test cases are written in a highly iterative manner, as described above. So, these research results support the need for this rapid iteration between test and production code to achieve the best benefits of TDD.

TDD shortens the decision-code feedback loop for the developer – in which the developer makes a decision on what to do, implements the decision, and is provided with feedback on this decision. Programmers who use TDD often become "test infected" [2] and really enjoy the security they get by repeatedly running an extensive set of automated tests on their code and seeing the results.

The lower cycle of Figure 1 involves acceptance testing. Acceptance testing will be discussed more in Section 4.

## 1.1   Test and Implementation Code as Design

In XP, TDD begins without any major/formal design effort occurring beforehand. Possibly, a pair of developers will decide to brainstorm a design and will sketch it on a whiteboard or a piece of paper. Alternately, the pair will decide to do a CRC card session (perhaps including a few more teammates in the activity.) But, either of these two activities is done informally without consuming much time. For the most part, a pair of developers looks at the user story and gets started iteratively writing tests and production code to satisfy the user story. Because the creation of automated unit test cases requires that the developer know the structure of code, the developer must decide what the code will look like in order to write the test(s). For example, the programmer will have to decide what method will be called, what parameters will need to be passed to this method, and what kind of value the method will return. Through these many small decisions, the pair of developers designs the production code as part of the TDD cycles.

## 1.2 Design before TDD

Alternatively, a team can spend some time and devise a documented design before starting the TDD cycles. Then, as developers implement code, they refer to this design to incrementally write test cases and production code. The initial design will tell them what methods are called, what parameters need to be passed, and what the return values need to be. Naturally, the developer can always change the initial design as part of the TDD cycles. No matter what development methodology is used, the initial design almost never exactly matches the actual design of the code that is implemented. This is also likely the case when developers do a design prior to starting TDD.

We will do an extensive TDD example in Section 3. In this example we will use the "Design before TDD" approach.

## 2  JUnit

*Never in the field of software development was so much owed by so many to so few lines of code.* -- Martin Fowler

JUnit[7] is an award-winning open source testing framework for Java written by Erich Gamma and Kent Beck. JUnit is used for white box testing. White box testing is testing that takes into account the internal mechanism of a system or component. [9] Therefore, you must know the internal structure of the code. The framework can be used for white box testing for both unit test and integration test. It is fairly easy to learn to use JUnit because it is a Java framework. You download the framework, put it in your classpath, and create test cases by inheriting from the classes in the framework.

In the next section of this chapter, we provide an extensive example of TDD and writing test cases with JUnit. The following list summarizes the steps for creating test cases. For your reference, Figure 2 provides a class diagram of the JUnit framework. These steps are demonstrated via extensive code examples in the next section of this chapter.

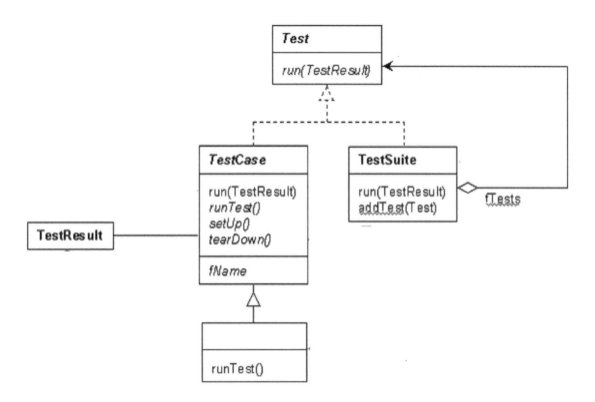

**Figure 2: UML class diagram for JUnit**

Define a subclass of TestCase. For instance, MyTest.

Override the setUp() method to initialize the object(s) and resources under test. setUp() runs before each individual test. Override the tearDown() method to release the object(s) and resources under test. tearDown() runs after each individual test. Each test runs in the context of its own fixture, calling setUp() before and tearDown() after each test method to ensure there can be no side effects among test runs.

Define one or more public testXXX() methods that exercise the object(s) under test and assert expected results. There are various forms of assert available in the tool. See Table 1 for a description of these. You will probably use assertTrue and assertEquals most often. The JUnit framework defines an error class called AssertionFailedError. All the assertion methods in the JUnit framework throw an AssertionFailedError whenever an assertion fails. The JUnit framework catches this error and reports that the test has failed. If the AssertionFailedError object has any detail about the failure, the user interface displays that information to the user. Alternatively, you can test whether the program throws an exception to verify that the test's execution path ends up inside the exception handler as expected using JUnit's fail() method.

JUnit provides both a textual and a Swing graphical user interface. Both user interfaces indicate how many tests were run, any errors or failures, and a simple completion status (a text message or a red/green bar). You specify your choice of interface in your main method. The simplicity of the user interfaces is the key to running tests quickly. You can run your tests and know the test status with a glance.

Optionally, define a static `suite()` method that creates a `TestSuite` containing all the `testXXX()` methods of `MyTest`. A `TestSuite` is a composite of other tests, either instances of `TestCase` subclasses or other `TestSuite` instances. The composite behavior of the `TestSuite` allows you to assemble test suites of tests and run all the tests automatically and uniformly to yield a single pass or fail status. Commonly, there is a one-to-one correspondence between classes in the implementation code and subclasses of `TestCase` (for example, the `Auction` class in the code hierarchy would have a corresponding `AuctionTest` class in the test code hierarchy). A `TestSuite` can be used to gather together all the `TestCase` instances and run their test cases.

**Table 1: JUnit Asserts**

| assert | Description |
|---|---|
| `assertEquals(a,b, delta)` | Asserts that a and b are equal. a and b could be Booleans, bytes, chars, doubles, floats, ints, longs, shorts, Strings, or any Java Objects. Doubles and floats require a third parameter, delta, which specifies the maximum variance under which a and b would be declared equal. |
| `assertTrue(a)` | Asserts that a Boolean condition, a, is true. |
| `assertFalse(a)` | Asserts that a Boolean condition, a, is false. |
| `assertNull(a)` | Asserts that an object, a, is null. |
| `assertNotNull(a)` | Asserts that an object, a, is not null. |
| `assertSame(a, b)` | Asserts that two objects, a and b, refer to the same object. |
| `assertNotSame (a, b)` | Asserts that two objects, a and b, do not refer to the same object. |

When you write JUnit test cases, you want to use all the white box testing strategies, such as boundary value analysis and equivalence class partitioning. You also should strive to get the maximum method, statement, branch, and condition coverage with your tests.

With automated testing, it is unnecessary to *instrument* the code. When you instrument code, you add lines of code to the program that are only intended to help in the testing – for example, adding a line that will print out a value. Instrumenting code is a concern because these extra lines of code could cause errors, affect performance, and/or may need to be commented out when testing is complete. A big advantage of the JUnit framework is that the test code is completely independent of the program being tested because it lives in a totally separate code hierarchy. Thus, you don't run the risk of introducing a bug just because you add a test.

## 3   Test-Driven Development Example

We will now go through a TDD example using our Monopoly game example to show you how JUnit works. For the example, we will use the "Design before TDD" version of TDD. We think this is an appropriate approach for this book because we want you to be able to follow our thought processes and understand where we are going.

## 3.1 Starting Point

First of all, let's have a simple starting point. What are the most essential things in a Monopoly game? The game board and the cells! After all, Monopoly is a board game. A game board has many cells, and a cell, regardless of the type (property, utility, railroad, etc.), has a name. We should be able to add cells to a game board. A cell has no reason to exist if not for the game board, so their interrelationship is a composition. This seems good enough to get started. Figure 3 is a UML class diagram that depicts the idea.

**Figure 3: A starting point of the Monopoly game**

Let's write a test for the game board. This test should be just enough to show our design.

```
public class GameboardTest extends TestCase {
    public GameboardTest(String name) {
        super(name);
    }

    public void testAddCell() {
        GameBoard gameboard = new GameBoard();
        assertEquals(0, gameboard.getCellNumber());
        Cell cell = new Cell();
        gameboard.addCell(cell);
        assertEquals(1, gameboard.getCellNumber());
    }
}
```

The test shows that when a game board is initialized, it has no cell. After we add a cell to the game board, it'll have one cell. The test does not pass the compiler because we do not have the GameBoard and the Cell classes created yet. From the class diagram, we want an addCell method in GameBoard, and a name attribute in Cell. From the test, we see that we need a method to get the number of cells from a GameBoard. We can write these two classes:

```
public class GameBoard {
    public void addCell(Cell cell) {
    }

    public int getCellNumber() {
        return 0;
```

```
        }
}
public class Cell {
      private String name;

      public String getName() {
            return this.name;
      }

      public void setName(String name) {
            this.name = name;
      }
}
```

The initial purpose of writing these two classes is just to pass the compiler. We can compile the program now. If we run thee test, we can see that we can pass the first assertion, but not the second one. This is because we simply return 0 in getCellNumber of GameBoard. We need to use some data structure to store the cells. We use ArrayList here, because the cells should be put in an ordered list. We don't want the cells to change their orders in the middle of a game. Therefore, GameBoard can be implemented as:

```
public class GameBoard {
      ArrayList cells = new ArrayList();

      public void addCell(Cell cell) {
            cells.add(cell);
      }

      public int getCellNumber() {
            return cells.size();
      }
}
```

We pass the first test now. Let's move on to the next step.

## 3.2   Let the Game Begin

We have a game board, and we can add cells to the game board. What is missing if we want to play the game? The players! Look at the requirements and find some requirements that are related to players. We start with the three requirements that seem to be easy:

1.  Before the game begins, one player shall enter the number of players and the names of the players.
2.  At the beginning of the game, all the players shall be at the Go cell.
3.  The players shall move based on the dice roll. When the player reaches the last cell of the game board, he shall cycle around the board and start from the Go cell again.

Even with these three "easy" requirements, we have some design considerations.

1.  What takes care of the players? Adding the players to the game board should work, but can we say that a game board has some players? It does not sound right. Therefore, we decided to create a new class to manage the players. We gave this class a cool name: the GameMaster.
2.  There is always only one GameMaster in the game. We can use a design pattern and make it a

94

singleton.

3. It is reasonable to let the GameMaster to move the players on the game board. Therefore, the GameMaster should have the knowledge of the players and the game board.

4. From the requirement, the Go cell is indispensable. When a game board is created, there should already be one Go cell.

5. What puts the players at the Go cell at the beginning of the game? Since there is guaranteed to be a Go cell in a game board, we decided to put a player at the Go cell as soon as the player instance is created.

6.  We created a simple game board so that we could test the player's movement. The simple game board looks like Figure 4. To simplify the situation, there are only a Go cell and five different property cells.  While later we can test with a more "realistic" game board – it is good to write the simplest test cases that can force the conditions we want to occur.  This Simple Game Board does that for us.

What is the difference between the Go cell and a property cell? Well, they are totally different cells actually, except that they both have names. Thus, we decided to make the Go cell and the property cell subclasses of the Cell class.

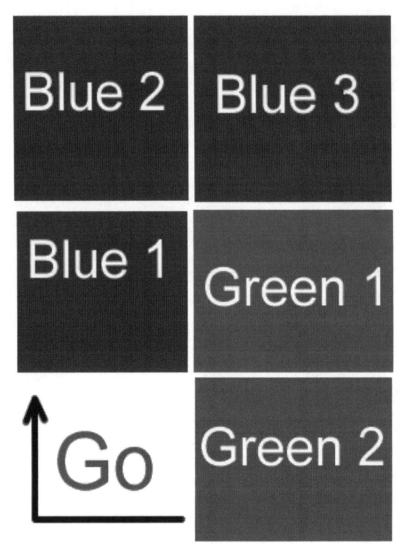

**Figure 4: The Simple Game Board**

These ideas are summarized in the UML class diagram in Figure 5. The rest of the JUnit example will show how to apply TDD to develop a system that satisfies these three requirements.

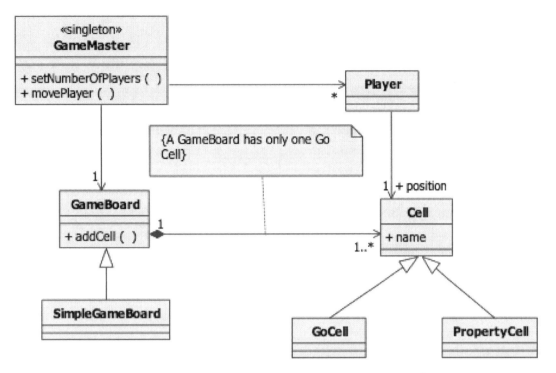

**Figure 5: System Design – Introducing GameMaster and Player.**

## *The One and Only GameMaster*

We want to apply the singleton design pattern to the GameMaster class. Singleton means there can be only one instance of this class. Whenever we request an instance from the singleton class, we will always get the same instance. We write our intent in a test case:

```
public class GameMasterTest extends TestCase{
    public void testSingleton() {
        GameMaster instance1 = GameMaster.instance();
        assertNotNull(instance1);
        GameMaster instance2 = GameMaster.instance();
        assertNotNull(instance2);
        assertSame(instance1, instance2);
    }
}
```

We need to create the GameMaster class, and also a static method instance, to make the test case compile. We may start this with a code skeleton for GameMaster:

```
public class GameMaster {
    public static GameMaster instance() {
        return null;
    }
}
```

Because we only return null in the instance method, we cannot pass the test case. There is a standard way to implement the singleton pattern in Java: create a static member for the singleton instance, and use lazy instantiation to initialize the instance. We modified GameMaster so that the singleton instance is always returned:

```
public class GameMaster {
      static private GameMaster singleton;

      public static GameMaster instance() {
            if(singleton == null) {
                  singleton = new GameMaster();
            }
            return singleton;
      }
}
```

The test passes, and we have a singleton instance of the GameMaster.

## *The Go Cell*

At this moment, the only thing special about the Go cell is that the name of the cell is always Go. We cannot change the name of the Go cell. We may do so by setting the name of the Go cell in GoCell's constructor, and override setName method so that this method does nothing:

```
public class GoCell extends Cell {
      public GoCell() {
            super.setName("Go");
      }

      void setName(String name) {
      }
}
```

The implementation is so easy that we do not even bother to write a test. Usually, we do not need to write tests for the accessor (getters and setters).

In our design, the game board has a Go cell when it is created. We need to modify the GameboardTest to show this. We also need to add a new test to make sure that the first cell is the Go cell.

```
public class GameboardTest extends TestCase {
      :
      public void testAddCell() {
            GameBoard gameboard = new GameBoard();
            assertEquals(1, gameboard.getCellNumber());
            Cell cell = new Cell();
            gameboard.addCell(cell);
            assertEquals(2, gameboard.getCellNumber());
      }

      public void testFirstCell() {
            GameBoard gameboard = new GameBoard();
```

```
        Cell firstCell = gameboard.getCell(0);
        assertSame(GoCell.class, firstCell.getClass());
    }
}
```

The compiler tells us that we need a getCell method for GameBoard. No problem:

```
public class GameBoard {
        :
    public Cell getCell(int index) {
        return (Cell)cells.get(index);
    }
}
```

Although we can compile the code now, we cannot pass the test. JUnit reports that testAddCell has an assertion error, and testFirstCell has an index out of bound exception. The reason for these errors is that the game board has no cell when it is created. We want the game board to have a Go cell when it is created. We can put the code in the constructor of GameBoard:

```
public class GameBoard {
    public GameBoard() {
        addCell(new GoCell());
    }
        :
}
```

Now the game board has a Go cell when instantiated. What about PropertyCell? For this time being, the PropertyCell does not have any special behaviors. Just making it a subclass of Cell is good enough:

```
public class PropertyCell extends Cell {
}
```

One may argue that we need a more detailed test for adding a new cell. When several cells are added to a game board, shouldn't we write a test to make sure that these cells are added in order? Looking at addCell method in GameBoard, we can see that it only calls a method of ArrayList. If we write a test to see that the cells are added in order, whether the test will pass depends on the correct implementation of ArrayList. This is not our intension. This is another example of unnecessary test.

## SimpleGameBoard

SimpleGameBoard is a subclass of GameBoard. It does not have additional methods or member variables. However, several cells are created and added to the game board when a new instance of SimpleGameBoard is created. The code of SimpleGameBoard is listed below. There is nothing worthy of testing in SimpleGameBoard since we already tested all that functionality before.

```
public class SimpleGameBoard extends GameBoard {
      public SimpleGameBoard() {
            super();
            Cell blue1 = new PropertyCell();
            Cell blue2 = new PropertyCell();
            :

            blue1.setName("Blue 1");
            blue2.setName("Blue 2");
            :

            addCell(blue1);
            addCell(blue2);
            :
      }
}
```

## The Player

Figure , the class diagram, shows that the player knows his or her position. Let's create the Player class, with a member variable and the accessors:

```
public class Player {
      private Cell position;

      public Cell getPosition() {
            return this.position;
      }

      public void setPosition(Cell newPosition) {
            this.position = newPosition;
      }
}
```

Again, we don't need to write tests for the accessors. However, we do need a test to show that when a player is created, the position is at the Go cell:

```
public class PlayerTest extends TestCase {
      public PlayerTest(String name) {
            super(name);
      }

      public void testStartPosition() {
            GameBoard board = new SimpleGameBoard();
            GameMaster.instance().setGameBoard(board);
            Player player1 = new Player();
            Player player2 = new Player();
            Cell go = board.getCell(0);
            assertSame(go, player1.getPosition());
            assertSame(go, player2.getPosition());
      }
}
```

First of all, the `GameMaster` needs a method to set up the game board:

```
public class GameMaster {
      :
      private GameBoard gameBoard;
      :
      public void setGameBoard(GameBoard board) {
            this.gameBoard = board;
      }
}
```

This test fails, because the players' positions are both null. We can initialize the player's position in the constructor of the `Player` class:

```
public class Player {
      :
      public Player() {
            position = GameMaster.instance().getGameBoard().getCell(0);

      }
}
```

The test passes now. This means when we create a new instance of `Player`, the position of the player is set to the Go cell (cell 0) of the current game board.

One of the requirements states that at the beginning of the game, the players shall enter the number of players. In our design, the players are initialized when calling `setNumberOfPlayers` on the `GameMaster`. We can write a test to show that after this call, we will have exactly the same number of players, all of which are at the Go cell.

```
public class GameMasterTest extends TestCase{
      :
      public void testPlayerInit() {
          master = GameMaster.instance();
          master.setGameBoard(new SimpleGameBoard());
          master.setNumberOfUsers(6);
          assertEquals(6, master.getNumberOfPlayers());
          Cell go = master.getGameBoard().getCell(0);
          for (int i = 0; i < 6; i++) {
              Player player = master.getPlayer(i);
              assertSame(go, player.getPosition());
          }
      }
}
```

The compiler is complaining about the missing methods. We need to add those methods to `GameMaster` to pass the compiler:

```
public class GameMaster {
      :
      public void setNumberOfPlayers(int number) {
      }

      public int getNumberOfPlayers() {
            return 0;
      }

      public Player getPlayer(int index) {
            return null;
      }
}
```

Again, this is just a code skeleton. It helps us pass the compiler. Since there is no real implementation in the code, the test fails. We need to think about how we may store the players in the game master. The players should be stored in order, so ArrayList would be a nice choice. When setting up the number of players, we can simply create several instances of Player and put them in the ArrayList. We may also get the number of players or query a player via an index from the ArrayList.

```
public class GameMaster {
      private ArrayList players;
      :
      public void setNumberOfPlayers(int number) {
            players = new ArrayList(number);
            for(int i = 0; i < number; i++) {
                  Player player = new Player();
                  players.add(player);
            }
      }

      public int getNumberOfPlayers() {
            return players.size();
      }

      public Player getPlayer(int index) {
            return (Player)players.get(index);
      }
}
```

The test passes. We now can specify the number of players, and these players are put at the Go cell. Finally, we are ready to deal with the player movement.

## Test Makes the Players Go Round

We have a game board. We have players. It's time to move the players. To make the example simpler, we will just write test cases to move a single player. First, let's consider the case in which the player does not reach the end of the game board:

```
public class GameMasterTest extends TestCase{
    :
    public void testMovePlayerSimple() {
        master = GameMaster.instance();
        master.setGameBoard(new SimpleGameBoard());
        master.setNumberOfUsers(1);
        Player player = master.getPlayer(0);
        master.movePlayer(0, 2);
        assertEquals("Blue 2", player.getPosition.getName());
        master.movePlayer(0, 3);
        assertEquals("Green 2", player.getPosition.getName());
    }
}
```

Because the player's movement is based on the dice roll, we put two parameters for movePlayer method. The first one is the index of the player; the second the value of the dice role. In this test, we move the first player two steps forward, and check if it lands on Blue 2; and then we move him three steps further, and check if it lands on Green 2. We need to add this method to make the test compile:

```
public class GameMaster {
    :
    public void movePlayer(int playerIndex, int diceRoll) {
    }
}
```

After the program compiles OK, we may run the test. We have not written anything in movePlayer, so the player always stays at the Go cell. Therefore, the test fails. How do we move the player? We can think of a straightforward algorithm:

Find out the player's position. (GameMaster can find out a player with an index. The player knows its position.)

Find out the index of the cell the player is in. (GameBoard has the knowledge. However, it doesn't have an interface for this.)

Add the index with the dice roll value. The result is the index of the cell the player is moving to.

Find the cell object with the index from step 3. (GameBoard already has an interface for this, the getCell method.)

Set the position of the player to the cell object.

The only missing piece in this algorithm is that we cannot find out the index of a certain cell. GameBoard knows all the cells, so it must know the index of every cell. We just need to add a method. With TDD, of course, we need to write a test first.

```
public class GameboardTest extends TestCase {
    :
    public void testGetCellIndex() {
```

```
                GameBoard gameBoard = new SimpleGameBoard();
                Cell blue2 = gameBoard.getCell(2);
                Int index = gameBoard.getCellIndex(blue2);
                assertEquals(2, index);
                Cell notExist = new Cell();
                Index = gameBoard.getCellIndex(notExist);
                assertEquals(-1, index);
        }
}
```

In this test, we not only state that GameBoard should have getCellIndex method, but also specify the behavior of this method. If the cell is found, the index is returned. However, if the cell is not found, the method returns -1. Actually this is easy if we are familiar with the ArrayList API:[8]

```
public class GameBoard {
        :
        public int getCellIndex(Cell cell) {
                return cells.indexOf(cell);
        }
}
```

Then we can finish the movePlayer method for GameMaster:

```
public class GameMaster {
        :
        public void movePlayer(int playerIndex, int diceRoll) {
                Player player = getPlayer(playerIndex);
                Cell playerPosition = player.getPosition();
                int oldIndex = gameBoard.getCellIndex(playerPosition);
                int newIndex = oldIndex + diceRoll;
                Cell newPosition = gameBoard.getCell(newIndex);
                player.setPosition(newPosition);
        }
}
```

We pass the test! However, we have not finished yet. When a player reaches the end of the game board, he or she shall cycle around. Let's write a test to test this situation:

```
public class GameMasterTest extends TestCase{
        :
        public void testMovePlayerCycle() {
                master = GameMaster.instance();
                master.setGameBoard(new SimpleGameBoard());
                master.setNumberOfUsers(1);
                Player player = master.getPlayer(0);
                master.movePlayer(0, 2);
                master.movePlayer(0, 5);
                assertEquals("Blue 1", player.getPosition.getName());
        }
}
```

In this test, we move the player two steps then five steps. The player should reach the end of the game board, and then start again from the Go cell, and finally land on Blue 1. When we try to run the test, we will run into an array index out of bound exception. This is because the value of the new index is 7, and there is no $8^{th}$ cell in the game board. We need to modify `movePlayer` in `GameMaster` to pass this test:

```
public class GameMaster {
    :
    public void movePlayer(int playerIndex, int diceRoll) {
        :
        int newIndex =
                (oldIndex + diceRoll) % gameBoard.getCellNumber();
        :
    }
}
```

Run the test again, and we can see that the implementation passes the test. Do we need to care about the situation when the player's position is not found on the game board? No, because it is not possible.

Looking at the `GameMasterTest`, we can see some repeated code to initialize the `GameMaster`. We can use the `setUp` method to remove the repetition. The `setUp` method is called before each test method is called. There is a similar method called `tearDown`. However, `tearDown` is called after each test method is called. It is usually used to free the resources that are allocated in `setUp` (such as file handle, network connection, or database connection). In this example, we do not allocate any resource in `setUp`, so `tearDown` is not needed. After the cleaning up, `GameMasterTest` looks like this:

```
public class GameMasterTest extends TestCase{
    GameMaster master;

    public void setUp() {
        master = GameMaster.instance();
        master.setGameBoard(new SimpleGameBoard());
    }
    :

    public void testPlayerInit() {
        master.setNumberOfUsers(6);
        assertEquals(6, master.getNumberOfPlayers());
        :
    }

    public void testMovePlayerSimple() {
        master.setNumberOfUsers(1);
        Player player = master.getPlayer(0);
        :
    }

    public void testMovePlayerCycle() {
        master.setNumberOfUsers(1);
        Player player = master.getPlayer(0);
        :
    }
}
```

## *What Have We Here?*

Let's take a look at what we have so far. Figure 6 shows the class diagram. The blue classes are test cases. Their super class, TestCase, is now shown in this diagram. Accessor methods are now shown in this diagram.

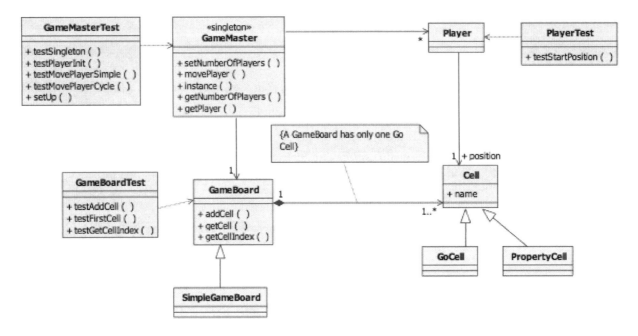

**Figure 6: A Snap Shot of Current System**

## 4. Acceptance Testing

Acceptance tests are black box test cases that are jointly written by a developer and a customer. An acceptance test is a concrete situation, or scenario, that the system might encounter when using the functionality of a user story. When an acceptance test case runs properly, this lets the customer know that the user story has been properly implemented – at least for the scenarios defined in the acceptance tests. Customers are generally not software engineers so they don't understand about equivalence class partitioning, boundary value analysis, test coverage, or the like. They usually provide one very basic "success" test case based on the requirements. So we must not take the acceptance test cases written by the customer as the only black box test cases we run. We must write all those test cases that test all the different combinations of bad and good things that users of our software might try to do.

Acceptance tests have the same four parts as all black box test cases: a test ID; a description that describes the preconditions of the test and the steps of the test; the expected results of running the test; and the actual results of running the test.

The dialog between the customer and the developer when the acceptance test cases are created usually leads to the discussion of many details about the user story – details the developer needs

106

to know about what is entailed in the user story. The conversation also helps the development team to understand how difficult a simple user story can get [1].

With XP, the progress of a development effort is often tracked by the number of acceptance test cases that run successfully. Additionally, in XP there is an emphasis on *automating* the acceptance test cases so that they can be run many times as the functionality of the program grows. We always want to have a level of confidence that the new functionality we just added did not break any of the functionality that used to work. Running the automated acceptance test cases often can help us do that.

A recommended tool for automating acceptance test of web applications is HttpUnit.[9]

## Summary

Several practical tips for automated test were presented throughout this chapter. The keys for successful automated test are summarized in Table 3.

**Table 3 Key Ideas for Automated Test**

| | |
|---|---|
| 🔑 | Download and learn to use the JUnit and the HttpUnit testing frameworks. If you don't code in Java, these tools are available for other languages. |
| 🔑 | Running automatic tests often will help you see if your new code broke any existing functionality. Collect all the tests from the entire time for the entire code base. Run these tests often – at least once per day. |
| 🔑 | Use the "key ideas" in black box testing and white box testing from prior chapters to create your automated tests. |
| 🔑 | In automating tests, consider the advice in the Test Automation Manifesto. |
| 🔑 | When a defect is found in your code, add automated tests to reveal the defect. Then, fix the defect and re-run the automated tests to make sure they all pass now. |
| 🔑 | Work with your customer to create acceptance tests – then automate them. You can use the number (or percent) of acceptance test cases that pass as the means of determining the progress of your project. |

The XP software development method uses two forms of automated testing -- white box unit tests that support the TDD practice and black box acceptance tests. In this chapter, you learned how to create both of these types of automated test cases. You can use these techniques and tools to develop automated tests in any software development process. These tests can help you identify defects in your code, can be used to ensure new changes don't cause problems with previously-working code, and can be used to help track project status. Remember that writing automated tests can be expensive, so be reasonable with the investment you make in automated tests.

**Glossary of Chapter Terms**

| Word | Definition | Source |
|---|---|---|
| acceptance test | formal testing conducted to determine whether or not a system satisfies its acceptance criteria (the criteria the system must satisfy to be accepted by a customer) and to enable the customer to determine whether or not to accept the system | [9] |
| mock object | debug replacement for a real-world object | [8] |
| regression testing | selective retesting of a system or component to verify that modifications have not caused unintended effects and that the system or component still complies with its specified requirements | [9] |
| white box testing | testing that takes into account the internal mechanism of a system or component | [9] |

# References

[1]    D. Astels, G. Miller, and M. Novak, *A Practical Guide to Extreme Programming*. Upper Saddle River, NJ: Prentice Hall, 2002.

[2]    K. Beck, *Test Driven Development -- by Example*. Boston: Addison Wesley, 2003.

[3]    B. Beizer, *Software Testing Techniques*. London: International Thompson Computer Press, 1990.

[4]    R. D. Craig and S. P. Jaskiel, *Systematic Software Testing*. Norwood, MA: Artech House, 2002.

[5]    L. Crispen and T. House, *Testing Extreme Programming*. Boston, MA: Addison Wesley Pearson Education, 2003.

[6]    E. Dustin, J. Rashka, and J. Paul, *Automated Software Testing*. Reading, Massachusetts: Addison Wesley, 1999.

[7]    B. George and L. Williams, "A Structured Experiment of Test-Driven Development," *Information and Software Technology (IST)*, vol. 46, no. 5, pp. 337-342, 2003.

[8]    A. Hunt and D. Thomas, *Pragmatic Unit Testing in Java with JUnit*. Raleigh, NC: The Pragmatic Bookshelf, 2003.

[9]    IEEE, "IEEE Standard 610.12-1990, IEEE Standard Glossary of Software Engineering Terminology," 1990.

[10]   C. Kaner, J. Bach, and B. Pettichord, *Lessons Learned in Software Testing*. New York: John Wiley and Sons, Inc., 2002.

[11]   R. C. Martin, *Agile Software Development: Principles, Patterns, and Practices*. Upper Saddle River, NJ: Prentice Hall, 2003.

[12]   G. Meszaros, S. M. Smith, and J. Andrea, "The Test Automation Manifesto," in *Extreme Programming and Agile Methods -- XP/Agile Universe 2003, Lncs 2753*, F. Maurer and D. Wells, Eds. Berlin: Springer, 2003.

[13]   M. M. Müller and O. Hagner, "Experiment about Test-first Programming," Conference on Empirical Assessment in Software Engineering (EASE), 2002, pp.

[14]   L. Williams, E. M. Maximilien, and M. Vouk, "Test-Driven Development as a Defect-Reduction Practice," IEEE International Symposium on Software Reliability Engineering, Denver, CO, 2003, pp. 34-45.

# Static Analysis

Static analysis is an important technique for removing certain types of defects prior to the software testing phase. In this chapter, we will explain the following:

> the basics of static analysis
>
> the capabilities of static analysis tools that automate static analysis
>
> the types of defects that are likely to be found by a static analysis tool

*Static analysis* is *the process of evaluating a system or component based on its form, structure, content, or documentation* [4], which does not require program execution. Inspections are an example of a classic static analysis technique; *inspections* are a *static analysis technique that relies on the visual examination of development products to detect errors, violations of development standards, and other problems* [4]. Tools are increasingly being used to automate the identification of anomalies that can be removed via static analysis, such as coding standard non-compliance, uncaught runtime exceptions, redundant code, inappropriate use of variables, division by zero, and potential memory leaks. The use of static analysis tools can be thought of as an automated code inspection. By using a static analysis tool, software engineers may be able to fix faults before they surface more publicly in inspections or as test and/or customer-reported failures – or, in the case of students, before these faults surface as problems in your project which result in a lower grade.

Complementary to static analysis is a practice known as dynamic analysis. *Dynamic analysis* is *the process of evaluating a system or component based on it behavior during execution* whereby static analysis does not involve execution. Dynamic analysis includes all types of testing techniques. Because analysis is achieved without actually running any code and automated testing focuses entirely on results the code achieves when running, it may be tempting to think of the two methodologies as opposites. This is not accurate. As will be discussed below, static and dynamic analysis find different types of defects [9] so including both in your development process is important.

## 1 Introduction and Background

Static analysis can be thought of as a spell/grammar checker for your code (see *Figs. 1a & 1b*). Spell checkers parse through the text of a word processing document and compare the language with known grammar rules and a dictionary to find possible errors. Any good spell checker will also make suggestions for how to improve various sentences' structures even when the sentences are perfectly legal from a grammatical standpoint.

110

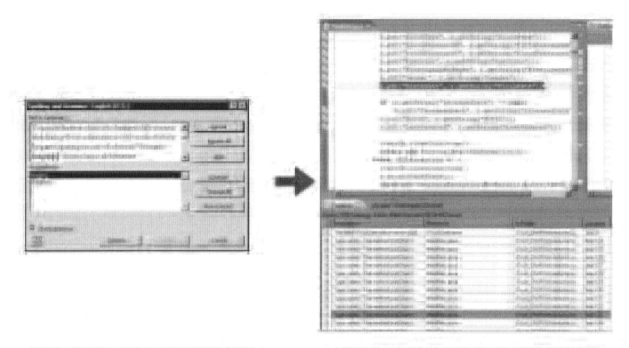

**Figure 1.1a: A Common Spell Checker**     **Figure 1.1b: Static Analysis with FindBugs**

A static analysis tool will "do spellcheck" on your code. A spell checker has a set of grammar patterns that are wrong and will flag a word processing document that contains these errors as well as occurrences of words that do not appear in the dictionary. Similarly, a static analysis will parse through your code, comparing each class definition to its set of bug patterns. A *bug pattern* is a *code idiom that is likely to be an error; occurrences of bug patterns are places where code does not follow usual correct practice in the use of a language feature* [3].

Have you ever had an experience with a spell/grammar checker that told you a word (such as a name) was spelled wrong, but you knew it was right? Well, the spell/grammar checker identified a false positive. A *false positive* happens when *a test incorrectly reports that it has found a positive result where none really exists* [7]. Unfortunately, current static analysis tools can give a significant number of false positives. Active research is taking place to reduce the number of false positives found by the tool. Often, static analysis tools can be customized and filters can be established so that certain classes of faults are not reported, reducing the number of false positives. But, it is better to have been warned about the possibility of a fault and after inspection, realize it is not a fault, than to be suffering the error and not knowing where it could come from.

## 2   But Why?

In automated testing of an application, the programmer writes code to check the source of the application. The results of an automated test frequently come down to a Boolean statement: Does the application produce the expected results? Static analysis is an excellent addition to your code reviewing arsenal because it contains a method that is a bit more robust than true or false.

Static analysis has the added benefit of not being as biased toward your system. One's own understanding of how the system being created works can influence him or her not to test for a particular error due to thoughts such as "Well, it will never happen that way." The bug patterns that static analysis tools look for have been gathered by developer's who have spent a long time analyzing code for the most frequently-occurring defects and have put patterns for them into the set that the tools look for.

With development kits that are as helpful as the compiler and automated software testing methods such as JUnit/test-driven development [1], one may wonder what the purpose of a tool that searches for simple and obvious fault is. The compiler already acts as a proofreader in its own right. When a resource such as a Java source code file compiled, it and feeds back all of the compile-time errors and even warnings to the console. What can static analysis offer that the warnings coming from the compiler do not? In the next section, we look at a couple of examples of errors that static analysis will catch that the Java compiler will not.

## 3 Examples

The example in Figure 2.1 is a demonstration of a common error programmers can run into when writing their first program dealing with Strings or human-readable text.

```
String a = "very similar strings";
String b = "very similar strings.";
if (a == b)
        //do something
```

**Figure 2.1: A Fault (not so) Easily Caught**

In the conditional, the programmer is trying to see if the two strings are equivalent—that is, if they contain the same sequence of characters. The semantics of the Java language, however, do not allow String content comparison with the == operator, because this operator is meant for dealing with *reference equivalence*. If the programmer were trying to determine if the references a and b both pointed to the same object in memory, this statement would be the one to use. However, since the goal is to determine if these two String objects **contain the same data**, the statement to use is if (a.equals(b)). This mistake would not be caught by the basic code checking features of the Java Development Environment because it is not a statement that requires a warning, nor is it syntactically incorrect! However, the use of == for string equivalence is a bug pattern caught by many static analysis tools.

An example of an error that is harder to catch is in Figure 2.2

```
int a = 3;
int b = 4;
if (a = b)
        //do something...
```

**Figure 2.2: A Less Obvious Error**

The programmer probably meant to write a == b for the if conditional, but there is nothing syntactically or otherwise wrong with the if statement as it stands. The code will compile and execute perfectly—the only problem is that every time the if statement is executed, a **will be set to equal** b and the condition will be true. When testing the code, the developer will discover that there is definitely something wrong with its behavior, but he or she may have a difficult time figuring out where the error occurred. Both examples are easily caught, of course, but try to imagine how many times it or something like it has happened to you.

The previous figures demonstrate two specific examples of faults. The most powerful ability of static analysis automation is that rather than looking for **one instance** of the formation of an idiom that is likely to be a fault, automation allows your favorite static analysis tool to search your code for **every** possible variation on the idiom that can be constructed. Thus, resulting in a *bug pattern*. In the example associated with Figure 2.2, for instance, the variable names could be different, the variables could have been declared on a different line of code or in a different class, the variables could **be** classes, the programmer may have not indented the line within the conditional or the programmer may have been using a while conditional instead of if. No matter what the surrounding code is, this example will be caught because it matches the pattern.

The authors of a commonly-used, open source static analysis tool FindBugs [3], have listed three reasons why obvious faults occur (in Java) and why you should use static analysis tools to catch them before they catch you:

    Everyone makes dumb mistakes
    Java offers many opportunities for latent bugs
    Programming with threads is harder than people think

## 4 An Example Static Analysis Tool Implementation

FindBugs[10] uses the following methods to check code for possible errors:

> **Class Structure and Inheritance Hierarchy**: this strategy looks at the hierarchy of classes in the project without looking at the code in the classes.
> **Linear Code Scan**: a linear scan of the bytecode is made, and a state machine is made of visited instructions.
> **Control Sensitive**: a control flow graph is made of the program, and the patterns are compared to the control flow graph. A control flow graph is a graph of all possible paths through the program.
> **Dataflow**: these patterns use the control flow and dataflow graphs generated from analyzing the program. A dataflow graph looks at when data is created, used, and destroyed.

These methods are executed using the Visitor pattern (see *Fig. 3.1*). The object code files for the Java classes you implement follow the pattern by allowing the Visitor to examine each object type's definition. The structure of each is then compared with patterns of known errors.

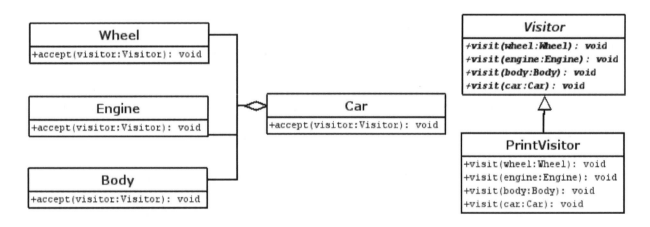

**Figure 3.1: The Visitor Pattern [7]**

The resulting execution finds six types of vulnerabilities:
>    correctness
>    internationalization
>    malicious code vulnerabilities
>    multithreaded correctness

performance
style

# 5  Different Types of Faults

After your first experience with static analysis, you may think that with proper rigorous testing and static analysis tool in place, you will be able to smite every fault in your code. This is not the case. While these tools are an excellent addition to the set, they do not cover everything—in fact, it is recommended that it is best to use more than one static analysis tool, because they will each catch something the others do not [6]. And, there is a range of programmer errors that can never be detected by any static analysis [5, 8] – so don't feel overly secure and continue with other validation and verification techniques.

Additionally, a static analysis study was conducted at Nortel Networks [9]. The faults found by static analysis and inspections and the test and customer-reported failures were counted and classified. Data analysis consisted of faults reported by over 200 inspectors and testers, and by customers, for over three million LOC written in C/C++. The classification scheme used was IBM's Orthogonal Defect Classification (ODC) [2]. The goal of ODC is to categorize defects such that each defect type is associated with a specific stage of development. ODC has eight defect types. Each defect type is intended to point to the part of the development process that needs attention. The relationship between these defect types and process associations are shown in Table 1, which adapted from [2]. Therefore, the ODC scheme can be used to indicate the development phase in which a defect was injected into the system.

**Table 1: ODC Defect Types and Process Associations, adapted from [2]**

| Process Association | Defect Type |
|---|---|
| Design | Function |
| Low Level Design | Interface, Checking, Timing/Serialization, Algorithm |
| Code | Checking, Assignment |
| Library Tools | Build/Package/Merge |
| Publications | Documentation |

The results indicate that static analysis tools predominantly identify two ODC defect types: Checking and Assignment – which would most likely be injected in the coding phase. Approximately 90% of all the faults identified by inspection belong to Algorithm, Documentation, and Checking faults. A large majority of test/customer-reported failures is in Function and Algorithm types.

**Table 12: Mapping of defects found by different filters to ODC defect types [adapted from [9]]**

| Defect Type | Static analysis tools (%) | Inspection (%) | Test (%) | Customer (%) |
|---|---|---|---|---|
| Function | 0 | 1.09 | **55.73** | **69.70** |
| Assignment | **72.27** | 4.37 | 3.82 | 0 |
| Interface | 0 | 0.87 | 0.20 | 0 |
| Checking | **27.73** | **20.52** | 0.80 | 0 |
| Timing/ Serialization | 0 | 0 | 0 | 0 |
| Build/Package/Merge | 0 | 1.77 | 1.81 | 0 |
| Documentation | 0 | **35.37** | 0 | 0 |
| Algorithm | 0 | **36.03** | **37.63** | **30.30** |

The bottom line is that it is prudent to use several different static analysis tools on your code and to continue with the full range of validation and verification techniques to get the most faults out of your code.

## 6   Summary

Several main ideas about static analysis were presented throughout this chapter. They are summarized in Table 1.

| | |
|---|---|
| 🔑 | Static analysis is to your code as a spell checker is to a word processing document. |
| 🔑 | Static analysis looks at your system's source code without executing it. |
| 🔑 | Everyone makes dumb mistakes, and static analysis tools are useful for catching them before they become really serious problems. |

| | Whereas automated testing is managed and created by the team itself, static analysis is based on a set of bug patterns that have been determined by a much larger group of programmers. |
|---|---|
| | Static analysis tools do not all look for the same errors—the use of more than one on a given system is highly recommended! |
| | Though tools for performing static analysis have a high rate of false positives, it is better to have a false positive than to not know about the fault. |

**Table 1: Key Ideas for Chapter**

## Glossary of Chapter Terms

| Term | Definition | Source |
|---|---|---|
| bug pattern | a code idiom that is likely to be an error; occurrences of bug patterns are places where code does not follow usual correct practice in the use of a language feature | [3] |
| dynamic analysis | The process of evaluating a system or component based on it behavior during execution. | [4] |
| false positive | A test incorrectly reports that it has found a positive result where none really exists. | [7] |
| inspection | static analysis technique that relies on the visual examination of development products to detect errors, violations of development standards, and other problems | [4] |
| object code | Computer instructions and data definitions in a form output by an assembler or compiler. | [4] |

| source code | Computer instructions and data definitions expressed in a form suitable for input to an assembler, compiler or other translator. | [4] |
|---|---|---|
| static analysis | the process of evaluating a system or component based on its form, structure, content, or documentation | [4] |

## References:

[1]    K. Beck, *Test Driven Development -- by Example*. Boston: Addison Wesley, 2003.

[2]    R. Chillarege, I. Bhandari, J. Chaar, M. Halliday, D. Moebus, B. Ray, and M. Wong, "Orthogonal Defect Classification -- A Concept for In-Process Measurements," *IEEE Transactions on Software Engineering*, vol. 18, no. 11, November 1992, pp. 943-956.

[3]    D. Hovemeyer and W. Pugh, "Finding Bugs is Easy," Conference on Object Oriented Programming Systems Languages and Applications (OOSPLA) Companion, Vancouver, BC, 2004 pp. 132-135.

[4]    IEEE, "IEEE Standard 610.12-1990, IEEE Standard Glossary of Software Engineering Terminology," 1990.

[5]    L. Osterweil (Eds.), *Integrating the Testing, Analysis, and Debugging of Programs*. North Holland: Elsevier Science Publishers, 1984.

[6]    N. Rutar, C. B. Almazan, and J. S. Foster, "A Comparison of Bug Finding Tools for Java," IEEE International Symposium on Software Reliability Engineering (ISSRE), St. Malo, France, 2004 pp. 245-256.

[7]    Wikipedia, "http://www.wikipedia.org/," no.

[8]    M. Young and R. N. Taylor, "Rethinking the taxonomy of fault detection techniques," International Conference on Software Engineering, Pittsburgh, Penn., 1989 pp. 53-62.

[9]    J. Zheng, L. Williams, W. Snipes, N. Nagappan, J. Hudepohl, and M. Vouk, "On the Value of Static Analysis Tools for Fault Detection," *IEEE Transactions on Software Engineering*, vol. 32, no. 4, 2006, pp. 240-253.

## Chapter Questions

1.  True or False: Static Analysis is accomplished using the Visitor pattern?

2.  True or False: Static Analysis and Automated Testing are counter opposite tools?

3.  How is static analysis like a spell checker?

4.  List three reasons static analysis should be used on your software project.

5.  If compilation of your program results in only a few warnings from the JDK, why should you run static analysis on it anyway?

6.  What is a bug pattern and how is it used?

7.  Name two of the vulnerabilities that FindBugs, a static analyzer, finds in software projects.

8.  How does your quality assurance manager exert a bias over the tests he or she writes for the software project?

9.  [Exercise] Go to the FindBugs bugs descriptions page (`http://findbugs.sourceforge.net/bugDescriptions.html`), and find a bug description that you like. Write a source code example that would be caught by this bug pattern.

# Requirements Engineering and Elicitation

This chapter gives an overall introduction to that part of the software development process in which you begin to learn what your customer needs built and why. In this chapter, we will explain the following:

    the definition of requirements engineering

    the different types of requirements

    how to gather requirements

    the components of a Software Requirements Specification

    strategies for managing requirements changing throughout development

Two college students walked out of their last final exam of a long, hard semester. They wanted to celebrate, but it was only 11:00 AM. A nice breakfast was the answer! They walked into a coffee shop and sat down. A waiter came over to their table. One student said, "I would like a chocolate-chocolate chip muffin, but I'm not sure what I want to drink." The other said, "I'd like a blueberry croissant, but I also don't know what I want to drink. I'm tired and need caffeine, but I'm really sick of just plain coffee." The waiter decided the best thing to do was to bring over the drink specialist who could help the students decide what to drink with their delectable treats.

The drink specialist then queried the students on the requirements for their beverages. "Hot or cold?" Hot. "Caffeinated?" Absolutely! "More like tea, coffee, or hot chocolate?" Coffee. "What else should I know?" The students shared that they wanted to celebrate, they wanted to feel pampered, plain coffee was definitely out. They wanted something sweet. One student said she heard you could have frothed milk on top – with cocoa powder. That sounded great. The other student said the frothed milk and the cocoa powder were definitely not for him. The drink specialist listened intently and then read back the students' requirements:

1. The beverage shall be hot.
2. The beverage shall be caffeinated.
3. The beverage shall have coffee in it, but should not be plain coffee.
4. The beverage shall make you feel pampered.
5. The beverage shall be sweet.
6. For one of you, the beverage shall have frothed milk and cocoa powder on top. For the other of you, there shall be no frothed milk or cocoa powder.

"Is this correct?" The students agreed. The drink specialist said he could surely satisfy those requirements, except for #4. He said he'd do his best to bring a drink that would make them feel pampered, but couldn't guarantee that one since it wasn't very specific and depended on their opinion. The students agreed to take a chance on the specialist's choice. On his way back he pondered what to make. Either a cappuccino or a latte (with some added cocoa power) would satisfy one student. An espresso or a Greek coffee would meet the second student's requirements. He decided to make a cappuccino and an espresso, his own personal favorites.

In most of the computer science classes you've taken so far, you've probably been given non-negotiable, fairly detailed specifications from your instructor. In reality, what is required in software development is not nearly so defined. In the coffee shop example above, the students knew their goal -- to celebrate the end of exams by relaxing with a leisurely breakfast. The drink specialist had to elicit their requirements for this breakfast. Ultimately, he had to make a judgment of what to serve the students to best satisfy their goal. This was much harder and subjective than if the students had come in and ordered a cappuccino and an espresso right away.

A software *requirement* is a *condition or capability needed by a user to solve a problem or achieve an objective* [14] and *that must be met or possessed by a system or system component to satisfy a contract, standard, specification, or other formally imposed document* [13]. In software development, the requirements are never explicitly "ordered." You must always *work hard* to determine exactly what the customers/users want so as to design a solution to meet their goals. This is challenging to do because requirements are often buried "deep beneath layers of assumptions, misconceptions, and politics [11]." Understanding what you need to do to satisfy your customer is essential because if you don't precisely know what problem you're solving, you may end up solving the wrong problem. You must never assume you know what your customer wants – you must ask and ask again later if you are unsure.

# 1    Requirements Engineering

*Requirements engineering is a systematic way of developing requirements through an iterative process of analyzing a problem, documenting the resulting observations, and checking the accuracy of the understanding gained.* [19] Software requirements engineering provides the techniques for understanding what a customer wants, analyzing it, assessing feasibility, negotiating a reasonable solution, specifying the solution unambiguously, validating the specification, and managing the requirements as they are transformed into an operational system [26].

Requirements engineering is comprised of two major tasks, analysis and modeling [17]. However, often these two steps are done so iteratively, it can be hard to distinguish one from the other. Requirements evolve at an uneven pace and tend to generate further requirements from the definition process. [25]

Requirements analysis is the process of studying user needs to arrive at a definition of system, hardware, or software requirements [13]. In the analysis task, sub-tasks include fact-finding, communication and fact-validation [17]. The output of the requirements elicitation step is a requirements document (of sorts.) This document should express requirements in a form that <u>customers can unambiguously understand</u> – and participate in validating. In the modeling task, sub-tasks include representation and organization [17]. Modeling is done based on the requirements statement produced by elicitation. Via modeling, the requirements are translated into a form that <u>software engineers can unambiguously understand.</u> Once they are elicited, validated, and modeled, requirements must be managed to identify, control, and track changes to requirements as they are transformed into an operational system.

This chapter will describe requirements engineering in general, the practice of requirements elicitation in particular, and will educate you on the plan-driven approach of requirements specification.

# 2    Stakeholders and Requirements Elicitation

> *The primary interest of customers is not in a computer system, but rather in some overall positive effects resulting from the introduction of a computer system in their environment.*
> [7]

Requirements elicitation involves the gathering of requirements. Gathering requirements sounds so easy, doesn't it? "The words "gathering" seems to imply a tribe of happy analysts, foraging for nuggets of wisdom that are lying on the ground all around them . . . . "Gathering" implies that requirements are already there – you merely find them, place them in your basket, and be merrily on your way [11]." As we've already impressed upon you, effectively devising requirements is not easy.

There are different types of requirements to consider and many ways of gathering them. Several different groups of people will have a vested interest in your system. For example, there may be a group of people who pays for your system, a group of people that actually uses your system, a group of people who will maintain your system, and so forth. We use the term *stakeholder* to refer to the *key representative of the groups who have a vested interest in your system and direct or indirect influence on its requirements.* For example, for the Monopoly game the stakeholders are the people who will play the game and the organization that is paying for the software development to be done. Generally, each stakeholder has different perspectives on the problem the software must solve and different needs that must be met. Each of these perspectives must be captured in the requirement elicitation. One of the first activities is to involve people who will act as stakeholders over the course of product development. The stakeholders are thus heavily involved in the requirements elicitation process.

Depending upon the development process chosen, stakeholder involvement may be most heavily weighted at the front-end of the development life cycle (a plan-driven process) or spread throughout the majority of the life cycle (an agile process).

## 2.1 Types of Requirements

There are three distinct but equally important kinds of requirements that need to be gathered from the stakeholders: functional and non-functional requirements, and constraints.

### Functional Requirements

*Functional requirements* are *requirements that specify a function that a system or system component must be able to perform* [13]. These types of requirements specify the services a system must provide, describing how the system should react to specified inputs and how the system should behave in specified circumstances. Sometimes, functional requirements also state what the system should <u>not</u> do. Below are some sample functional requirements from our Monopoly game:

> When a player passes or lands on the Go cell, the player shall get paid $200.
> When a player lands on the Free Parking cell, nothing shall happen.
> When a player lands on an available property cell, the player shall have a chance to purchase it. The price shall be the land value of that property.

### Non-functional Requirements

*Non-functional requirements* are *requirements which are not specifically concerned with the functionality of a system but place restrictions on the product being developed* [16]. In general, non-functional requirements are emergent properties that relate to the system as a whole rather than to individual system functions. The majority of non-functional requirements are of the following five types:

*Security.* Security is the protection of information and data so that unauthorized persons or systems cannot read or modify them and authorized persons or systems are not denied access to them [6]. Depending upon the purpose of the system and the data it interacts with/transmits, the security needs vary widely. Security requirements are discussed further later in this section.

*Privacy.* The Law of Torts (1988) defines privacy as "the right to be let alone." Depending upon the sensitivity of the data the system interacts with/transmits, the needs for protecting the privacy of the data varies widely. Privacy requirements are discussed further later in this section.

*Usability.* The ease with which a user can learn to operate, prepare inputs for, and interpret outputs of a system or component [13]. Usability requirements consider human factors, aesthetics, ease of learning, and similar factors.

*Reliability.* The ability of a system or component to perform its required functions under stated conditions for a specified period of time [13]. Depending upon the purpose of the system and its functions, the reliability requirements (the acceptable frequency and severity of failures) will vary widely. For example, the manufacturer of a cellular phone might consider the auxiliary games to be a low-reliability functionality whereas the calling functionality would be considered a high-reliability functionality.

*Availability.* Availability is the degree to which a system or component is operational and accessible when required for use [13]. In addition to reliability, certain types of systems must be available or

functioning acceptably for a large majority of the time.
   *Performance.* The degree to which a system or component accomplishes its designated functions within given constraints, such as speed, accuracy, or memory usage [13].

Even though functional requirements may not be obvious, they are easier to elicit than non-functional requirements. Functional requirements reflect the things the stakeholders want to be able to do. Non-functional requirements are properties – properties the stakeholders often forget about until they actually try the system – and the transactions take too long . . . or the system is too difficult to use. Failure of a functional requirement generally means that an individual function the user wants does not work. In contrast, failure of a non-functional requirement might make not just an individual function unusable but the whole system unusable. Even worse, fixing non-functional defects are often prohibitively expensive, requiring "back to the drawing board" redesign. It can be exceedingly difficult, if not impossible, to make an insecure system secure or to make an unreliable system reliable.

To prevent these critical non-functional requirements from being overlooked, you must make a greater effort to elicit them from the stakeholders. Rather than wait, <u>ask</u> your customer if the data used in the application is sensitive, who can have access to the data, if it needs to be encrypted during the transaction, how much memory is available, what is the expected transaction time, and so forth. Many software engineers find it helpful to develop a domain-specific taxonomy or checklist of questions about non-functional requirements to ask during requirements elicitation activities.

Non-functional requirements often are born as vaguely-expressed concerns. These concerns need to be translated to statements with *<u>measurable</u>* properties. Ideally, non-functional requirements need be expressed as quantitatively as possible so that they can be tested with a definite "pass" or "fail" result.

   Bad: The system shall be responsive to any user input.
   Good: The system shall respond to any user input within 0.01 seconds.

## Constraints

*Constraints* are *a type of non-functional requirement that is imposed by the client that restricts the implementation of the system or the development process.* These can include things such as the implementation language, the development platform (e.g. Linux, Windows, .NET) or the hardware configuration. Additionally, required process steps, such as automated testing and documentation, could be stated as constraints.

An easy way to distinguish constraints from functional and general non-functional requirements is that constraints usually have no direct effect on the <u>users' view</u> of the system.

## *2.2   Security and Privacy Requirements*

The development of secure systems that protect the rights of individuals is very important. However, the need for information security and privacy is fairly recent concern. Technology and the Internet have made it much easier for intruders and criminals to steal, corrupt, and/or exploit data – from the private information of individuals to mission-critical assets of major corporations. As with most non-functional requirements, it is not easy to magically sprinkle privacy or security dust on an application to fix the built-in vulnerabilities. It is critical that security and privacy requirements are elicited from stakeholders early and for these essential requirements to be designed into our systems from the start. We therefore take a more detailed look at the security and privacy requirements we mentioned in the previous sections.

## Using an Organization's Security and Privacy Documents

In developing a set of security and privacy requirements, the engineer should focus on [22] identifying:

> <u>What</u> needs to be protected

> <u>From whom</u> those things need to be protected

> For <u>how long</u> protection is needed

The astute engineer will also examine the organization's security and privacy policies as a prompt for requirements. An organization's privacy policy should state the privacy rights of users and defines how information is collected, stored, used, and shared. If you've never seen a privacy policy, click on the Privacy Policy link of most any web page. An organization's security policy define how both internal and external users interact with systems in the organization, how the computer architecture topology is implemented, and where computer assets will be located.

It is more difficult to find an example of a security policy because these are generally considered a confidential asset of an organization. However, developers of computer systems have a need to read the security policy and should ask to see it.

## Asking Questions during Requirements Elicitation

Examining these two documents is very important for two reasons:

> Understanding the policies of the organization will enable the engineer to ask the right questions during requirements elicitation. For example, you might ask: *Your privacy policy would indicate that the private information not be revealed. Does this mean you would only like the name displayed on the screen and not the serial number?*

> Understanding the policies of the organization will enable the engineer to spot inconsistencies between the policy and the requirements that are being requested. For example, you might ask: *You said the data can be immediately changed in the database without any transaction logging. However, you security policy specifically states that all transactions must be traceable. I suggest we add a transaction log. What do you think?*

A system need for security and/or privacy may start as a non-functional requirement. Ultimately, these types of requirements should be formulated as a functional requirement if at all possible. For example, in discussing the security needs of an application, the customer might state that only employees of the company can access certain data. This will lead to a functional requirement to add password authentication.

## 3  How to Gather Requirements

In requirements elicitation activities, the software engineers and the stakeholders communicate to determine what the software system needs to be comprised of. In these elicitation activities, it is important to discover the underlying reason <u>why</u> users want a particular thing, rather than just their expression of <u>what</u> they want. Your system has to solve their business problem, not just meet their stated requirements. Documenting the reasons behind requirements will give your team invaluable information when making implementation decisions.

In this section, we provide you information on nine different ways to solicit requirements information from your stakeholders. Before reading these, it is important to familiarize yourself with the potential problems often found when embarking on these activities in Figure 1.

**Figure 1:  Ten Problems of Requirements Elicitation**

You should work to overcome as many of these problems and use a combination of these nine techniques for effectively eliciting your requirements. The first six of these techniques are used for initial requirements capture. The last three are used to collect feedback and additional requirements during the development process.

## 3.1 Interviews

The most common form of requirements elicitation technique is to interview stakeholders to gain their perspective on what the system needs to do. There are two forms of interviews, structured interviews and unstructured interviews. Before a *structured interview*, the software engineer prepares a list of pre-determined questions and a clear, planned agenda. The questions are designed to gain an understanding of real problems and potential solutions. The prepared questions can be open-ended (allowing the interviewee to say what they want) and/or closed-ended (interviewee chooses from a selection of choices, such as multiple choice, ranking, rating questions). The questions should be carefully designed not to be opinionated, biased, or leading. An example of a leading question is, "You don't do it this way, do you?" Having only structured interviews may lead the stakeholders down the wrong, pre-determined path. Structured interviews should be augmented with some *unstructured* interviews. No questions are prepared for an unstructured interview. The interviewee instead takes the conversation wherever he or she wants.

Interviews are very effective for collecting requirements. However, after the interviews are completed, the engineer has the difficult task of integrating different interpretations, goals, objectives, communication styles, and use of terminology into a single set of requirements. The structured interviews can be planned in such a way to facilitate this compilation and analysis.

## 3.2 Observation

One method of learning about system requirements is for the software engineer to observe business activities. This observation can either be passive or active [20]. With passive observation, the engineer observes business activities without interruption or direct involvement or via studies audio/video recordings of business activities. With active observation, the engineer "lives the requirements" by actually participating in the activities and/or becoming part of the team.

Observation is an expensive elicitation technique because it needs to be carried out over a prolonged period of time, at different time intervals, at different workloads, times of day, and times of year. You must also consider that people tend to behave differently when they are watched. They might do things like hide work shortcuts.

## 3.3 Examining Documents and Artifacts

A very effective means of collecting requirements is to examine existing documents and systems. Look at anything you can to gain insight about how things are currently done – such as forms and any automation. Don't forget to gather any policies, such as privacy and security policies.

## 3.4 Joint Application Design Sessions

Joint Application Design or JAD [28] sessions have been used by IBM since the mid 1970s as an effective means for getting the right people involved from the start of the project. The purpose of a JAD session is to guide user or subject matter experts through defining requirements, process, data models, and screen mock-ups.

JAD sessions can be held over a few hours or a few days but should not involve more than 25 to 30 people. There are six roles of the JAD participants:

1. **Executive Sponsor:** The executive who supports and/or pays for the project. He or she must be

high enough in the organization to be able to make decisions and to provide the necessary resources for the project. His/her presence at the session (often only the opening and closing segments) is an indication to the team of the importance of the project.

2. **Facilitator**: The facilitator moderates the meeting, keeping the group on the meeting agenda. The facilitator initiates interactive techniques, such as brainstorming, communication, and consensus building. The facilitator generally understands the business domain but is not a stakeholder. The facilitator does not contribute technical or domain information to the meeting.

3. **Project Leader:** The leader of the application development team answers questions about the project regarding scope, time, coordination issues, and resources.

4. **Participants:** Stakeholders provide the information about their requirements and objectives of the system to be developed. Engineers help users formulate problems and explore solutions.

5. **Scribe:** The scribe records and publishes the proceedings of the meeting. The scribe does not contribute information to the meeting.

6. **Development Team Members**: The development team members sit behind the participants and silently observe the JAD sessions, gathering information.

## 3.5 Groupware

Unavoidably and increasingly, software development teams are geographically separated from each other and from their stakeholders. Organizations have global joint ventures and geographically distributed teams, and sometimes software teams from other countries perform subcontract work. In these situations, frequent face-to-face meetings, even for requirements elicitation, can be impractical and prohibitively expensive. Software tools, such as *groupware*, to help the development collaboratively formulate the requirements have been shown to be effective for distributed requirements gathering [18]. These groupware tools support communication through video conferencing, audio conferencing, interactive chat, email, and specialized tools to capture the interactions and decisions of the teams. The teams can use the tools to interact together at the same time (synchronously). The tools can also allow asynchronous collaboration, whereby the teams do not work at the same time but instead pass back and forth documents (like tokens) and enter information into systems. Research has shown that synchronous requirements elicitation is preferred in a distributed setting [18].

Additionally, groupware tools can also be used by teams that can meet face-to-face. These tools can be used for decision making and negotiation. A very successful groupware tool, WinWin [3], allows the stakeholders to state their product and process objectives, explore their interactions, and negotiate mutual agreements on the specifics of the new project being contracted.

## 3.6 Questionnaires

Another effective means of gathering requirements is to design and distribute a questionnaire to stakeholders. Questionnaires enable the development team to reach a wider range of people than would be possible otherwise and have the advantage of providing a means for obtaining honest, anonymous input.

As with interviews, the questions should be carefully designed not to be opinionated, biased, or leading. The questions can be a mixture of closed-ended and open-ended. However, if the questionnaire has wide circulation, open-ended questions can make analysis more difficult. One disadvantage of questionnaires is that there is less control over the results. For example, one can often not go back to gain clarification on possible misunderstandings.

Questionnaires should be in addition to, not in lieu of, more active, personal elicitation activities.

## *3.7 Prototypes*

A prototype is a partially-developed, demonstration system that can be used to show end-users and/or stakeholders what facilities the system can provide. Users and/or stakeholders can interact with the prototype in an actual environment; this interaction is very helpful when requirements are vague or poorly understood. Stakeholders can then refine their ideas and be more specific of their requirements.

There are two possible approaches to developing prototypes [24]:

1. A paper prototype, which is a drawn or screen-shot mock- up of the system. Engineers and stakeholders can run through the types of functions that need to be handled using the paper mock-ups as props.
2. An automated prototype, developed using a fourth-generation language or other rapid development environment. Languages/tools such as Visual Basic, HTML, and Java are popular for automated prototypes. Automated prototypes are more expensive than paper prototypes, but are considered to be more effective at eliciting crisp feedback and requirements because the requirements are "animated."

## *3.8 Customer Focus Groups*

An excellent means for reviewing interim results is the customer focus group (CFG) [10]. In a CFG, customer decision makers explore a working application (not the documentation) in a facilitated environment. A CFG is run similar to a JAD session – where a facilitator runs the meeting, the customers interact with the system, and the development team quietly watches and listens.

The result of the CFG is (1) feedback on the quality and effectiveness of system so far from the stakeholder's perspective; (2) documented requirements changes, and (3) prioritization on future work. CFGs also help to form a trust bond between the development team and the customers.

## *3.9 On-Site Customer (and Variations Thereof)*

We don't want to conduct product development in a vacuum once the requirements have been defined. Therefore, it is excellent to have customer or stakeholder available nearby (preferably in the same room or cubicle suite) the development team. The customer would then be able to clarify requirements questions and to provide feedback to team members as the need arises, on a minute-by-minute basis. Experience has shown that when a customer is nearby, only about 10% of his or her time is actually taken by the development team. The rest of the time can be spent on the customer's "normal" work. In the absence of such an on-site customer, developers often make assumptions when a requirement is not adequately defined, a sure-fire recipe for failure. Yet another alternative is to have a customer who is committed to being responsive to email, instant messaging, and telephone calls by the development team and also who periodically makes personal visits to the team.

## 4 Requirements Specification

The project requirements must be clearly and concisely documented. As a result, organizations often adopt templates, standard forms for specifying requirements. When an organization shares and uses such a template, readers come to expect and understand the format of the document and can more easily understand it. Additionally, the engineers creating the requirements specification (also called a requirements document) will be less likely to leave out important information; the template jogs their memory as to what is needed. A software *requirements specification* is a *document that specifies the requirements for a system or component* [13]. In this section, we present a template for a Software Requirements Specification (SRS), a means for documenting the requirements of a software project.

No single ideal requirements process exists because what needs to be done is dependent upon several factors. Software projects have differing amounts of requirements volatility, in addition to other important considerations, such as the type and size of the project and the size and experience level of the team. As a result, we will teach you three ways to document your requirements. The form of SRS we present in this chapter is consistent with an IEEE standard [12] and has been adapted from the SRS of a published evolutionary process [1]. This form of SRS is considered to be an excellent means of documenting requirements for projects that are relatively large with fairly stable requirements.

This example SRS shows the requirements for the Monopoly game.

**On-line Monopoly Game
System Requirements Specification**

**Version 1.1
July 22, 2004**

**Project Team:**
    Chih-wei Ho, Team Lead
    Hema Srikanth, Quality Assurance Manager
    Nachi Nagappan, Requirements Analyst            Lucas
Layman, Project Manager
    Mark Sherriff, Development Manager

**Document Author(s):**
    Nachi Nagappan, Requirements Analyst

**Customer Representative(s):**
    Michael Gegick, Raleigh

**I. Introduction**

This system is an on-line Monopoly board game. This game provides several features we can see in the board game version. This document describes the requirements of this program.

## II. Functional Requirements

### FR0. Game Initialization

FR0 provides the initialization of the game.

> FR0.1 Enter Player's Information
>
> > There shall be two dice in the game. Each dice shall have six faces. The player's movement shall be based on the dice roll. If the dice roll is two, the player shall move forward two cells; if the dice roll is three, the player shall move forward three cells; etc.
> >
> > Origin:  Interview with Mr. Gegick on May 1, 2004 (Interview #I03SC01).
> > Priority:  1
> > Implementation Completed Date:  July 9, 2004

### FR1. Player Movement

FR1 describes the rules of the movement.

> FR1.1. Roll Dice
> > There shall be two dice in the game. Each dice shall have six faces. The player's movement shall be based on the dice roll. If the dice roll is two, the player shall move forward two cells; if the dice roll is three, the player shall move forward three cells; etc.
> >
> > Origin:  Interview with Mr. Gegick on May 1, 2004 (Interview #I03SC01)
> > Priority:  1
> > Implementation Completed Date:  July 9, 2004

> FR1.2. Play in Turn
> > Monopoly is a turn-based game. The players shall play in turns in this game. Player sequence shall be determined by the order the names are entered before the game starts. A player's turn shall end when the player presses the End Turn button.
> >
> > Origin:   Interview with Mr. Gegick on May 1, 2004 (Interview #I03SC01)
> > Priority:  1
> > Implementation Completed Date: July 9, 2004

### FR2. Cells

FR2 describes the rules of different types of cells that are used in the game.

FR2.1. Pass Go Cell

When the player passes or lands on the Go cell, the player shall get paid $200.
Origin: Interview with Mr. Gegick on May 1, 2004 (Interview #I03SC01)
Priority: 1
Implementation Completed Date: July 14, 2004

FR2.2. Jail Cell

If a player is sent to jail by either landing on the Go to Jail cell or drawing a go to jail card, the player shall pay $50 in bail money to get out of jail at their next turn. If a player lands on jail as the result of a dice roll, nothing shall happen.
Origin: Interview with Mr. Gegick on May 1, 2004 (Interview #I03SC01)
Priority: 2
Implementation Completed Date:

FR2.3. Do Nothing on Free Parking

When the player lands on the Free Parking cell, nothing shall happen.
Origin:  Interview with Mr. Gegick on May 1, 2004 (Interview #I03SC01)
Priority: 2
Implementation Completed Date:

FR2.4. Go to Jail

When the player lands on the Go to Jail cell, the player shall be sent to the Jail cell. The player shall not receive $200 if she or he passes the Go cell on the way to the Jail cell.
Origin: Interview with Mr. Gegick on May 1, 2004 (Interview #I03SC01)
Priority: 2
Implementation Completed Date:

FR2.5. Buy Property

When the player lands on a tradable cell, including properties, railroads, and utilities, she or he shall have a chance to buy that cell given that the cell is available. If the player clicks on the Buy button, the cell shall be sold to the player. See FR3 for the price rules of the properties, railroads, and utilities.
Origin: Interview with Mr. Gegick on May 1, 2004 (Interview #I03SC01)
Priority: 1
Implementation Completed Date: July 14, 2004

FR2.6. Draw Card

When the player lands on a card cell, including Community Chest and Chance, she or he shall click on the Draw Card button and draw a card from the Community Chest or Chance. The player shall perform the actions specified in the cards. See FR4 for the rules of the cards.
Origin: Interview with Mr. Gegick on May 1, 2004 (Interview #I03SC01)
Priority: 1

<u>Implementation Completed Date</u>:

## FR3. Tradable Cells

Tradable cells are properties, utilities, and rail roads. When a player lands on an available tradable cell, she or he shall have a chance to buy that cell. If player A lands on a tradable cell that is owned by player B, A shall pay rent to B.

FR3.1. Buy Properties

When a player lands on an available property cell, the player shall have a chance to purchase it. The price shall be the land value of that property.

<u>Origin</u>:  Interview with Mr. Gegick on May 1, 2004 (Interview #I03SC01)

<u>Priority</u>: 3

<u>Implementation Completed Date</u>:

FR3.2. Buy Utilities

When a player lands on an available utility cell, the player shall have a chance to purchase it. The price shall be $150.

<u>Origin</u>:   Interview with Mr. Gegick on May 1, 2004 (Interview #I03SC01)

<u>Priority</u>: 3

<u>Implementation Completed Date</u>:

FR3.3. Buy Rail Roads

When a player lands on a rail road cell, the player shall have a chance to purchase it. The price shall be $200.

<u>Origin</u>:  Interview with Mr. Gegick on May 1, 2004 (Interview #I03SC01)

<u>Priority</u>: 3

<u>Implementation Completed Date</u>:

FR3.4. Pay Rent to Properties

When a player (A) lands on a property cell owned by another player (B), A shall pay rent to B. If there is no house on the cell, A shall pay the base rent of the cell. If there are n houses on the cell, the rent shall be (base rent * (number of houses + 1)).

 <u>Priority</u>:  3

<u>Implementation Completed Date</u>:

FR3.5. Pay Rent to Utilities

If player A lands on player B's utility, player A shall pay rent to player B based on a dice roll and the number of utilities player B owns.  If player B owns one utility the system shall charge player A rent of 4 times the dice roll.  If player B owns two utilities the system shall charge player A rent of 10 times the dice roll.  The game board shall have no more than two utility cells.

<u>Origin</u>:  Interview with Mr. Gegick on May 1, 2004 (Interview #I03SC01)

<u>Priority</u>:  3

Implementation Completed Date:

### FR3.6. Pay Rent to Rail Roads

If player A lands on player B's rail road, A shall pay rent to B based on the number of railroads B owns. The base rent of railroads shall be $50. If the number of the railroads B owns is $N$, the amount of rent A shall pay B is $\$50 * 2^{N-1}$.

Origin: Interview with Mr. Gegick on May 1, 2004 (Interview #I03SC01)

Priority: 3

Implementation Completed Date:

### FR3.7. Build Houses

A player has the monopoly of a color group if she or he owns all the property cells in the color group. During a player's turn, before she or he rolls the dice, the player shall have a chance to buy houses for the monopolies she or he owns. A player shall not build more than five houses on one cell.

Origin: Interview with Mr. Gegick on May 1, 2004 (Interview #I03SC01)

Priority: 1

Implementation Completed Date: July 14, 2004

## FR4. Cards

There shall be two decks of cards in the game: Community Chest and Chance. When a player lands on a Community Chest cell or a Chance cell, the player shall draw a card from the top of the Community Chest cards or Chance cards, respectively.

### FR4.1. Draw jail card

If the player draws a jail card, the system shall move the player to jail. If this move causes the player to pass the Go cell, the player shall not receive the $200 salary from the system.

Origin: Interview with Mr. Gegick on May 1, 2004 (Interview #I03SC01)

Priority: 2

Implementation Completed Date: July 9, 2004

### FR4.2. Draw lose money card

If the player draws a lose money card, the system shall decrease the player's money by the amount specified on the card.

Origin: Interview with Mr. Gegick on May 1, 2004 (Interview #I03SC01)

Priority: 3

Implementation Completed Date: July 9, 2004.

### FR4.3. Draw gain money card

If the player draws a gain money card, the system shall increase the player's money

by the amount specified on the card.
Origin:  Interview with Mr. Gegick on May 1, 2004 (Interview #I03SC01)
Priority:  2
Implementation Completed Date: July 9, 2004.

FR4.4. Draw move player card
If the player draws a move player card, the system shall move the player to the specified cell.  If this move causes the player to pass the Go cell, the player shall receive $200 salary from the system.
Origin:  Interview with Mr. Gegick on May 1, 2004 (Interview #I03SC01)
Priority:  2
Implementation Completed Date: July 9, 2004

**FR5. Trading**

A player (A) shall have the chance to buy properties from another player (B) during A's turn, before A rolls the dice. The trading shall begin when A clicks the Trade button. A shall select which player to trade with, and which tradable cell to buy. A dialog shall pop up to ask B whether he or she agrees with the price. If B clicks the Yes button in the dialog, the amount of money they agreed upon shall be transferred from A to B, and the selected tradable cell shall belong to A. If B clicks No, nothing shall happen.
Origin:  Interview with Mr. Gegick on May 1, 2004 (Interview #I03SC01
Priority:  3
Implementation Completed Date: July 9, 2004

**III. Nonfunctional Requirements**

**NR1. Performance**

The system shall wait for all user inputs, and execute only the necessary functions given a user input to the system.  All functions shall be completed quickly.

NR1.1. User response
The system shall respond to any user input within 0.01 seconds.
Origin: Interview with Mr. Gegick on May 1, 2004 (Interview #I03SC01
Priority: 3
Implementation Completed Date: July 9, 2004.

NR1.2. Update user data
The system should update user data within 0.01 seconds.
Origin:  Interview with Mr. Gegick on May 1, 2004 (Interview #I03SC01

Priority: 3
Implementation Completed Date: July 9, 2004.

## NR2. Usability

A user shall be able to determine quickly what player options they have to perform.

### NR2.1. Player options

A user shall only have access to functionality that is allowed to them at a given time.
Origin: Interview with Mr. Gegick on May 1, 2004 (Interview #I03SC01
Priority: 3
Implementation Completed Date: July 9, 2004.

### NR2.2. User Interface

The system shall allow a user to interface with it through mouse events on buttons and drop down boxes and keyboard events on text fields. The amount of user keyboard input shall be minimized by the system to include only entering the number of players, player names, and a trade price.
Origin: Interview with Mr. Gegick on May 1, 2004 (Interview #I03SC01
Priority: 1


Implementation Completed Date: July 29, 2004.

### NR2.3. User Errors

The system shall catch improper input from all text fields in the system.
Origin: Interview with Mr. Gegick on May 1, 2004 (Interview #I03SC01
Priority: 1
Implementation Completed Date: July 9, 2004.


## IV. Constraints

All code development shall be done with the Java programming language.
All testing shall be done using JUnit and FIT.


# V. Requirements Dependency Traceability Table

The matrix is used to identify dependencies between requirements to identify when one

requirement must be completed before another can be implemented.

| | Is dependant upon requirement |
|---|---|

| | F0.1 | F1.1 | F1.2 | F2.1 | F2.2 | F2.3 | F2.4 | F2.5 | F2.6 | F3.1 | F3.2 | F3.3 | F3.4 | F3.5 | F3.6 | F3.7 | F4.1 | F4.2 | F4.3 | F4.4 | F5 | N1.1 | N1.2 | N2.1 | N2.2 | N2.3 |
|---|---|---|---|---|---|---|---|---|---|---|---|---|---|---|---|---|---|---|---|---|---|---|---|---|---|---|
| F0.1 | | | | | | | | | | | | | | | | | | | | | | | | | X | X |
| F1.1 | X | | | | | | | | | | | | | | | | | | | | | X | X | X | X | |
| F1.2 | X | | | | | | | | | | | | | | | | | | | | | | | X | X | |
| F2.1 | X | X | | | | | | | | | | | | | | | | | | | | | X | | | |
| F2.2 | X | X | | | | | | | | | | | | | | | | | | | | X | X | X | X | |
| F2.3 | X | X | | | | | | | | | | | | | | | | | | | | | X | | | |
| F2.4 | X | X | | X | | | | | | | | | | | | | | | | | | | X | | | |
| F2.5 | X | X | | | | | | | | X | | | | | | | | | | | | X | X | X | X | |
| F2.6 | X | X | | | | | | | | | | | | | | | | | | | | X | X | X | X | |
| F3.1 | X | | | | | | | X | | | | | | | | | | | | | | X | X | X | X | |
| F3.2 | X | | | | | | | X | | | | | | | | | | | | | | X | X | X | X | |
| F3.3 | X | | | | | | | X | | | | | | | | | | | | | | X | X | X | X | |
| F3.4 | X | | X | | | | | X | | X | | | | | | | | | | | | X | X | | | |
| F3.5 | X | | X | | | | | X | | | X | | | | | | | | | | | X | X | | | |

135

| | | | | | | | | | | | | | | | | | | | | | | | | |
|---|---|---|---|---|---|---|---|---|---|---|---|---|---|---|---|---|---|---|---|---|---|---|---|---|
| F3.6 | X | | X | | | | X | | | X | | | | ░ | | | | | | | X | X | | |
| F3.7 | X | | | | | | X | | X | | | | | | ░ | | | | | | X | X | X | X |
| F4.1 | X | | | X | | X | | | | | | | | | | ░ | | | | | | X | | |
| F4.2 | X | | | | | | | X | | | | | | | | | ░ | | | | | X | | |
| F4.3 | X | | | | | | | X | | | | | | | | | | ░ | | | | X | | |
| F4.4 | X | | | | | | | X | | | | | | | | | | | ░ | | | X | | |
| F5 | X | | X | | | | X | | X | X | X | | | | | | | | | ░ | X | X | X | X X |
| N1.1 | X | | | | | | | | | | | | | | | | | | | | ░ | | X | X |
| N1.2 | X | | | | | | | | | | | | | | | | | | | | | ░ | | X |
| N2.1 | X | | | | | | | | | | | | | | | | | | | | | | ░ | X |
| N2.2 | X | | | | | | | | | | | | | | | | | | | | | | ░ | X |
| N2.3 | X | | | | | | | | | | | | | | | | | | | | | | X | ░ |

## VI. Development and Target Platforms
1. Windows XP Operating System
2. Intel Pentium IV processors
3. Eclipse IDE

**VII. Project Glossary**

**cell:** a box on the game board on which the players land. Cells can be houses, utilities, rail roads, jail, or "pick a card" slots.

**VIII. Document Revision History**

| Version | 1.1 |
|---|---|
| Name(s) | Laurie Williams |
| Date | July 22, 2004 |
| Change Description | Updated priorities and dependency chart |
| Version | 1.0 |
| Name(s) | Dright Ho and Sarah Smith |
| Date | July 19, 2004. |
| Change Description | Original creation of the SRS. |

# 5 Requirements Validation

As you are documenting your requirements, you must write them in such a way that both the development team and the customer can unambiguously understand and agree to the requirements (via the validation process; more about validation later). Ultimately, the requirements document must reflect a consensus between the development team and the stakeholder on the system that will be produced. In this section, we will discuss characteristics of properly written requirements and the validation and prioritization of these requirements.

Well-written requirements have several important characteristics. Keep these in mind not only as you document requirements, but in your elicitation activities too. You need to ask the right questions! Adapted from IEEE 830-1998 [12], the following are characteristics of well-written requirements.

## 5.1 Understandable

The purpose of the requirements document is to document and validate the stakeholders' desires for the system. The requirements are a formal or informal contract between the stakeholders and the development team for what will be produced. Two mistakes are common:
1. The requirements are full of domain-specific language and terms the development team does not understand. This causes problems because the team does not really understand what they are committing to and does not know what to design/implement.
2. The requirements are full of technical terms the stakeholders don't understand. If the stakeholders can't understand the document, it will either need to be rewritten (so the stakeholders can understand it) or the team is doomed to surprise the stakeholders with something they really don't want.

The best guideline is to write your requirements at an elementary school level, using short, declarative statements. Remember, the development team and the stakeholders will likely contain several people whose first language is not the same as yours. It is a valuable and desirable to have examples and figures and/or tables for clarification.

## 5.2 Non-prescriptive

The requirements should state everything about what the customer wants and nothing about how the programmer(s) will do it. You define the "how" when you start modeling and designing. The requirements should be design-free.

## 5.3   Correct and Complete

To no surprise, the requirements must be a precise reflection of what the stakeholders want.  The requirements must also be an exhaustive list of what they want including what should happen in exceptional and/or undesirable situations.  However, it is difficult to ensure that the requirements are correct and complete before the system is developed, tested, and delivered to the customer.  One can never guarantee or prove the requirements to be correct and complete.  Despite this difficulty, we must strive for correctness and completeness and perform a thorough validation of the requirements.

## 5.4   Concise

Be to the point.  Avoid rambling text that does not contribute to the understanding of what is necessary.  There are two reasons you need to be concise.  First, the requirements document needs to be validated by the customer.  The longer the document, the more tired the stakeholders and development team reviewing the document will get, resulting in defects not being caught.  Additionally, developers may tend to skim long requirements statement and pass over the most important information.  Use the KISS principle (Keep it Short and Sweet).  Remember the famous words:

> *Perfection is achieved, not when there is nothing left to add, but when there is nothing left to take away . . .* [8]

## 5.5   Consistent Language

For ease of reading and for efficient identification of problems, it is best for you to express all your requirements in a similar format.  Requirements are often stated as "shall" statements.  For example:

> When the player passes or lands on the "Go" cell, the player shall get paid $200.

The use of shall statements indicates a "contract" or mandatory, binding provision to provide that capability.  Desirable but optional or non-binding propositions can be stated as "should" or "may" statements.  For example:

> The system should update user data within 0.01 seconds.

The use of shall, should, and may will feed into the requirement prioritization process, as will be discussed below.

## 5.6   Unambiguous and Testable

The requirements need to be written so that there can be only one interpretation of what is desired – exactly one system can be specified.  The reduction of ambiguity is helped tremendously by considering exactly how the system can be precisely tested to ensure the requirement is met.  Remember back to the coffee shop example at the beginning of this chapter.  The students specified "testable" things such as that their beverage had to be hot, sweet, caffeinated, but not plain coffee.  They also said they wanted to "feel pampered."  This last requirement was ambiguous, hard to satisfy reliability, and could not be tested – a bad requirement.  Requirements must be both <u>unambiguous</u> and <u>testable</u>.

The following is an ambiguous but testable requirement.

> Players can buy utility properties.

The following is an unambiguous <u>and</u> testable requirement.

> When a player lands on an available utility cell, the player shall have a chance it.  The price is $150.

Writing <u>test cases</u> during the requirements process is an excellent means of ensuring your requirements are unambiguous and testable. Very often, you will realize that you don't understand enough about a requirement to write a test case. This is a strong signal you had better ask more questions! You can use the following three ways [23] to make your requirements more testable:

1. Specify a quantitative description for each adverb and adjective so that the meaning of qualifiers is clear and unambiguous.
2. Replace pronouns with specific names of entities.
3. Make sure that every noun is defined in exactly one place in the requirements document.

It is valuable to involve your customer in this early test-writing process. Ask you customer what kind of test they would run if they wanted to make sure this requirement was implemented properly. Consider this test case a "customer acceptance test case" – the customer will accept your system if these test cases run properly. We advocate that the test cases based on the requirements are written before you proceed to modeling and/or designing your product.

## 5.7 Consistent

Requirements are inconsistent when two or more different requirements contradict each other. For example:

When a player lands on the Free Parking cell, nothing shall happen.
When a player lands on the Free Parking cell, that player gets all the money in the kitty.

This may be a simplified example, but problems like these can easily creep into the set of requirements. How can this happen? You interview two different stakeholders. The user might want the ability to get a big pile of cash when landing on Free Parking. The person marketing representative might think it is more important to get the game out on the market than to have the Free Parking kitty functionality in the product.. Both requirements must not be recorded – the inconsistency must be surfaced and resolved with the users. Inconsistencies can also result in large requirements documents – these can be written by several people (one interviewed the red/green user, the other interviewed the purple/pink user) or be a single person who cannot keep track of all the interrelationships between all the requirements.

## 5.8 Traceable

Requirements must be able to be traced back to a stated need by the customer. Assign requirements unique identifiers. These identifiers help you in discussion. Fore example, you might call up a customer for clarification on Requirement 4.1. These identifiers also allow traceability in future stages. For example, you can trace a test case back to the requirement it verifies.

## 5.9 Feasible

Stakeholders can specify requirements that cannot feasibly be implemented within realistic constraints. Sometimes infeasible requirements can surface during the initial elicitation phase – and this should be explained to the stakeholder right away. Often a requirement may be deemed infeasible during the analysis or design phases. In this case, the stakeholder must be notified and the requirements documentation must be updated.

## 5.10 Ranked for Importance and Stability

Not all requirements should be treated equally. Some requirements are essential for an operational system; others are "nice to have." In order to prioritize the use of resources of a software development team, you must be very clear which requirements are the most important and at the core of the system. As a result, your requirements should be documented with a measure of importance or ranking. The team should jointly decide the importance rating scheme – whether it be high/medium/low or a rank. Be aware that the stakeholders will tend to indicate that all requirements are essential. Part of the requirements negotiation process should be to determine their realistic priorities.

Requirements stability is a related issue. Requirements stability is a measure of how likely a requirement is to change. The stakeholders can indicate how sure they are of the specific details of a requirement. If the details are quite crisp and the stakeholder is confident that these details are stable, the requirement should be annotated with a high stability rating. If the details are sketchy and/or the stakeholder is not sure that the requirement is necessary, a low stability should be indicated. Again, the team should jointly decide the stability rating scheme – whether it be high/medium/low or a rank.

It is advisable to begin development with the most important and stable requirements, though there are other important considerations, such as dependencies between requirements (e.g., when one requirement must be completed before another requirement can be started).

## 6   Requirements Validation Review

We have seen that requirements gathering and documentation is not an easy task. However, these requirements become the basis for the entire development effort. Errors in the requirements ultimately are "committed" into the implementation of the project. Requirements errors can be especially insidious because we may even have an automated test case that may verify that the "wrong" requirement works perfectly. It is essential that our requirements represent the stakeholders' true need and that these requirements exhibit the characteristics that were listed in the prior section.

We must remove as many requirements defects as possible as early as possible. An effective technique for this data removal is the requirements review. A *requirements review* is *a process or meeting during which the requirements for a system, hardware item, or software item are presented to project personnel, managers, users, customers, or other interested parties for comment or approval* [13]. The objective of such a review is to ensure the document clearly and accurately reflects the actual requirements. Requirements reviews are run as are any technical reviews. In a requirements review, the team of engineers that developed the SRS and the stakeholders gather in a room for a neutral but formal meeting. Someone other than the author of the requirements reads the SRS. The review team determines if what is read represents a clear description of the system and if there are any potential problems. By having the requirements read by another person who may have different "interpretation" of requirements – problems caused by misinterpretation or ambiguities can be identified [2]. The goal of the meeting is to resolve problems. As problems are discovered, no blame should be attached to any person.

It is helpful for the review team to use validation checklists to remind people what to look for in the SRS. The checklists focus on the criteria discussed in the previous section of this chapter. Additionally, it is useful for the review team to have in hand copies of the organization's security and privacy policies.

The review team must be realistic about how much can be validated in one meeting. Experience has shown [24] that probably about 40 requirements can be inspected per hour. Beyond that, the team is likely to get tired and gloss over errors.

## 7   Requirements Volatility

*Requirements volatility* is *the amount of change in the software requirements between the beginning and end of a software development project* [4], particularly once coding has begun. The complexity of managing the volatility is increased when a change to one requirement has a cascading impact on other requirements.

In most software projects, stable requirements do not often exist, though the actual change rate varies by project. Here are some points of reference:

A study at IBM Santa Teresa Laboratory in the mid-1970's found that, in a sample size of 1 million lines of code, the average project experiences a 25 percent change in requirements during development. [4, 6] Technology and expectations seem to have been more stable in the 1970's than they are currently.

Capers Jones indicates the U.S. average rate of "creeping requirements" (changes after the initial set of requirements is defined) is approximately 2% per month during the design and coding phases. This equates to changing almost 25% of the system on a year-long project. Jones has seen creep exceed 150%. [15]

During the time it takes to develop a system, the users' needs may mature because of increased knowledge brought on by the development activities, or they may shift to a new set of needs because of unforeseen organizational or environmental pressures [7].

## 7.1 Taming Requirements Volatility: Iteration

Because of this inevitable change, it is important to have requirements elicitation activities that are iterative in nature. You should not formulate the requirements, then carry on with development without reexamining the requirements with your stakeholders periodically. When the whole development process is iterative, mistaken assumptions can be detected faster and corrected sooner because the customer provides feedback on the developer's interpretation of the requirements. The developer can then correct the problems as they are found.

If a team does formulate the requirements only once, you run the risk of delivering exactly what the stakeholders initially asked for, but not what they actually want, as shown in Figure 2. Such activity supports an efficient process for missing your desired target in an environment where requirements are volatile.

**Figure 2: One-Time Requirements Formulation**

Instead, formulating requirements in an iterative way allows the requirements to evolve through time, synchronized with the design process [7]. Such an iterative practice will more likely result in a software development team delivering what the customer actually wants, as shown in Figure 3.

**Figure 3: Iterative Requirements Formulation**

Figure 2 indicates an efficient, straight path from the starting point to the completion point. Figure 3 indicates a meandering path; this path is less efficient than a straight line path from the starting point to the desired completion. Undoubtedly, some efficiency is lost when change is allowed into the process. There may be some design, implementation, or test planning that needs to be reworked and/or scrapped due to a requirements change. In a perfect world, we would not need to deal with such change, but in the world we live in, we must. In order to deliver a product that will be most valuable to the stakeholders, we must learn to deal with the inefficiencies of change and have software development practices that deal with these changes.

## 7.2 Additional Ways of Taming Requirements Volatility

There are other practices that can be used to reduce and/or control the degree of requirements volatility.

### Change Control Boards

In large system development, development organizations may have *change control boards*. A change control board is a group of managers, client representatives, and technical personnel who meet and decide what proposed changes should be accepted or rejected. If a proposed change to the system would likely cause too much cascading rework, the board may elect to reject the change. However, they must trade off the risk of rejecting the change and the likelihood that the stakeholders may not ultimately be fully satisfied with the product without the alteration.

### A Structured Process

Another means for reducing requirements volatility is to follow a defined methodology for requirements analysis and modeling [29], such as those discussed in this chapter. By creating and validating requirements in conjunction with the stakeholders, the Software Requirements Specification is more likely to reflect their true needs to start with. As much as we hate to admit this, some development teams proceed with development without a clear picture of the requirements that is obtained by creating and validating an SRS. In these cases, a great deal of the volatility can be attributed to the fact that the team was developing what they thought the stakeholders wanted – acting upon assumptions.

### Frequent Communication

Change occurs just to reset the project, often incrementally, from the assumptions to the real customer requirements. Communicating with the customer throughout the requirements elicitation phase helps to tame requirements volatility. A major study suggests that the more frequent developers and customers communicate with each other during the requirements elicitation phase, the less volatile the customer's requirements will be [29].

### Explicit Tradeoffs

The team must also have a structured means for not catering to every whim of the stakeholders. Scope creep must be controlled. *Scope creep* means that new or expanded requirements have "crept" into the project after everyone though the requirement were defined [9]. Gerald Weinberg refers to an ever-growing requirements document as being "perpetually pregnant." [27] An effective means of controlling scope creep is to ensure the stakeholders understand the cost of the changes and therefore must make explicit tradeoff decisions. For example, an engineer might say the following to a customer:

> *The original requirement was that no money would be given to anyone who lands on Free Parking. Now, you have said you would like for their to be a Free Parking kitty of money that players get if they land on Free Parking. It will take us three months to make this change. We have several options: (1) delay the whole project; (2) keep on schedule and add this requirement in the next release; (3) keep on schedule by adding this requirement but moving the "Free Parking" functionality to the next release. Which of these options do you prefer?*

Often these kind of tradeoff decisions, relating to budget and/or schedule renegotiation, will cause the stakeholder to translate a *must have* requirement to a *nice to have* requirement.

## Fast Process

Finally, elicitation, specification, and verification should not be too time consuming. If this process spans several months, the validated requirements could be obsolete before the design process starts.

## 8 Summary

*The hardest single part of building a software system is deciding precisely what to build . . . . No other part of the work so cripples the resulting system if it is done wrong. No other part is more difficult to rectify later.* [5]

Several practical tips for requirements engineering and elicitation were presented throughout this chapter. The keys for successful requirements engineering are summarized in Table 1.

| | |
|---|---|
| 🔑 | Gathering requirements is hard work. It is good to communicate with a variety of stakeholders to gain as many different perspectives of their goals as possible. It is also good to use <u>several</u> of the following techniques to get the best picture of what is needed: interviews, observations, examining documents and artifacts, Joint Application Development sessions, groupware, questionnaires, prototypes, customer focus groups, and the presence of an on-site customer. |
| 🔑 | Develop a domain-specific taxonomy of questions which can guide questions to stakeholders about their non-functional requirements. Non-functional are often not discussed in the elicitation process. It can be devastating to a product if the non-functional requirements are missed since rework for new non-functional requirements is so difficult. |
| 🔑 | Examine an organization's security and privacy policies to obtain important information about security and privacy requirements. |
| 🔑 | Create a requirements specification to record the requirements that have been gathered. |
| 🔑 | Examine the requirements document for the characteristics of properly-written requirements: understandable, non-prescriptive, correct and complete, concise, consistent language, unambiguous and testable, traceable, feasible, and ranked for importance. |
| 🔑 | Many requirements problems can be alleviated by having a requirements review with stakeholders. |

| 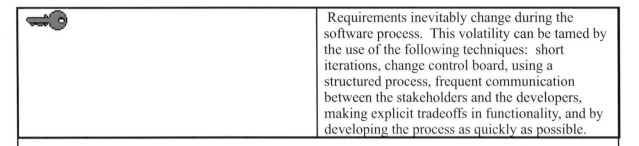 | Requirements inevitably change during the software process. This volatility can be tamed by the use of the following techniques: short iterations, change control board, using a structured process, frequent communication between the stakeholders and the developers, making explicit tradeoffs in functionality, and by developing the process as quickly as possible. |
|---|---|

**Table 1:  Key Ideas for Requirements Engineering and Elicitation**

**Glossary of Chapter Terms**

| Term | Definition | Source |
|---|---|---|
| Constraint | a type of non-functional requirement that is imposed by the client that restricts the implementation of the system or the development process | |
| Functional requirement | requirements that specify a function that a system or system component must be able to perform | [13] |
| Non-functional requirement | requirements which are not specifically concerned with the functionality of a system but place restrictions on the product being developed | [16] |
| requirement | (1) a condition or capability needed by a user to solve a problem or achieve an objective; (2) a condition or capability that must be met or possessed by a system or system component to satisfy a contract, standard, specification, or other formally imposed document. | [13] |
| requirements analysis | The process of studying user needs to arrive at a definition of system, hardware, or software requirements. | [13] |
| Requirements engineering | a systematic way of developing requirements through an iterative process of analyzing a problem, documenting the resulting observations, and checking the accuracy of the understanding gained | [19] |

| requirements review | A process or meeting during which the requirements for a system, hardware item, or software item are presented to project personnel, managers, users, customers, or other interested parties for comment or approval. | [13] |
|---|---|---|
| Requirements specification | A document that specifies the requirements for a system or component. | [13] |
| Requirements volatility | the amount of change in the software requirements between the beginning and end of a software development project | [4], |
| Stakeholder | key representative of the groups who have a vested interest in your system and direct or indirect influence on its requirements | |

# References

[1]    A. Anton, R. Carter, J. Earp, and L. Williams, "EPRAM:  Evolutionary Prototyping Risk Analysis and Mitigation," North Carolina State University, Raleigh, NC, no. CSC TR-2001-08, 2001.

[2]    B. Boehm, "Verifying and validating software requirements and design specifications," *IEEE Software,* no. pp. 75-88, January 1984.

[3]    B. Boehm, A. Egyed, J. Kwan, D. Port, A. Shah, and R. Madachy, "Using the WinWin Spiral Model:  A Case Study," *IEEE Computer,* vol. 31, no. 7, pp. 33-44, July 1998.

[4]    B. W. Boehm, *Software Engineering Economics.* Englewood Cliffs, NJ: Prentice-Hall, Inc., 1981.

[5]    F. P. Brooks, "No Silver Bullet," *IEEE Computer,* vol. 20, no. 4, pp. 10-19, 1987.

[6]    T. Climis, "Software Cost Estimation," in *NSIA Software Workshop*, Buena Park, CA, February 1979.

[7]    M. G. Cristel and K. C. Kang, "Issues in Requirements Elicitation," Software Engineering Institute, no. CMU/SEI-92-TR-12 7, September 1992.

[8]    A. de Saint-Exupéry, *Wind, Sand, and Stars*: Harvest Books, 1939.

[9]    E. Gottesdiener, *Requirements by Collaboration.* Boston: Addison-Wesley, 2002.

[10]    J. Highsmith, *Adaptive Software Development.* New York, NY: Dorset House, 1999.

[11]    A. Hunt and D. Thomas, *The Pragmatic Programmer.* Reading, Massachusetts: Addison-Wesley, 2000.

[12]    IEEE, "IEEE Recommended Practice for Software Requirements Specifications," no. IEEE Standard 830-1998, 1998.

[13]    IEEE, "IEEE Standard 610.12-1990, IEEE Standard Glossary of Software Engineering

Terminology," 1990.

[14]   IEEE, "IEEE Standards Collection:  Glossary of Software Engineering Terminology,"  no. IEEE Standard 610.12-1990, 1993.

[15]   C. Jones, *Estimating Software Costs*: McGraw-Hill Professional, 1998.

[16]   G. Kotonya and I. Sommerville, *Requirements Engineering:  Processes and Techniques*. Chichester: John Wiley and Sons, 1998.

[17]   J. C. Leite and P. Freeman, "Requirements Validation through Viewpoint Resolution," *IEEE Transactions on Software Engineering,* vol. 17, no. 12, pp. 1253-1269, December 1991.

[18]   W. J. Lloyd, M. B. Rossen, and J. D. Arthur, "Effectiveness of Elicitation Techniques," in *IEEE Joint Internation Conference on Requirements Engineering (RE '02)*, Essen, Germany, 2002.

[19]   P. Loucopoulos and R. Champion, "Knowledge-Based Support for Requirements Engineering," *Information and Software Technology,* vol. 31, no. 3, pp. 123-135, April 1989.

[20]   L. A. Maciaszek, *Requirements Analysis and System Design*. Harlow, England: Addison-Wesley, 2001.

[21]   J. A. McDermid, "Requirements Analysis: Problems and the STARTS Approach," *IEE Colloquium on 'Requirements Capture and Specification for Critical Systems' (Digest No. 138), 4/1-4/4,* no. November 1989.

[22]   G. McGraw, "On Bricks and Walls:  Why Building Secure Software is Hard," *Cutter IT Journal,* vol. 15, no. 5, pp. 5-14, May 2002.

[23]   J. Robertson and S. Robertson, *Complete Systems Analysis:  The Workbook, the Textbook, the Answers*. New York: Dorset House Publishing, 1994.

[24]   I. Sommerville and P. Sawyer, *Requirements Engineering:  A good practice guide*. Chichester: Wiley, 1997.

[25]   K. Southwell, J. James, B. A. Clarke, B. Andrews, C. Ashworth, M. Norris, and V. Patel, "Requirements Definition and Design.," in *The STARTS Guide*, Second ed. vol. 1: National Computing Centre, 1987, pp. 177-313.

[26]   R. H. Thayer and M. Dorfman, *Software Requirements Engineering*, Second ed.: IEEE Computer Society Press, 1997.

[27]   G. M. Weinberg, "Just Say No! Improving the Requirements Process.," *American Programmer,* vol. 8, no. 10, pp. 19-23, October 1995.

[28]   J. Wood and D. Silver, *Joint Application Design: How to Design Quality Systems in 40% Less Time*. New York: Wiley, 1989.

[29]   D. Zowghi and N. Nurmuliani, "A Study of the Impact of Requirements Volatility on Software Project Performance," in *Nineth Asia-Pacific Software Engineering Conference (APSEC 2002)*, 2002.

# Chapter Questions

1. From the perspective of requirements analysis, why is it important to know the organization's security and privacy policy?

2. What are the properties of well-stated requirements?

3. Describe, in your own words, what software stakeholders are. What is the difference between a stakeholder and a user from the aspect of requirements elicitation?

4. Rapid application development (RAD) is a software process model that emphasizes an extremely short (60-90 days) development cycle. At the end of the development cycle, the software team delivers workable software, often with some compromises. What requirements problems can be mitigated if the software team uses RAD? Justify your answer.

5. Are these requirement statements testable? If not, why not?
   A. The system shall support 100 simultaneous users.
   B. The database shall respond to a query in 100 milliseconds.
   C. The result image shall have soft-focus effect.
   D. The sound after the process shall not exceed 40db.
   E. The UI shall be user friendly.
   F. The query result shall be represented in XML format.

6. A requirement is traceable if the origin of the requirement is clear. What can be the origin of a requirement statement? Give at least 5 examples.

7. Take Microsoft Word for example. Who are the stakeholders of this software? If you were a requirements analyst in charge of this software, who and what would you consult when gathering the requirements? How would you collect the requirements?

8. Listed below is the requirements specification of a web-based bulletin board system. Identify the problems with the specification.
   Functional Requirements:
   FR1.     The administrator shall add new boards to the system.

   FR2.     The administrator may remove old boards from the system.

   FR3.     All boards shall be listed in the welcome page.

   FR4.     When a user clicks on the name of the board in the welcome page, he/she shall enter the board page.

   FR5.     All the articles in a board shall be listed in the board page.

   FR6.     When a user clicks on the name of the article in the board page, he/she shall enter the article page.

   FR7.     The article page shall list the detail of a specific article.

   FR8.     Any user shall read all the articles, but only registered user shall post an article.

   FR9.     Only the author of the article, or the board manager, shall remove an article from the board.

   FR10.    Each board has a board manager to maintain the articles in the board. The board manager shall be selected by the system administrator.

   Non-functional Requirements:
   NR1.     The system shall be able to handle high-volume of transactions.

   NR2.     The users' information shall be encrypted in the database.

   NR3.     The user interface for posting an article shall be easy enough so that even 8-year old kids know how to use it.

   Constraints:

C1. The system shall run on Red Hat Linux 9, on Pentium 4 boxes with 1GB of RAM.

9. Suppose you are going to develop an online shopping web site. During the requirement analysis, in order to make sure that you can have a complete set of nonfunctional requirements, it is a good idea to have a checklist about the nonfunctional properties of the system. Develop the checklist that helps you to gather nonfunctional requirements.

10. In some software process models, like the waterfall model, requirements are "frozen" after the requirements analysis phase. What are to pros and cons if the requirements are allowed to change after the requirements analysis phase? What projects are suitable to apply such process models?

11. Consider the following statement:

    *After the user logs in, the system shall assign the resources to the user according to the role. If the user is a Privileged User, the service shall be provided by High-Performance Cluster. Otherwise, the service shall be provided by the PC cluster.*

    Is this a function requirement, nonfunctional requirement, or constraint? Justify your answer.

    Sometimes it is not easy to classify a requirement. How should a requirement analyst (or the software team) deal with such situation?

12. Traceability matrix becomes difficult to manage when there are many requirements. What can we do to reduce the problem?

13. Use your knowledge about vending machines. Develop an SRS document for a vending machine that sells soft drinks.

14. Build a paper prototype for the Monopoly case study.

15. Discuss the skills that are required for a good requirements analyst.

## Appendix: Software Requirements Specification

# [Project Name] Requirements Specification
[Template adapted from [1]]

**[Document Version Number]**
**[Date]**
**Project Team:**
[Name] [Role]
    [Name] [Role]
    [Name] [Role]
[Name] [Role]

**Document Author(s):**
[Name] [Role]
    [Name] [Role]

**Customer Representative(s):**
[Name]

## I. Introduction
The requirements document specifies the services that the system will provide and the constraints under which the system must operate.

## II. Functional Requirements
Enumerate all functional requirements in this section. It is generally a good idea to organize the functional requirements according to the modules into which the system has been decomposed by the system architect. Don't forget to provide traceability information such as where the requirement originated and a unique identifier, what the priority is, a definition of different priority levels, how stable the requirement is, and a definition of different stability levels.

Example:

### V.1. Communication with Server.
V.1.1.

The system shall be able to communicate with the Zephyr server.

Description: Messages, location of other users, and class subscriptions must all be handled through communication with the server.

Origin: Use cases III.2.1., III.2.2., III.2.5., III.2.12., III.2.13., III.2.14., and III.2.15. Customer interview from November 11, 2000.

Priority: 2          Stability: 2

## III. Nonfunctional Requirements

Enumerate all nonfunctional requirements in this section. Again, it is best to organize the nonfunctional requirements according to the modules into which the system has been decomposed by the system architect. Don't forget to provide traceability information such as where the requirement originated and a unique identifier, what the priority is, a definition of different priority levels, how stable the requirement is, and a definition of different stability levels.

Example:

### VI.1. Timing

VI.1.1.

WindowGrams sent by WinZephyr shall be received at the destination in an amount of time comparable to Unix Zephyr.

Description: The time to receive a WindowGram is described as nearly instantaneous. Messages consisting of 200 characters (roughly three lines of text) shall be sent to and received from the server in an average of two seconds.

Origin: Zephyr on Athena Manual.

Priority: 3                                     Stability: 1

## IV. Constraints

Enumerate all constraints.

## V. Requirements Dependency Traceability Matrix

Provide a cross-reference matrix showing related requirements as shown in the example below. The matrix is used to identify dependencies between requirements to identify when one requirement must be completed before another can be implemented.

| Is dependent on requirement | | | | |
|---|---|---|---|---|
| | Req1 | Req2 | Req3 | Req4 |
| Req1 | | X | | |
| Req2 | | | | |
| Req3 | | | | X |
| Req4 | X | | | |

## VI. Development and Target Platforms

Describe in full detail the expected development and target platforms including software/ hardware types, versions, and so on.

# VII. Project Glossary

Define any terms that are used throughout the requirements document. There will be many domain terms that have specific meaning in context. It is important to have all these terms defined in one place so that their meaning is clear to all readers.

# VIII. Document Revision History

This section includes a list of significant changes that have been made to this document after the 1.0 version has been submitted for assessment. The revision history should contain a dated list of revisions to the document consisting of: the date of each change, the person responsible for the change, and a description of the change. You should be able to trace changes to the individual who completed the modification. Changes are to be listed in reverse chronological order, recording the following information for changes:

| Version | File version number. |
|---|---|
| Name(s) | Name of individual(s) responsible for the change. |
| Date | Date of change. |
| Change Description | Description of the changes made to the file. |

# Use Case-based Requirements

This chapter gives an overall introduction to documenting requirements using use cases. In this chapter, we will explain the following:

> the symbols found in a use case diagrams
>
> the relationships between the symbols in a use case diagram
>
> the textual description of a use case, the use case flow of events

It is quite likely that you have written code in an object-oriented language, such as Java or C++. In these object-oriented languages, you have come to create your programs in terms of classes where each class has its own data (via variables/attributes) and its own behavior (via the class methods). In your programs, you create instances of these classes, called objects. As your program runs, these objects interact with each other to implement the system functionality.

In this chapter we will discuss a means of documenting your stakeholder functional requirements in a way that will more easily lead you to discover what classes you will need to implement. This approach is called the *use cases* approach [5]. When you document your requirements using use cases, these use cases are then valuable during the next steps in your project development – such as in the design and testing activities. Also, it will be easier to write your user manual if you have documented your requirements by means of use cases.

When we document requirements using use cases, we use textual description along with use case diagrams. The use case diagram is a part of the Unified Modeling Language [10], more commonly referred to as UML. In this chapter, we will first introduce you to UML. Then, we will show you how to document your requirements using use cases.

## 1   An Introduction to UML

UML is a modeling language or graphical/diagrammatic notation for object-oriented programming – a way to express the "blueprints" of your system. Within UML, there are several types of diagrams. Some of them are:

> Use case diagrams for requirements
>
> State diagrams for object-oriented analysis
>
> Class diagrams and sequence diagrams for object-oriented design

As a software engineer, you need to become well-versed in these UML diagrams. As you head towards your professional life, your peers will simply assume that you know these diagrams. When you brainstorm together, your co-workers will quickly draw one of these diagrams on a whiteboard without explaining the symbols or notations, fully expecting that you understand. Or, you might receive UML-based requirements, analysis, or design documents that you will need to work with.

Once you know UML, you can also communicate with your peers using the diagrams too. You know the old adage, "A picture is worth a thousand words." You can spend a few moments reviewing a use case, class, or sequence diagram and have a pretty good understanding of what even large programs do. UML diagrams are also very understandable to non-technical stakeholders. So, these diagrams are useful for validating requirements.

## 2 Scenario-based Requirements Elicitation

Before jumping into use cases themselves, we will first describe a scenario, which is a subset of a use case. A *scenario* is a *sequence of actions that illustrates behavior. A scenario may be used to illustrate an interaction or the execution of a use case instance.* [10] Scenarios are used in a scenario-based requirements elicitation, a technique of asking questions related to a descriptive story in order to ascertain the design requirements. For example, consider the following scenario for the Monopoly game:

> *Player 1 lands on Blue 3. This house is owned by Player 2, and the rent is $25.*
> *Player 1 gives Player 2 $25.*

The above scenario specifically describes, step-by-step, what happens on one of Player 1's turns.

With scenario-based requirements elicitation, we query the stakeholders for the kinds of things they want to be able to do. We ask them to describe how they envision the system in use. We then map these system problem statements into a system specification; the specification is represented as a set of actors and use cases, as we discuss below. We work with the customer to get a complete set of scenarios, which we document in our natural language (as opposed to using any formal notation) using customer's terminology. A complete set of scenarios should describe everything the system is intended to do. Scenarios have proven useful for eliciting, validating, and documenting requirements [7]. Scenario-based approaches help to bridge the gap between the user/stakeholder view and the functional view of the future system so that the future system will meet the requirements of its users [8]. Scenario-based approaches are widely used within industry [13].

## 3 Elements of a Use Case

A *use case* is a *specification of sequences of actions, including variant sequences and error sequences, that a system, subsystem, or class can perform by interacting with outside actors* [10]. Scenarios are a set of scenarios tied together by a common user goal [4] or a sequence of transactions performed by a system that yields an outwardly visible, measurable result of value for a particular actor. A use case typically represents a major piece of functionality that is complete from beginning to end and captures a contract between the stakeholders of a system about its behavior [3].

## 3.1    Use Case Is Made Up of Scenarios

As you will see, several related scenarios are joined together in one use case.    For example, consider the following two scenarios:

*A player is in Jail.  The player clicks the "Get out of Jail" button.  $50 is decremented from their money.  The player can then roll the dice and continue with the game.*

*A player is in Jail.  The player clicks the "Get out of Jail" button.  The player has less than $50.  The player becomes bankrupt and all the tradable cells he or she owns becomes available in the game.  The player is out of the game.*

Both scenarios have the common user goal of getting out of jail.  The first scenario is the simplest, all-goes-well scenario.  The second has some alternatives that specify what should happen if the player does not have enough money to get out of jail.  As you will see, we will build these two related, alternative scenarios into one use case.

## 3.2    Basic UML Symbols

In UML, a use case is represented by an oval, as shown in Figure 1.  In our Monopoly game, the names of some use cases are: Draw Card, Get Out of Jail, and Switch Turn.  It is best to express your use case title/label in a few words (generally no more than five words).  These few words must begin with a present-tense verb phrase in active voice, stating the action that must take place (notice: **Draw** Card, **Get Out** of Jail, and **Switch** Turn).

**Figure 1:  The UML symbol for a use case**

An *actor* is *an entity that interacts with the system and/or needs to exchange information with the system.*   The actor is *not* part of the system itself and should be included to represent anyone or anything that interacts with the system in the following ways:

supplies input information to the system
receives information from the system
both supplies input information to and receives information from the system

The total set of actors in a use case model includes everyone and everything that needs to exchange information with the system [9]. In UML symbols, an actor is represented as a stickman, shown below in Figure 2. In our Monopoly game, the actors include the a player and a bad player. As you see, actors can be people or they can be other systems. An actor is always a <u>noun</u> in the scenario.

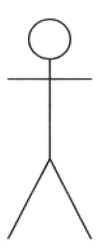

**Figure 2: The UML symbol for an actor**

You should think of the actors as roles, not as "individuals." For example, you might know that several players will play the game. However, they would all be represented by one actor because they all have the same role. Similarly, if you happen to know that one person might take on several roles, such as player and bad player, you might be tempted to combine those roles into one actor. However, you should keep each separated into their appropriate roles. Do not confuse actors with people and/or job titles.

## 3.3    *Identifying the Actors*

Often, people find it easiest to start the requirements elicitation process by identifying the actors. The following questions can help you identify the actors of your system [11]:

Who uses the system?

Who installs the system?

Who starts up the system?

Who maintains the system?

Who shuts down the system?

What other systems use this system?

Who gets information from this system?

Who provides information to the system?

Does anything happen automatically at a present time?

## *3.4  Identifying the Use Cases*

Then, the scenario-based requirements elicitation process continues by asking what outwardly visible, measurable result of value that each actor desires.  The following questions can be asked to identify use cases, once your actors have been identified [11]:

What functions will the actor want from the system?

Does the system store information?  What actors will create, read, update or delete this information?

Does the system need to notify an actor about chances in the internal state?

Are there any external events the system must know about?  What actor informs the system of those events?

## *3.5  Identifying the Boundary*

It is important to clearly define the boundary of your system.  Things inside the boundary of the system are things you need to worry about creating.  In a UML use case diagram, the *system boundary* is denoted by a rectangle, as in Figure 3.

## *3.6  Use Case Diagram*

A *use case diagram* is a visual representation of the relationships between actors and use cases together that documents the system's intended behavior.  A simple use case diagram is shown below in Figure 3.

Arrows and lines are draw between actors and use cases and between use cases to show their relationships.  We will discuss these relationships more later on in the chapter.  The default relationship between an actor and a use case is the *«communication»* relationship, denoted by a line with a small circle.  For example, the actor in Figure 3 is communicating with the use case.

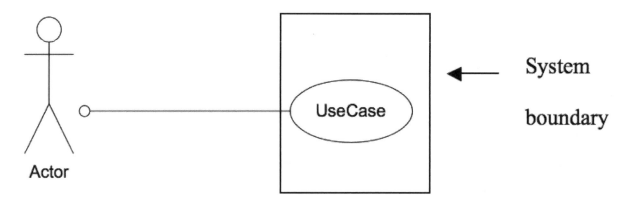

**Figure 3:  A UML use case diagram**

Use case diagrams are often developed incrementally.  When you feel that you are done with your use case diagram, any remaining actors that do not communicate with any use cases should be removed from your system.

# 4   Use Case Flow-of-Events

The use case diagram is important for visualizing a system. However, a textual description of the sequence of transactions of a use case is also needed for us to understand what really happens in a use case. In this section, we will use the use case *flow-of-events,* a description of what the system should do. The flow-of-events is written in terms of <u>*what the system should do*</u>, <u>not</u> <u>how</u> the system does it.

## *4.1   Templates for a Use Case Flow of Events*

Many different templates are available for writing a use case flow of events. The exact structure of these templates can vary slightly from author to author. In this book, we use the format that was described by Quantrani [6]. This template is shown in Figure 4 followed by an example of a completed flow of events for the Simulate a Configuration use case.

**X Flow-of-Events for the <name> Use Case**

**X.1 Preconditions**. *What needs to happen (in another use case) before this use case can start? What state must the system be in before the use case?*

**X.2 Main Flow**. *The main flow is a series of declarative steps.*

X.3 Sub-flows. *Sub-flows break down the main flow and other sub-flows to improve document readability.*

**X.4 Alternative Flows**. *The alternative flows define exceptional behavior that can interrupt the normal flow. Often alternative flows indicate what is to be done under error conditions. To determine alternative flows, ask yourself, "What could possibly go wrong?" for each of the actions in the main flow and the sub-flows.*

*Note: X is a unique identifier for each use case.*

**Figure 4:  Use Case Flow-of-Events Template**

## *4.2   An Example Flow of Events*

Below is an example flow-of-events for the Simulate a Configuration use case. The example uses the template of Figure 4 to structure the flow of events.

**UC8   Flow of Events for the *Buy House* Use Case**
**8.1   Preconditions:**

1. It is the player's turn.
2. The player has not rolled the dice.
3. The player has monopoly on one or more color groups.

## 8.2 Main Flow:

When a player has all the tradable cells in a color group, this player is said to have monopoly on the color group. A player may build house(s) in the property cells in the color groups the player has monopoly on by pressing the Buy House button before he or she rolls the dice [S1] [E1 – E2]. The price of the house is determined by the cell. After buying the house(s), the status of the player is updated and displayed on the game board [UC13].

## 8.3 Subflows:

[S1]   When the Buy House button is clicked, the Buy House dialog shows up. The player selects the monopoly color group and the number of houses from that dialog. After clicking on OK in the dialog box, the player pays the fee, and the houses are created. All the property cells in the selected color group have the same number of houses.

## 8.4 Alternative Flows:

[E1]   Nothing happens if the player does not have enough money.

[E2]   The player can build at most five houses in a cell.

Let us now dissect this flow of events.

The use case *precondition* indicates that before the use case can begin, it must be the player (who wants to buy a house)'s turn. The player has not rolled the dice, and the player must have a monopoly by owning all properties in a color group.

The *main flow* lists the sequence of events.

   o   When a main flow or sub-flow has an event marked such as [Sx], this indicates that a sub-flow of this use case must be "run." When that sub-flow completes, "control" is passed back. For example, the buy house dialog shows up [S1]. Once the dialog box is clicked, control is passed back to the main use case and the house is purchased.

   o   When a main flow or sub-flow has an event marked such as [Ex], this indicates that an exceptional condition might occur. If it does occur, the appropriate alternative flow explains how the situation should be handled.   For example, if the player does not have enough money or has more than five houses [E1-E2], the buy house dialog will not show up.

   o   When a main flow or sub-flow has an event marked such as [UCx], this indicates that another use case must be "run." When that use case completes, "control" is passed back to this use case.   For example, once the house purchase is complete, the status of the player is updated and displayed.   [UC13]

The *sub-flows* list individual sequences of the main flow.  Sub-flows can also handle the "calling" of other use cases, other sub-flows, and alternative flows similarly to the main flow.

*Alternative flows* list individual sequences of how exceptional situations should be handled.

All sub-flows and all alternative flows must be "called" from the main flow or from sub-flows(s) by an indication such as [Sx] or [Ex]. If they are not called, they have no purpose because they can never be executed.

## 4.3 A Scenario as One Flow Through a Flow of Events

As we said, multiple scenarios are handled by one use case. Consider the following two scenarios of this use case.

*The player has all the tradable cells in a color group and wants to buy a house for the color group. The player has enough money to buy the house and is shown the number of houses own in that group [S1], and purchases the house. The player's status is displayed [UC13].*

*The player has all the tradable cells in a color group and wants to buy a house for the color group. The player does not have enough money to buy the house. The player's status is displayed [UC13].*

Both of these scenarios and a multitude of others are represented with this use case. *A scenario is just one flow through the use case flow-of events.*

## 4.4 Writing a Flow of Events

A flow-of-events is generally written in an iterative manner. First, just a brief description of the normal flow of the use case is written. More details are added gradually and iteratively, including the alternative flows. The complete flow-of-events emerges by the end of the requirements specification phase.

By using a formal flow-of-events template, you can be sure that you include all the information you need in a use case. However, you should be sure use the entry 'none' as appropriate when you are filling out the template. There is no need to come up with something to fill each slot if the information is not needed. Only fill in items with added information.

The use case flow-of-events is very useful for formulating your test cases. When formulating these test cases, choose a variety of scenarios extracted from the use case, particularly those that include the alternate flows.

## 5 Use Case Relationships

There are several different kinds of relationships between actors and use cases. Earlier, we said that the default relationship is the *communication* relationship. The communication relationship indicates that one of these entities initiated communication or invoked request of the other. Obviously, an actor communicates with use cases because actors want measurable results. It might not be quite as obvious that use cases can communicate with other use cases. This happens when a use case needs information from or to initiate action of another use case. When a line or an arrow is draw on a diagram and there is no label on the arrow, it is, by default, a communication relationship.

There are two other kinds of relationships between use cases (not between actors and use cases) that you might find useful. These are the include relationship and the extend relationship, both of which we will describe in this section.

## 5.1    The include Relationship

The include relationship signifies that one use class is included in another's functionality. You use the include relationship when a chunk of behavior is similar across more than one use case and you don't want to keep copying the description of that behavior [4]. This is similar to breaking out re-used functionality in a program into its own methods that other methods invoke for that functionality. For example, suppose many actions of a system require the user to log into the system before the functionality can be performed. These use cases would *include* the Login use case. Here's a hint. *You should not break out a use case to be included by other use cases unless more than one other use case will include it (i.e. in a case diagram there should be more than one arrow coming into the included use case).*

The include relationship is not the default relationship. Therefore, in a use case diagram, the arrow is labeled with «include» when one use case makes full use of another use case, as shown in Figure 5. The Draw Card and the Buy House both use the View Information functionality. *Whenever a use case includes functionality of another use case, the use case flow-of-events will call the included use case.* In the example Buy House flow-of-events in the last section, the View Information [UC13] use case was called from the main flow.

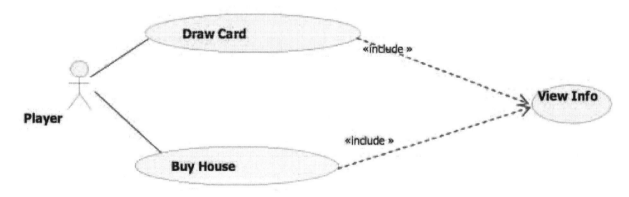

**Figure 5:  The Include Relationship between Use Cases**

## 5.2    The extend Relationship

160

You use the *extend* relationship when you are describing a variation on normal behavior or behavior that is only executed under certain, stated conditions. You might wonder how this is different from simply stating alternative flows. The extend relationship is similar to the alternative flows of a use case. However, the extend relationship is used when the alternative flow is fairly complex and/or multi-stepped, possibly with sub-flows and alternative flows. For example, consider an earlier scenario of the chapter.

*A player moves on the board because he or she has to go to jail.*
*A player moves on the board because he or she has to go to Free Parking.*

This scenario involves a player moving. However, sometimes a player has to deal with "exceptional" situations – rather than just moving to a new property cell. Therefore, we can extend the Move use case with the Go to Jail and the Go to Free Parking use case (and some others) as shown in Figure 6. In this diagram the extend relationship is signified by writing «extend» below a dotted line whose arrow points toward the use case that is being extended.

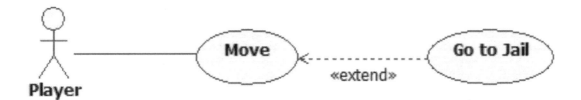

**Figure 6: The Extend Relationship between Use Cases**

The Start Individual Train use case would include a sub-flow to close the door. The Clear Door Obstacles flow-of-events activates only if any door is blocked. If a door is blocked, the train sounds an announcement for passengers to clear the doorways, waits for 10 seconds, and then tries to close the doors again. If the doors are not closed after three such cycles, a train operator is dispatched to find the problem. This is a multi-step alternative flow or sub-flow, best handled by separating the functionality out into a separate, extended use case. As with the including use cases, a use case flow-of-events must specifically call its extending use case(s). By doing so, the additional sequence of steps of the extended use case would be inserted in the base use case under certain, stated conditions.

## 5.3    *include Versus extend*

Frequently, software developers are confused as to whether to use the include relationship or the extend relationship. Consider the following distinctions between the two:

Use Case X *includes* Use Case Y:
X has a multi-step subtask Y. In the course of doing X or a subtask of X, Y will *always* be completed.

Use Case X *extends* Use Case Y:

Y performs a sub-task and X is a similar but more specialized way of accomplishing that subtask (e.g. going to jail is a sub-task of Y; X provides an alternate means of moving). *X only happens in an exception situation.* Y can complete without X ever happening.

In general, the extend relationship makes use cases difficult to understand. It is suggested that developers use this relationship sparingly.

## 6   Misuse Cases

Privacy and security requirements are also included as a special kind of use case, the misuse case. A misuse case is a use case from the point of view of an actor hostile to the system; the actor is a hacker deliberately threatening the security of the system and/or the privacy of the users of the system [1]. In the diagram in Figure 7 a black ellipse is used to denote a misuse.

**Figure 7:  Misuse Case**

We should carefully consider misuse cases in our requirements stage. Misuse cases are used to plan for mitigating threats; we deliberately list our mitigation steps in the flow-of-events. An example of a complete misuse case flow-of-events (based on a template from [12]) is found in the next section of this chapter.

## 7   Use Cases and the Software Requirements Specification

Organizations that use the use cases requirements approach insert the use cases into an SRS document in place of the functional requirements. This is called a *use case-based software requirements specification*. Although some requirements engineers view use cases as requirements [3], others caution that use cases are not requirements [11]. They feel instead that an SRS should contain formal statements of requirements that can be used as the conditions of system acceptance [2]; the use cases (with a traceability mapping to the formal requirements) can be added to the SRS if desired as an add-on.

# Monopoly Requirements Specification

**Version 1.0**

**May 16, 2004**

**Project Team:**

Chih-wei Ho, Team Lead
Hema Srikanth, Quality Assurance Manager
Nachi Nagappan, Requirements Analyst
Lucas Layman, Project Manager
Mark Sherriff, Development Manager

**Document Author(s):**

Nachi Nagappan, Requirements Analyst

**Customer Representative(s):**

Michael Gegick

# I. Introduction

The goal of this project is to create a Java-version of Monopoly board game. This game provides several features we can see in the board game version. This document describes the requirements of this program.

# II. Use Cases

| UC1 | Enter Player Info |
|------|-------------------|
| UC2 | Move |
| UC3 | Pass Go Cell |
| UC4 | Go to Jail |
| UC5 | Visit Jail |
| UC6 | Go to Free Parking |
| UC7 | Purchase Tradable Cell |
| UC8 | Buy House |
| UC9 | Pay Rent |
| UC10 | Draw Card |
| UC11 | Roll Dice |
| UC12 | Switch Turn |
| UC13 | View Information |
| UC14 | Get Out of Jail |
| UC15 | Trade |

| UC16 | Play More Than One Turn in a Round |
|------|-----------------------------------|

## UC1  Flow of Events for the *Enter Player Info* Use Case

### 1.1  Preconditions:

None.

### 1.2  Main Flow:

Right after the game gets started, the Player Information dialog will show to prompt the players enter the number of players for the game [E1] and the name of each player [E2] [E3].

### 1.3  Subflows:

None.

### 1.4  Alternative Flows:

[E1]  The number of players is a whole number between 2 and 8. If the players do not enter a whole number, or the number is not between 2 and 8, the game asks the player to retype the number of players again.

[E2]  The name cannot be an empty string. If a player enters an empty string, the game asks the player to retype his/her name.

[E3]  When the Cancel button is pressed, the Player Information dialog closes and the game ends.

## UC2  Flow of Events for the *Move* Use Case

### 2.1  Preconditions:

The players have entered their information in the Player Information dialog.

### 2.2  Main Flow:

The game is turn based. The first player's turn starts when the players' information is entered. The movement is based on the player's dice roll [UC11]. If the dice roll is 2, the player moves forward 2 steps; if the dice roll is 3, the player moves forward 3 steps; etc. What happens to the player depends on the cell the player lands on [S1] and whether the movement passes the Go cell [UC3]. The new position and information of the player is displayed on the game board [UC13]. The turn ends when the player hits the End Turn button [UC12]. Then the next player's turn begins.

### 2.3  Subflows:

[S1]  After the player moves to a new cell, based on the type of the cell, he or she may stop at the Go cell [UC3]; proceed to the Jail cell [UC4]; stop at the Jail cell [UC5]; stop at Free Parking [UC6]; pay rent to the cell owner [UC9]; draw a card from Community Chest or Chance [UC10]; or purchase an available tradable cell [UC7].

### 2.4  Alternative Flows:

None.

## UC3  Flow of Events for the *Pass Go Cell* Use Case

### 3.1  Preconditions:

1. It is the player's turn.

164

2. The player has rolled the dice.

### 3.2 Main Flow:

If the player passes the Go cell during the movement, or if the player lands on the Go cell after the movement, the player gains $200 [E1].

### 3.3 Subflows:

None.

### 3.4 Alternative Flows:

[E1] If the player passes the Go cell because he or she is sent to Jail, the player cannot collect the money. A player can be sent to Jail either because he or she draws a Go to Jail card, or because he or she lands on the Go to Jail cell.

## UC4  Flow of Events for the *Go to Jail* Use Case

### 4.1 Preconditions:

1. It is the player's turn.
2. The player has rolled the dice
3. The player lands on the Go to Jail cell.

### 4.2 Main Flow:

The player is sent to the Jail cell directly. When a player is sent to the Jail cell, he or she is said to be *in jail*.

### 4.3 Subflows:

None.

### 4.4 Alternative Flows:

None.

## UC5  Flow of Events for the *Visit Jail* Use Case

### 5.1 Preconditions:

1. It is the player's turn.
2. The player has rolled the dice.
3. The player lands on the Jail cell.

### 5.2 Main Flow:

The player visits the Jail. Nothing happens to the Jail visitors.

### 5.3 Subflows:

None.

### 5.4 Alternative Flows:

None.

## UC6  Flow of Events for the *Go to Free Parking* Use Case

### 6.1 Preconditions:

1. It is the player's turn.
2. The player has rolled the dice.
3. The player lands on the Free Parking.

**6.2  Main Flow:**

Nothing happens to a player landing on the Free Parking cell.

**6.3  Subflows:**

None.

**6.4  Alternative Flows:**

None.

## UC7  Flow of Events for the *Purchase Tradable Cell* Use Case

**7.1  Preconditions:**

1. It is the player's turn.
2. The player has rolled the dice.
3. The player lands on an available tradable cell.

**7.2  Main Flow:**

There are three types of tradable cells in this game: property cells, railroad cells, and utility cells. A tradable cell is available if it has no owner. When a player lands on an available tradable cell, he or she may buy the cell by clicking the Purchase button [E1]. The price the player needs to pay is the land value of the tradable cell [E2]. Player's information displayed on the game board is refreshed to show the cells and the amount of money a player owns [UC13].

**7.3  Subflows:**

None.

**7.4  Alternative Flows:**

[E1]  Nothing happens if the player does not have enough money for buying the cell.

[E2]  The price for a railroad cell or a utility cell is fixed. Railroad cells all cost the same. So do utility cells.

## UC8  Flow of Events for the *Buy House* Use Case

**8.1  Preconditions:**

1. It is the player's turn.
2. The player has not rolled the dice.
3. The player has monopoly on one or more color groups.

**8.2  Main Flow:**

When a player has all the tradable cells in a color group, this player is said to have monopoly on the color group. A player may build house(s) in the property cells in the color groups the player has monopoly on by pressing the Buy House button before he or she rolls the dice [S1] [E1 – E2]. The price of the house is determined by the cell. After buying the house(s), the status of the player is updated and displayed on the game board [UC13].

**8.3  Subflows:**

[S1]  When the Buy House button is clicked, the Buy House dialog shows up. The player selects the monopoly color group and the number of houses from that dialog. After clicking on OK in the dialog box, the player pays the fee, and the houses are created. All the property cells in the selected color group have the same number of houses.

**8.4 Alternative Flows:**

[E1] Nothing happens if the player does not have enough money.

[E2] The player can build at most five houses in a cell.

# UC9 Flow of Events for the *Pay Rent* Use Case

**9.1 Preconditions:**

1. It is the player's turn.

2. The player has rolled the dice.

3. The player lands on a tradable cell that is owned by another player.

**9.2 Main Flow:**

The player pay rent to the owner of the cell. The rate of the rent depends on the type of cell the player lands on [S1 – S3] [E1].

**9.3 Subflows:**

[S1] The rent of a property cell is defined in the property attribute. Each cell may have different rent rate. If the cell is in the owner's monopoly color group, the rent doubles.

[S2] If the cell is a utility cell, the player rolls the dice again [UC11]. If the owner owns one utility cell, the player pays three times the dice roll; if the owner owns two utility cells, the player pays ten times the dice roll.

[S3] If the cell is a railroad cell, and the owner owns $N$ railroad cells, the amount of rent the player needs to pay is $\$50 * 2^{N-1}$.

**9.4 Alternative Flows:**

[E1] If the player does not have enough money to pay the rent, the player is bankrupt. He or she needs to give all the tradable cells to the owner, and is out of the game.

# UC10 Flow of Events for the *Draw Card* Use Case

**10.1 Preconditions:**

1. It is the player's turn.

2. The player has rolled the dice.

3. The player lands on a card cell.

**10.2 Main Flow:**

There are two types of card cells in this game: Community Chest and Chance. Each type of card cell is associated with a pile of cards. When the player lands on a card cell, he or she draws a card by clicking the Draw Card button. A card is drawn from the top of the Community Chest card pile or the Chance card pile, depending on the type of cell the player lands on. The player performs the actions described on the card [S1 – S4]. After that, the card is put back to the bottom of the card pile, and the status of the player is updated and displayed [UC13].

**10.3 Subflows:**

[S1] If the card says the player can collect some certain amount of money, that amount of money is given to the player.

[S2] If the card says the player loses some certain amount of money, that money is subtracted from the player [E1].

[S3] If the card says the player goes to jail, the player is sent to the Jail cell immediately.

[S4] If the card says the player goes to some cell, the player is sent to that cell immediately.

**10.4 Alternative Flows:**

[E1] If the player does not have enough money, he or she is bankrupt. He or she needs to give up all his / her money, and all the tradable cells he / she owns become available. The player is out of the game.

## UC11 Flow of Events for the *Draw Card* Use Case

**11.1 Preconditions:**

It is the player's turn.

**11.2 Main Flow:**

The player rolls the dice by clicking on the Role Dice button. The Dice Roll dialog pops up to indicate the value of the dice roll. In this game, there are two six-faced dice.

**11.3 Subflows:**

None.

**11.4 Alternative Flows:**

None.

## UC12 Flow of Events for the *Switch Turn* Use Case

**12.1 Preconditions:**

1. It is the player's turn.

2. The player has rolled the dice, and moved to the new cell.

**12.2 Main Flow:**

The player's turn ends when he or she clicks on the End Turn button.

**12.3 Subflows:**

None.

**12.4 Alternative Flows:**

None.

## UC13 Flow of Events for the *View Information* Use Case

**13.1 Preconditions:**

None.

**13.2 Main Flow:**

The players can see their status, including their names, money, and properties, on the game board. The attributes of the cells, including the names, the owners, the number of houses, and the price, is displayed on the game board, too.

**13.3 Subflows:**

None.

**13.4 Alternative Flows:**

None.

## UC14 Flow of Events for the *Get Out of Jail* Use Case

### 14.1 Preconditions:

1. It is the player's turn.

2. The player has not rolled the dice.

3. The player is in jail.

### 14.2 Main Flow:

Before the player can roll the dice, he or she needs to click on Get Out of Jail button. Upon clicking the button, the player pays $50, and is no longer in jail [E1].

### 14.3 Subflows:

None.

### 14.4 Alternative Flows:

[E1] If the player does not have enough money, he or she is bankrupt. He or she needs to give up all his / her money, and all the tradable cells he / she owns become available. The player is out of the game.

## UC15 Flow of Events for the *Trade* Use Case

### 15.1 Preconditions:

1. It is the player's turn.

2. The player has not rolled the dice.

### 15.2 Main Flow:

The player may ask another player to sell his or her tradable cells. If the player wants to trade with another player, he or she clicks on the Trade button. The Trade Property dialog pops up and the player enters the player (the seller) he or she wishes to trade with, the cell he or she wishes to buy, and the amount of money he or she wish to pay [E1 – E2]. Then another dialog box shows up to ask the seller if the seller agrees with the deal. The seller clicks on Yes in the dialog box, and the cell is sold to the player for that amount of money [E3].

### 15.3 Subflows:

None.

### 15.4 Alternative Flows:

[E1] If the player clicks on Cancel button, the dialog closes and the deal is cancelled.

[E2] If the player does not have enough money, the deal is cancelled.

[E3] If the seller says no to this deal, the deal is cancelled.

## III. Misuse Cases

## UC16 Flow of Events for the *Play More Than One Turn in a Round* Use Case

### 16.1 Preconditions:

The player has completed moving, except for clicking on the End Turn button.

### 16.2 Main Flow:

Instead of the End Turn button, the player clicked on the Roll Dice button so that he or she can play another turn in the same round [E1].

**16.3  Sub-flows:**

None.

**16.4  Alternative Flows:**

[E1]  The Roll Dice button is disabled after the player rolls the dice. The player cannot click on it until the next turn.

# IV. Nonfunctional Requirements

### NR1. Performance

The system shall wait for all user inputs, and execute only the necessary functions given a user input to the system.  All functions shall be completed quickly.

    NR1.1. User response

        The system shall respond to any user input within 0.01 seconds.

        <u>Origin</u>: Interview with Mr. Gegick on May 1, 2004 (Interview #I03SC01

        <u>Priority</u>: 3

        <u>Implementation Completed Date</u>: July 9, 2004.

    NR1.2. Update user data

        The system should update user data within 0.01 seconds.

        <u>Origin</u>:  Interview with Mr. Gegick on May 1, 2004 (Interview #I03SC01

        <u>Priority</u>: 3

        <u>Implementation Completed Date</u>: July 9, 2004.

### NR2. Usability

A user shall be able to determine quickly what player options they have to perform.

    NR2.1. Player options

        A user shall only have access to functionality that is allowed to them at a given time.

        <u>Origin</u>:  Interview with Mr. Gegick on May 1, 2004 (Interview #I03SC01

        <u>Priority</u>: 3

        <u>Implementation Completed Date</u>: July 9, 2004.

    NR2.2. User Interface

        The system shall allow a user to interface with it through mouse events on buttons and drop down boxes and keyboard events on text fields.  The amount of user keyboard input shall be minimized by the system to include only entering the number of players, player names, and a trade price.

        <u>Origin</u>:  Interview with Mr. Gegick on May 1, 2004 (Interview #I03SC01

        <u>Priority</u>: 1

        <u>Implementation Completed Date</u>: July 29, 2004.

    NR2.3. User Errors

        The system shall catch improper input from all text fields in the system.

Origin:  Interview with Mr. Gegick on May 1, 2004 (Interview #I03SC01
Priority: 1
Implementation Completed Date: July 9, 2004.

## IV. Constraints

All code development shall be done with the Java programming language.
All testing shall be done using JUnit and FIT.

## VI. Requirements Dependency Traceability Table

| | UC1 | UC2 | UC3 | UC4 | UC5 | UC6 | UC7 | UC8 | UC9 | UC10 | UC11 | UC12 | UC13 | UC14 | UC15 | UC16 | NR1.1 | NR1.2 | NR2.1 | NR2.2 | NR2.3 |
|---|---|---|---|---|---|---|---|---|---|---|---|---|---|---|---|---|---|---|---|---|---|
| UC1 | | | | | | | | | | | | | | | | | | | | | |
| UC2 | | | | | | | | | | | X | X | X | | | | | | | | |
| UC3 | | X | | | | | | | | | | | | | | | | | | | |
| UC4 | | X | | | | | | | | | | | | | | | | | | | |
| UC5 | | X | | | | | | | | | | | | | | | | | | | |
| UC6 | | X | | | | | | | | | | | | | | | | | | | |
| UC7 | | X | | | | | | | | | | | X | | | | | | | | |
| UC8 | | | | | | | X | | | | | | X | | | | | | | | |
| UC9 | | X | | | | | X | | | | X | | | | | | | | | | |
| UC10 | | X | | | | | | | | | | | X | | | | | | | | |
| UC11 | X | | | | | | | | | | | | | | | | | | | | |
| UC12 | X | | | | | | | | | | | | | | | | | | | | |
| UC13 | X | | | | | | | | | | | | | | | | | | | | |
| UC14 | | | | X | | | | | | | X | | | | | | | | | | |
| UC15 | | | | | | | X | | | | | | | | | | | | | | |
| UC16 | | | | | | | | | | | X | X | | | | | | | | | |
| NR1.1 | | | | | | | | | | | | | | | | | | | | | |
| NR1.2 | | | | | | | | | | | | | | | | | | | | | |
| NR2.1 | | | | | | | | | | | | | | | | | | | | | |
| NR2.2 | | | | | | | | | | | | | | | | | | | | | |
| NR2.3 | | | | | | | | | | | | | | | | | | | | | |

## VII. Development and Target Platforms
1. Windows XP Operating System
2. Intel Pentium IV processors
3. Eclipse IDE

## VIII. Project Glossary
**cell:** a box on the game board on which the players land.  Cells can be houses, utilities, rail roads, jail, or "pick a card" slots.

## IX. Document Revision History

| Version | 1.0 |
|---|---|
| Name(s) | Dright Ho and Sarah Smith |
| Date | July 19, 2004. |
| Change Description | Original creation of the SRS. |

# 8 Summary

Several practical tips for use case-based requirements engineering were presented throughout this chapter. The keys for producing use-case based requirements specifications are summarized in Table 1.

| | |
|---|---|
| 🔑 | Identify all the actors of the system. |
| 🔑 | Think about all the functionality that the actors want from the system. |
| 🔑 | Consider what the various functions the actors are asking have in common. Abstract these as «include» use cases. |
| 🔑 | Avoid the «extend» relationship because it can make the use cases overly complex. |
| 🔑 | A picture is worth a thousand words. Use case diagrams help to visualize what the system has to do. But, more importantly, the use case flow-of-events gets much more specific about what the customer wants – the variations and the exceptions. |

**Table 1: Key Ideas for Use Case Requirements**

Use cases have proven helpful for the elicitation of, communication about, and documentation of requirements [13]. Many stakeholders feel more comfortable with describing scenarios than with describing an operational SRS that focuses on "The system shall..." requirements. [12]. Additionally, the simple and intuitive diagrams may provide nice overviews of system functionality. There is an element of personal preference when comparing the two forms of the SRS, the formal SRS and the use case SRS. As we said earlier, some requirements engineers feel that the formal version of the SRS is necessary in all cases, with the use cases adding additional support, if desired. Both forms of SRS provided so far can be used for building a verifiable SRS, exhibiting the characteristics of properly-written requirements – understandable, non-prescriptive, correct, complete, concise, consistent, unambiguous, testable, traceable, and feasible.

## Glossary of Chapter Terms

| Term | Definition | Source |
|---|---|---|

172

| actor | An abstraction for entities outside a system, subsystem, or class that interact directly with the system. An actor participates in a use case or coherent set of use cases to accomplish an overall purpose. | [10] |
|---|---|---|
| Scenario | A sequence of actions that illustrates behavior. A scenario may be used to illustrate an interaction or the execution of a use case instance. | [10] |
| Stereotype | A new kind of model element defined within the model based on an existing kind of model element. Stereotypes may extend the semantics but not the structure of pre-existing metamodel classes. | [10] |
| Use case | The specification of sequences of actions, including variant sequences and error sequences, that a system, subsystem, or class can perform by interacting with outside actors. | [10] |

# References

[1]    I. Alexander, "Misuse Cases:  Use Cases with Hostile Intent," *IEEE Software*, vol. 20, no. 1, pp. 58-66, January/February 2003.

[2]    A. I. Anton, J. H. Dempster, and D. F. Siege, "Deriving Goals from a Use-Case Based Requirements Specification for an Electronic Commerce System," *Requirements Engineering Journal*, vol. 6, no., pp. 63-73, May 2001.

[3]    A. Cockburn, *Writing Effective Use Cases*. Reading, Massachusetts: Addison-Wesley, 2000.

[4]    M. Fowler, *UML Distilled*. Reading,  Massachusetts: Addison Wesley, 2000.

[5]    I. Jacobson, M. Christerson, P. Jonsson, and G. Övergaard, *Object-Oriented Software Engineering:  A Use Case Driven Approach*. Wokingham, England: Addison-Wesley,

1992.

[6]     T. Quatrani, *Visual Modeling with Rational Rose and UML*. Reading, Massachusetts: Addison Wesley, 1998.

[7]     J. Ralyté, "Reusing Scenario Based Approaches in Requirement Engineering Methods: CREWS Method Base," 1st International Workshop on the Requirements Engineering Process, Florence, Italy, 1999, pp. 305-309.

[8]     J. Ralyté, C. Rolland, and V. Plihon, "Method Enhancement with Scenario Based Techniques," 11th International Conference on Advanced Information System Engineering (CAISE'99), Heidelberg, Germany, 1999, pp. 103-118.

[9]     D. Rosenberg and K. Scott, *Use Case Driven Object Modeling with UML: A Practical Approach*. Reading, Massachusetts: Addison-Wesley, 1999.

[10]   J. Rumbaugh, I. Jacobson, and G. Booch, *The Unified Modeling Language Reference Manual*. Reading: Addison Wesley, 1999.

[11]   G. Schneider and J. P. Winters, *Applying Use Cases: A Practical Guide*. Reading, Mass.: Addison Wesley, 1998.

[12]   G. Sindre and A. L. Opdahl, "Templates for Misuse Case Description," 7th International Workshop on Requirements Engineering: Foundation for Software Quality, Interlaken, Switzerland, 2001, pp.

[13]   K. Weidenhaupt, K. Pohl, M. Jarke, and P. Haumer, "Scenario Usage in System Development: A Report on Current Practice," *IEEE Software*, no., March 1998.

## Chapter Questions

1. Stakeholder are the key representatives of the groups who have a vested interest in a system and direct or indirect influence on its requirements. Are stakeholders the same as actors during use case analysis?

2. What are the questions we should ask ourselves when finding the actors in a system?

3. Tom installed a pupil scanner at the front door. The scanner is connected to a central unit, which stores the pupil patterns of Tom. Describe the scenario (in words) whenever Tom wants to get in from the front door.

4. After a use case model is built, if we find that there are two actors associating with similar use cases, what does it possibly mean? Should we take some action if such situation arises?

5. In a bulletin board system, only a registered user can post an article. If an unregistered user tries to post an article, he or she will be asked to register. Consider the following diagrams:

Are they equivalent? If not, which one better captures the requirements? Justify your answer.

6. Tiger Wiggler is a supermarket. Customers of Tiger Wiggler may apply for a VIP card. When the customer shows the VIP card at the counter, the he will get a special discount. Following is the flow of event of the use case which describes the process when the cashier scans the VIP card. What are the problems with the description?

---

### UC3: Cashier Scanning VIP Card

#### 3.1 Preconditions:
The cashier has logged in the POS system.

#### 3.2 Main Flow:
The cashier scans the VIP card [S1-S2]. The card information goes into the CRM system, and the products the customer buys are added into the shopping record.

#### 3.3 Subflows:
S1. The card reader reads the information on the card. The POS system checks the personal information from the CRM system [E1].

S2. If the reader does not recognize the card, the cashier asks the customer to reapply a new VIP card.

#### 3.4 Alternative Flows:
E1. If the membership expires, the cashier asks the customer to renew the membership.

E2. If there is no shopping record for the customer, a new record is created.

---

7. Use the use case analysis methods introduced in this chapter to analyze the requirements of a soft drink vending machine's software. What are the actors? What are the use cases? Are there any relationships between the use cases?

8. "Select an Item" is a use case for the vending machine's software. Describe the flow of event of this use case.

9. Suppose you are given a task to design the use cases for software run in a vending machine which sells soft drink. Identify a misuse case for the vending machine's software. Also, give a textural description for the misuse case.

10. So far, we have learned two methods to specify requirements. Discuss when the use case method is preferred, and when it is not.

11. Suppose we are writing a simple browser. This browser can read a "static" HTML file, and show the content on the screen. A static HTML file is a plain HTML file that contains neither dynamic scripts such as JavaScript, nor server side scripts such as JSP. This browser only displays the content. It does not have forward or backward buttons. Consider only the functional requirements.
    A. Develop a use case SRS document.
    B. Develop a formal SRS document.
    C. Comparing these two artifacts. Which one do you think is better for this project? Why?

12. Use your knowledge about ATM. Describe the possible misuse cases for the ATM. Also, develop a formal SRS document that focuses on security and privacy concerns. Do the misuse cases help to identify these security and privacy requirements? In your opinion, which is the better way to describe the security and privacy requirements? Justify your answers.

# User Story-Based Requirements Elicitation

Sometimes it is very difficult or not economical to produce a complete, verifiable set of requirements. In this chapter, we explain:

The circumstances when traditional and/or use case requirements specifications may not be appropriate

The practices of producing low-ceremony, high-level requirements that are predicted to change throughout development.

*The hardest part of the software task is arriving at a complete and consistent specification, and much of the essence of building a program is in fact the debugging of the specification.* — Fred Brooks, 1987 [4]

There are many benefits to devising and verifying a software requirements specification. The requirements guide the rest of the software development – so it can be exceedingly costly and/or devastating to the project if the requirements are incorrect or incomplete. Additionally, the requirements can act as a contract between the customer and the software development.

**Traditional Versus Agile Approaches**

As you've probably realized, though, it takes a lot of hard work to develop a verifiable set of requirements—sometimes it can even seem impossible. As you can see from the above quote, presumably the world's most famous software engineer, Fred Brooks, agrees! He goes even further to say that once you are done with this hardest task of arriving at a complete and consistent specification, you end up spending a great deal of time debugging the creation you worked so hard on. These difficulties have led to a "don't even bother" philosophy when working on a project that is expected to have a lot of requirements changes. With the agile software development model, on the other hand, a high-level, low-ceremony version of the requirements specification is produced; the agile team is ready to respond to the inevitable changes in these requirements.

**Context Determines the Approach**

Both the agile approach and the verifiable approaches to requirements engineering are appropriate in their own context. Projects with a lot of change that need to get out to the market quickly might be best done with high-level, low-ceremony requirements practices. Stable projects with safety-critical implications could best be done with a plan-driven, well-documented specification.

# 1 Essential Aspects of Agile Requirements

*Agile practices are based on the belief that neither the customer nor the developers have full knowledge in the beginning and that the important consideration is having practices that will allow both [the customer and the developer] to learn and evolve as that knowledge is gained—without ongoing recrimination.* [6]

Those software developers who use agile methods believe that the statement of requirements will evolve through the whole project. As a result, a verifiable, documented form of the requirements (that would exhibit the characteristics of being understandable, non-prescriptive, correct, complete, consistent, concise, unambiguous, testable, traceable, and feasible) is never produced. Instead, agile requirements are expressed as high-level, brief written statements of the best information fairly easily available.

## 1.1 Frequent, Personal Interactions

Because the requirements are just short statements of the best information easily available, an *essential aspect* of agile requirements is to have *frequent, personal interactions with customers and/or stakeholders*. These interactions are necessary for the developers to understand the details of what the customers really want. Best case, a customer is available on-site and resides with the development team. This ability for a developer to easily have personal interaction with a customer makes the difference between (1) the software developer finding out what the customer really wants and (2) the software developer making assumptions about what the customer probably wants. Acting on the latter of these two options is dangerous – so the readily-available customer is critical for the success of the project. In the case of "shrink-wrapped" software (such as Microsoft Office) that is distributed to hundreds, thousands, or even millions or customers, it can be difficult to get a real customer to sit with the team. Instead, "proxy users" are inserted between the developers and the "real" customers. These proxy users are business analysts and/or systems analyst who work directly with real users and can hopefully communicate the wishes of the majority of customers.

## 1.2 Frequent Delivery of Software

Another essential aspect of agile requirements is to have *frequent delivery of software to customers*. Most agile teams provide a new version of the working system to customers every two weeks. Only when the customer can actually use the evolving project can he or she provide vital feedback on what has been done and a new, refreshed view of follow-on requirements based on the progress so far. Additionally, frequent delivery helps to keep the momentum of customers working with developers.

*There is nothing that focuses requirements better than seeing the nascent system come to life. Therefore, capturing the specific details about the requirement long before it is implemented is likely to result in wasted effort and premature focusing. Therefore, if requirements are developed on an as-you-go basis, in an agile approach, the development can be more efficient in the long run than if requirements were elicited up front. [7]*

### 1.3 Expressing Requirements as Features

In varying form, agile methods use high-level, low-ceremony requirements practices. For example, the Feature-Driven Development [5] and Scrum methodologies [9] express their requirements as features. A *feature* is *a small, client-valued function expressed in the form <action.><result><object> (e.g. calculate the total of a sale)* [8]. An example of a Monopoly feature might be:

> Purchase available property.

With such a short description of the requirement, it is essential that software developers and stakeholders talk often to clarify exactly what is needed for each feature.

## 2   The Basics of User Stories

Of the agile methodologies, the Extreme Programming [2] (XP) methodology specifies its requirements practices with the most detail and rigor. Therefore, in this chapter we will discuss the XP form of requirements in great deal with an extensive example. XP specifies its requirements in the form of user stories. A *user story represents a feature customers want in the software* [3]. User stories are written by a customer, maybe with the assistance of the developers. Formal requirements and use cases are often documented in an archived document, available to the development team via a hardcopy document or online. Sometimes user stories are entered into an online system, but most often the stories are written on index cards.

### 2.1   Using Index Cards

The index cards are passed to the team member(s) who will work on the requirements and/or they are pinned to a "big visible board" in the area where the team works. As with features, the few sentences on the card are not enough for a developer to really understand what the customer wants. Instead these cards are a "mnemonic token of an ongoing conversation" [7] and the customer and the developer must converse often to gain a thorough understanding of what is desired.

### 2.2   Estimating Ideal Development Time

After the customer writes the stories, the developers estimate how long the stories might take to implement. Consider a team that has two-week iterations. Then, each story will get an estimate of days of ideal development time. *Ideal development time* describes how long it would take to implement the story in code if there were no distractions, no other assignments, and you knew exactly what to do [2]. If a story would take longer than two weeks, the story must be broken down into multiple smaller stories. If a story takes less than one day, the story is too detailed a level and should be combined with other small stories.

# 3   Gathering User Stories

The initial requirements should be gathered during a small, preferably offsite meeting. The meeting is attended by software developers and a small group of customers who bring domain expertise and are representative of the user population. There are two ways of gathering user stories, the goal oriented approach and the scattergun approach.

With the *goal-oriented approach* [1], the meeting starts with a goal of the system, such as "Players can move around the board." The group then considers what steps the user takes when trying to achieve this goal. These steps are written as user stories.

Conversely, with the *scattergun approach* [1], user stories are generated as expectations arise in the conversation. No structure is imposed on the way the meeting progresses.

Story writing is iterative and interactive. Customers propose a story. The developers consider if the story can be tested and/or estimated. If not, the team converts the story into one that can be tested and estimated. Then the developers estimate the story, asking the customer many questions of clarification to do this. If the story is too big or too small, the story is split or combined.

# 4   How to Write an Agile Requirement User Story

Here is an example of a user story for the Monopoly game. From it we can extract some criteria to guide us in our writing of a user story. The user story appears on an index card like this:

| Title: **Draw Lose Money Card** | | |
|---|---|---|
| Acceptance Test: **communityChest2** | Priority: **3** | Story Points: **1** |
| When a player lands on a Community Chest or Chance cell, the player draws a card from the Community Chest or Chance. If the card is a lose money card, the player pays the money to the bank. If he does not have enough money, he is out of the game, and the cells he owns become available without any houses. | | |

### 4.1 Index Card Elements
Now let us dissect this user story:

> *Title.* Write a two or three word title for this user story. The title should begin with a present-tense verb phrase in active voice (similar to the name of a use case). Write this title in the middle of the top line of an index card.
>
> *Acceptance Test.* List the unique identifiers of the acceptance tests for the user story. The unique identifier can be a word (such as LoginTest in the example above) or a alphanumeric string.
>
> *Priority.* The customer must decide how important each of the stories is so that the most important stories can be done first. We are using a 1-2-3 priority scheme where a 1 is given to the most important stories.

*Story Points.* The number of days of ideal development time.

*Description:* Write 1–2 sentences in the main space of the index card. These describe a single step toward achieving the goal.

## 4.2 Criteria for User Stories

Here are some important points to remember when writing user stories [3]:

*Stories must be understandable to the customer.* The stories should be written in the natural language of the customer, not in any kind of technical language or form.

*Each story must provide value to the customer.* Therefore, there are no stories for things such as designing databases or developing an infrastructure. Databases and infrastructure do not provide value to the customer. Instead, the first story that needs the database would need to include the resources for designing and developing the database needed to complete the story.

*Developers do not write stories.* As developers, we might think we know about requirements the customer hasn't thought of yet. However, the customer needs to be involved in every story. So, if the developer thinks he or she has thought of something the customer hasn't yet thought of, this must be discussed with the customer before a story can be written.

*Stories need to be of a size that several of them can be completed in each iteration.* At the end of each iteration (generally every two weeks), new functionality must be demonstrated (and perhaps delivered) to the customer. This functionality needs to be of value to the customer.

*Stories should be as independent of each other as possible.* By this we mean that it should not be necessary for one story to be completed before the development of another can start. It is not possible to completely remove dependencies between stories, but we should strive to minimize dependencies as much as possible. By minimizing the dependencies, we can have the freedom to schedule the work in any order, giving the customer maximum flexibility for scheduling their priorities.

*Each story must be testable.* We need to definitely know whether or not we are done with a story. This prevents ambiguous stories, such as "The betting process must be easy to understand." The phrase "easy to understand" is ambiguous because whether or not this story is implemented depends on the interpretation of the tester. We'll discuss this more in the next section.

# 5   Acceptance Tests

In the agile approach, in addition to gathering requirements, writing user stories, another important step is the development of acceptance test cases to verify the implementation of the user story.

An *acceptance test* is a test case written by the customer (in partnership with the developers). When the customer runs the test case and it runs, he or she can feel confident that the team has, indeed, implemented the desired functionality. One or more automated acceptance tests must be created to verify the user story has been correctly implemented.

The details about the user stories are captured in the form of acceptance tests specified by the customer. Often details of the requirements are worked out as the test case is written. Together, the user stories plus the corresponding acceptance test case(s) are used to verify that the system is behaving as the customers have specified. [7]

Ideally, the acceptance test cases are automated by the development team. Then, the suite of automated acceptance test cases can grow over the course of development. The test suite can be run again and again (at least daily) to ensure that no new functionality/code has broken the previously working user stories.

There should be traceability between the user story and the acceptance test(s) used to verify that user story. Then, if an acceptance test works, this is "proof" that the story is working under the specific conditions of the test; if an acceptance test does not work, the story has not been implemented to properly work under the conditions of the test. Often, agile developers will state that there should be at least one acceptance test case per use story. Sufficient testing would necessitate using many more than one test case per requirement. Usually there is one acceptance test—a basic, "everything goes smoothly" success test—just scratching the surface.

## 6    Documenting Non-Functional Requirements and Constraints

Use cases and user stories are functional requirements. As you know, functional requirements are only part of the story. In the process of eliciting user stories, you must all pay special attention to understanding and documenting the non-functional requirements, security and privacy requirements, and constraints. Because so much of the conversation will be focused on the user stories, you must make a dedicated effort to understand the customers' usability, reliability, availability, and performance needs. Additionally, you must understand the security and privacy concerns of the project and, as much as possible, translate these concerns into user stories. For example, the players of the Monopoly game will not like to wait for very long for the dice to "roll" or for their game piece to move.

Most often the user story cards are augmented with a simple listing of the non-functional requirements (including security and privacy) and the constraints. Although non-functional requirements and constraints can't really be written as use stories, they impact many stories. For example, if a non-functional requirement was that all transactions must be performed in under 1 second, every transactional user story must understand this criteria. Or, if the system must be 96% reliable, the whole team is impacted in everything they do by the need for high reliability and the need to meet this criteria for customer satisfaction with the system. Therefore, the user story cards should be augmented with a listing of non-functional requirements and constraints.

## 7    Examples of User Stories—Online Monopoly Game

We will now show you a selection of user story cards with corresponding acceptance test cases followed by some example non-functional requirements and constraints for the online auctions management system.

**Table 1:  User Story Summary**

| User Stories | Priority | Points | Acceptance Tests |
|---|---|---|---|
| Move Player | 1 | 1 | playerMovement1 |
| Move Player in Turns | 1 | 1 | playerMovement2 |
| Pass Go | 2 | 2 | passGo |
| Free Parking | 2 | 1 | freeParking |
| Go to Jail | 2 | 2 | jail1 |
| Get Out of Jail | 2 | 2 | jail2 |
| Purchase Property | 1 | 2 | purchasingProperty1 |
| Pay Rent | 3 | 1 | payRent1 |
| Pay Rent and Bankruptcy | 3 | 2 | payRent2 |
| Trade Properties | 3 | 3 | tradeAccept, tradeDecline |
| Buy Railroad | 3 | 1 | railroad1 |
| Pay Rent to Railroad | 3 | 2 | railroad2 |
| Buy Utility | 3 | 1 | util1 |
| Pay Rent to Utility | 3 | 2 | util2 |
| Buy House | 1 | 2 | buyHouse1 |
| Draw Jail Card | 2 | 2 | communityChest1 |
| Draw Lose Money Card | 3 | 1 | communityChest2 |
| Draw Gain Money Card | 2 | 1 | communityChest3 |
| Dra31w Move Player Card | 3 | 2 | communityChest4 |
| **Total Story Points** | | 31 | |

## 7.1 Functional Requirements

The functional requirements of the Monopoly game are now listed as user stories.

| Title: Move Player | | |
|---|---|---|
| Acceptance Test: playerMovement1 | Priority: 1 | Story Points: 1 |
| A player moves based on the dice roll (two dice, each with six faces). When the user reaches the end of the board, he cycles around. | | |

| Title: Move Players in Turns | | |
|---|---|---|
| Acceptance Test: playerMovement2 | Priority: 1 | Story Points: 1 |
| The players should play in turns. | | |

| Title: Pass Go | | |
|---|---|---|
| Acceptance Test: passGo | Priority: 1 | Story Points: 2 |
| When a player passes or lands on the GO cell, the bank gives the player $200. | | |

| Title: Free Parking | | |
|---|---|---|
| Acceptance Test: freeParking | Priority: 2 | Story Points: 1 |
| When a player lands on Free Parking, nothing happens. | | |

| Title: Go To Jail | | |
|---|---|---|
| Acceptance Test: jail1 | Priority: 2 | Story Points: 2 |
| When a user lands on the "Go to Jail" cell, the player goes directly to jail, does not pass go, and does not collect $200. | | |

| Title: Get Out of Jail | | |
|---|---|---|
| Acceptance Test: jail2 | Priority: 2 | Story Points: 2 |
| When a player is in Jail, he must pay 50 dollars to get out of jail in the next turn. If he does not have enough money, he is out of the game, and the cells he owns become available without any houses. | | |

| Title: Purchase Property | | |
|---|---|---|
| Acceptance Test: purchasingProperty1 | Priority: 1 | Story Points: 2 |
| When a player lands on a property cell, and it is available, the player may purchase it. The price is the land value of that property. | | |

| Title: Pay Rent | | |
|---|---|---|
| Acceptance Test: payRent1 | Priority: 3 | Story Points: 1 |
| When a player (A) lands on a property owned by another player (B), A must pay rent to B. The level of rent paid is a base level of rent, unless the owner has a monopoly or houses/hotel. | | |

| Title: Pay Rent and Bankruptcy | | |
|---|---|---|
| Acceptance Test: payRent2 | Priority: 3 | Story Points: 2 |
| If player B owes player A more money than player B currently has, player B is bankrupt, and must give all of their property to player A . | | |

| Title: Trade Properties | | |
|---|---|---|
| Acceptance Test: tradeAccept, tradeDecline | Priority: 3 | Story Points: 3 |
| If player 2 wishes to purchase a property from player 1, player 2 will name an amount of money to pay player 1 for the property they wish to own. Player 1 can decide to accept or decline the offer. | | |

| Title: Buy Railroad | | |
|---|---|---|
| Acceptance Test: railroad1 | Priority: 3 | Story Points: 1 |
| The land value of the railroads is the same. | | |

| Title: Pay Rent to Railroad | | |
|---|---|---|
| Acceptance Test: railroad2 | Priority: 3 | Story Points: 2 |
| When player A lands on player B's railroad, A pays rent to B based on the number of railroads B owns. If the base rent of a railroad is R, and the number of the railroads B owns is N, the amount of rent A needs to pay B is $R * 2^{N-1}$. | | |

| Title: Buy Utility | | |
|---|---|---|
| Acceptance Test: util1 | Priority: 3 | Story Points: 1 |
| The land value of the utilities is the same. | | |

| Title: Pay Rent to Utility |
|---|

| Acceptance Test: util2 | Priority: 3 | Story Points: 2 |
|---|---|---|

When player A lands on player B's utility, A pays rent to B based a dice roll. If player B owns 1 utility, A pays 4 times the dice roll. If player B owns 2 utilities, A pays 10 times the dice roll. There can only be two utilities on a game board.

| Title: Buy House | | |
|---|---|---|
| Acceptance Test: buyHouse1 | Priority: 1 | Story Points: 2 |

A player has monopoly when he purchases all the properties of a color group. When a player has a monopoly of a color group, he can buy houses for those properties at the beginning of his turn. Player cannot purchase more than 5 houses on any given monopoly.

| Title: Draw Jail Card | | |
|---|---|---|
| Acceptance Test: communityChest1 | Priority: 2 | Story Points: 2 |

When a player lands on a Community Chest or Chance cell, the player draws a card from the Community Chest or Chance. If the card is a Jail card, the player goes to Jail without getting paid when passing the Go cell.

| Title: Draw Lose Money Card | | |
|---|---|---|
| Acceptance Test: communityChest2 | Priority: 3 | Story Points: 1 |

When a player lands on a Community Chest or Chance cell, the player draws a card from the Community Chest or Chance. If the card is a lose money card, the player pays the money to the bank. If he does not have enough money, he is out of the game, and the cells he owns become available without any houses.

| Title: Draw Gain Money Card | | |
|---|---|---|
| Acceptance Test: communityChest3 | Priority: 2 | Story Points: 1 |

When a player lands on a Community Chest or Chance cell, the player draws a card from the Community Chest or Chance. If the card is a gain money card, the player gets the money from the bank.

| Title: Draw Move Player Card | | |
|---|---|---|
| Acceptance Test: communityChest4 | Priority: 2 | Story Points: 2 |

> When a player lands on a Community Chest or Chance cell, the player draws a card from the Community Chest or Chance. If the card is a move player card, the player goes to the specified cell. If the player passes go, he or she is paid $200 from the bank.

**7.2 Non-functional requirements**
1. A user shall respond to any user input within 0.01 seconds.
2. The system shall update user data within 0.01 seconds.
3. The system shall catch improper input from all text fields

**7.3 Constraints**
1. The system shall be developed using Java.
2. The system shall be tested using the JUnit and FIT frameworks.

**7.4     Sample Acceptance Tests**

For illustrative purposes, two sample test cases for two of the user stores are given below in Table 2.

**Table 2:  Sample acceptance test cases**

| Test ID | Description | Expected Results | Actual Results |
|---|---|---|---|
| | | | |

| util1* | Precondition: Game is in test mode.<br>Number of players: 2<br>    Enter 2 in # of player's dialog | 1 has $1350<br>2 has $1500<br>1 is located at Electric Company | |
|---|---|---|---|
| | Enter player 1's name as 1<br>Enter player 2's name as 2<br>Press 1's Roll Dice button<br>Enter dice roll of 12<br>Press 1's Purchase Property button<br>Press 1's End Turn button | 2 is located at Go<br>1 owns Electric Company<br>2 does not own any property | |
| purchasingProperty1* | Precondition: util1 has passed<br>    Press 2's Roll Dice button<br>    Enter dice roll of 3<br>    Press 2's Purchase Property button<br>    Press 2's End Turn button | 1 has $1350<br>2 has $1440<br>1 is located at Electric Company<br>2 is located at Baltic Avenue<br>1 owns Electric Company<br>2 owns Baltic Avenue | |

## 6 Summary

Several practical tips were provided for documenting requirements in a low-ceremony, high level manner – and when it was appropriate to use this type of requirement documentation rather than traditional or use case requirements. These tips are summarized in Table 3.

| | |
|---|---|
| | Agile requirements are appropriate for projects with short cycle times/iterations and volatile requirements. |
| | Because agile requirements are not stated completely, developers must have regular access to customers so the specifics of the requirements can be clarified as necessary. |
| | Each user story should have at least one acceptance tests. The acceptance test helps to determine the specifics of what the customer wants. |

| | Acceptance test cases are written by the customer in partnership with the developer. The customer uses the acceptance test cases to determine if a user story has been completed. |
|---|---|

**Table 3: Key Ideas for Agile Requirements**

## Glossary of Chapter Terms

| Term | Definition | Source |
|---|---|---|
| Feature | a small, client-valued function expressed in the form <action.><result><object> (e.g. calculate the total of a sale) | [8]. |
| User story | a feature customers want in the software | [3] |

# References

[1] D. Astels, G. Miller, and M. Novak, *Prentice Hall*. Upper Saddle River, NJ: Prentice Hall, 2002.

[2] K. Beck, *Extreme Programming Explained: Embrace Change*. Reading, Mass.: Addison-Wesley, 2000.

[3] K. Beck and M. Fowler, *Planning Extreme Programming*. Reading, Massachusetts: Addison Wesley, 2001.

[4] F. P. Brooks, "No Silver Bullet," *IEEE Computer*, vol. 20, no. 4, pp. 10-19, 1987.

[5] P. Coad, E. LeFebvre, and J. DeLuca, *Java Modeling in Color with UML*: Prentice Hall, 1999.

[6] J. Highsmith, *Agile Software Development Ecosystems*. Boston, MA: Addison-Wesley, 2002.

[7] R. C. Martin, *Agile Software Development: Principles, Patterns, and Practices*. Upper Saddle River: Prentice Hall, 2003.

[8] S. R. Palmer and J. M. Felsing, *A Practical Guide to Feature-Driven Development*. Upper Saddle River, NJ: Prentice Hall PTR, 2002.

[9] K. Schwaber and M. Beedle, *Agile Software Development with SCRUM*. Upper Saddle River, NJ: Prentice-Hall, 2002.

## Chapter Questions

1. AgileGo is a development team that practices agile methodologies. After several successful projects, they found out that the team's velocity is 20 story points per week (which means they can finish 20 story points every week). AgileGo has just got a new project recently. After working with the customer, they had an initial version of user stories. These stories weighted 230 points totally.

    A. Based on experience, how long will AgileGo need to finish the project?
    B. The client needs the software working in two months. How many story points can AgileGo finish in two months?
    C. What can AgileGo do to deliver the software in two months?

2. It is important to have an on-site customer if we practice Extreme Programming. However, we cannot find the real customers for shrink-wrapped software like Microsoft Office. How shall we develop the requirements for such software?

3. Agile methods are said to fit into software projects of turbulent requirements. List the features of agile requirements elicitation, and discuss, from the perspective of requirement elicitation, why agile methods are suitable for e-commerce projects.

4. When writing user stories, the development team uses velocity to estimate performance. Velocity is the number of story points the team can finish in a period of time, e.g. 20 points/week. If you participated in an agile software project, how do you estimate the performance of yourself, and your team? (Hint: Agile developers always use the easiest way to solve problems.)

5. The students need to do a term project in the Operating Systems course. This is a teamed project, and each team consists of 4 students. In the project, the students are asked to write a memory management system. The students can choose their own algorithm or memory management scheme. The final score of the project is given based on the effectiveness of the program. Given a fixed amount of memory, if a team's program can load more data, the team will get a higher score.

    If you were a student in this course, will you use user stories to manage the requirements of this project? Justify your answer. If this is not a school project, but a commercial project, will you change your answer? Why?

6. In this chapter, we've learned about agile requirements elicitation. We know that agile practices are best used with projects which have volatile requirements. Suppose we were developing a software product using an agile approach. One day, the customer wants to change a feature, which is described in a user story card and has been developed and tested. Worse still, this feature is related to several other features. Discuss the things we need to do to make this change.

7. There is an interesting comparison of traditional and agile processes. Traditional plan-driven processes are like "ready, ready, ready, …, aim, aim, aim, …, fire!" and hope the bullet hit the target. Agile processes are like "ready, aim, fire, ready, aim, fire, …, fire," and the bullet

will hit the target at last. In this chapter, we know that agile processes are used to address volatile requirements, or "moving targets." Actually, in real life, we can see some sports, like golf, which have a fixed target and still require the "ready, aim, fire, ready, aim, fire, …, fire" technique. Is there any software project that does not have volatile requirements and still is suitable for agile processes? Discuss the considerations, other than requirements volatility, that the developers take to employ agile processes.

You are going to write user stories for the systems below. There are two ways to do so:

1. As teamed exercise. Each team has 3 or 4 people. One of them is the customer, and the others are developers. The customer needs to understand the problem domain. The developers will work collaboratively with the customer for the user stories. This simulates how we do things in an agile way.

2. As individual exercise. You will work on the exercise alone, following the steps:
   a. List the specification of the system. You will act as the role of customer, so the specification should be written using natural language.
   b. Write the user stories based on the specification from step a. You will act as the role of developer. If you have a problem with a user story, read the specification and recall what you have thought about it in step a.
   c. During step b, if you think the specification is not correct, correct it and make sure the user story and the specification is consistent.
   d. Evaluate the size of each user story.
   e. Prioritize each user story.

This is not how agile developers do the requirements, however. In real agile projects, developers and the customer work together, and the user stories are developed in an iterative fashion.

Be sure to evaluate and prioritize each user story. Also, you need to consider the nonfunctional requirements.

8.

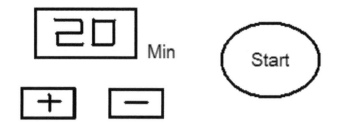

Above is a sketch of the control panel of a drier machine. The panel has three buttons and a display. The display can show any two-digit number. The purpose of the + and – buttons is to set up the timer. When the + or – button is pressed, the drying time is increased and decreased, respectively, by five minutes. This drier allows the user to select the drying time from 5 minutes to 60 minutes. The selected drying time is shown in the display.

When the user pushes the start button, the machine starts running. The display then shows the remaining time. The display only shows the minute. For example, if there are 19 minutes and 20 seconds left, the display shows 20. If there are 19 minutes and 0 second left, the display shows 19. The machine stops when the selected time is up.

The drying machine has a safety feature. If the door is opened when the machine is running, the machine will stop immediately. The timer remains unchanged, though. Therefore, the user can close the door again and push the start button, and the machine will run until the timer counts to zero.

9. A university uses a campus-wide card – it is called CampusPass. With this card, the students, faculties, and staff of the university can deposit money in their accounts, and use it in the grocery stores and food courts in the university. Recently, to deposit money, the card holders need to go to the cashier's office.

   To make the deposit process easier and more accessible, several kiosks are going to be deployed at several spots. They are connected to the central database. The card holders can deposit money at the kiosks. A software team is assigned a task of developing the software for the deposit stations. Make necessary assumptions, and develop the user stories for the software.

   Also note that the money deposited in the kiosk is locked in a safe. The software does not need to worry about how the money is drawn.

10. Suppose you are going to start a web-based business. You have got a new idea: an online book shelf. A user can pay little amount of money and enjoy ubiquitous access to a limited Internet hard disk space. (Of course, the user can always pay more money to buy more space.) The user can upload files as long as he or she has Internet connection. Additionally, the user can have these files printed and shipped to his/her home or office, with additional charge. Write the user stories for this web site.

# A Survey of Plan-Driven Development Methodologies

Plan-driven methodologies have been utilized by organizations for many years. In this chapter, we provide an overview of three prominent, modern plan-driven methodologies:

the Personal Software Process
the Team Software Process
the Rational Unified Process

Software methodologists incorporate the general characteristics of a software development model (a *software development model* is a *simplified, abstracted description of a software development process*) into specific software development processes that adhere to the spirit of these models. A *software development process* is the *process by which user needs are translated into a software product. The process involves translating user needs into software requirements, transforming the software requirements into design, implementing the design in code, testing the code, and sometimes installing and checking out the software for operational use. Note: these activities might overlap or be performed iteratively.* [13] While software development models have general characteristics, such as "having strong documentation and traceability mandates across requirements, design and code" [1], software development processes have *specific practices* (a *software development practice* is a *disciplined, uniform approach to the software development process* [13]) that need to be followed, such as code inspection. You can think of the relationship between software models and software processes as an abstract superclass–subclass relationship. The model specifies generally the common techniques and philosophies, while the methodology "overrides" and specializes these general specifications with details of specific practices.

In this chapter, we will describe the practices of the most prominent methodologies that have plan-driven characteristics:[11] the Personal Software Process (PSP) [7], the Team Software Process (TSP) [10], and the Rational Unified Process® (RUP®).[17] The class diagram in Figure 1 shows these methodologies in the spirit of the superclass–subclass relationship. For each of these methodologies, we will present an overview, the main roles involved in the methodology, the documents and artifacts produced, the development process, and a final discussion.

**Figure 1: Plan-Driven Methodologies**

Before beginning, it is important to understand that there is not a sharp dichotomy between plan-driven and agile software development methodologies. So, these three methodologies have some elements of agility to them or can be slightly modified to incorporate agility. The PSP is probably the most plan-driven. The TSP could be used to structure team development of agile teams. Finally, versions of the RUP have been created that could distinctly be classified as agile; this

194

will become more clear when we discuss RUP in Section 3. Let us review some common characteristics of plan-driven methodologies, though these guidelines are more relaxed in smaller projects [1]:

Focus on repeatability and predictability

Defined, standardized, and incrementally improving processes

Thorough documentation

A defined software system architecture defined up-front

Detailed plans, workflow, roles, responsibilities, and work product descriptions

Process group containing resources for specialists: process monitoring, controlling, and educating

On-going risk management

Focus on verification and validation

# 1    Personal Software Process<sup>SM</sup> (PSP<sup>SM</sup>)

The PSP [7, 8] is a process to be followed by an individual programmer, not a team of programmers—hence, the name *Personal* Software Process. While many software processes are followed by a whole team, an individual programmer can practice the PSP even if his teammates are not using those practices. It certainly helps when others are using the practices as well, though.

## *1.1    Overview*

The PSP is a structured framework of forms, guidelines, and procedures developed by Watts Humphrey of the Software Engineering Institute.[12] The framework guides an engineer in using a defined, measured, planned, and quality controlled process. However, another purpose of the framework is to help engineers understand their own skills so they can modify the process to meet their personal needs and preferences and to improve their own personal performance.

PSP training follows an evolutionary improvement approach. An engineer learning to integrate the PSP into his or her process begins at Level 0 and progresses in process maturity to Level 3 (See Figure 2). Each level incorporates new skills and techniques into the engineer's process— skills and techniques that have been proven to improve the quality of the software process. Each level has detailed scripts, checklists, and templates to guide the engineer through required steps. The scripts, checklists, and templates are only a starting point, however. The PSP provides measurement-based feedback that helps each engineer improve her own personal software process. Thus, Humphrey encourages the customization of these scripts and templates as the engineer receives this feedback and gains an understanding of his or her own strengths and weaknesses.

**Figure 2: The levels of the personal software process.**

PSP has several strong tenets. The first is that the longer a software defect remains in a product, the more costly it is to detect and remove it. Therefore, thorough design and code reviews are performed for efficient defect removal. The second philosophy is that defect prevention is more efficient than defect removal. Careful designs are developed and data is collected to give additional input on where the programmer should adjust their own personal software process to prevent future defects.

## 1.2 Documents and Artifacts

The artifacts in the PSP are the scripts, forms, templates, standards, and checklists. Each of these is discussed in this section.

**Script**. The scripts provide an orderly structure of steps the engineer should go through to complete the process step and refer the engineer to the relevant standards, forms, templates, guidelines, and measures. The PSP has six different kinds of scripts. In many cases, there is a different version of the script for every relevant level (PSP0, PSP0.1, PSP1, PSP1.1, PSP2, PSP2.1, and PSP3).

> Process script—lays out the inputs and the steps to complete a process. By following the script, the engineer can ensure she has all the required inputs and understands the requirements of the job. The completeness of the process is checked via stated exit criteria. A sample process script is shown in Figure 3.
>
> Planning script—provides instructions for planning development activities, such as making size and time estimates.
>
> High-level design script—provides instructions for creating a high-level design (for PSP3 only).
>
> High-level design review script—provides instruction for reviewing the PSP3 high level design.
>
> Development script—outlines the steps for design, code, compile, and test.
>
> Postmortem script—provides the instructions for analyzing and summarizing the data collected in the forms and templates.

**PSP Process Script**

| | Purpose: | To guide you in developing small programs. |
|---|---|---|
| | Inputs Required | - The problem description<br>- PSP Project Plan Summary form<br>- A copy of the Code Review Checklist<br>- Actual size and time data for previous programs<br>- Time Recording Log<br>- Defect Recording Log |
| 1 | Planning | - Obtain a description of the program functions.<br>- Estimate the Max., Min., and total LOC required.<br>- Determine the Minutes/LOC.<br>- Calculate the Max., Min., and total development times.<br>- Enter the plan data in the Project Plan Summary form.<br>- Record the planning time in the Time Recording Log. |
| 2 | Design | - Design the program.<br>- Record the design in the specified format.<br>- Record design time in the Time Recording Log. |
| 3 | Code | - Implement the design.<br>- Use a standard format for entering the code.<br>- Record coding time in the Time Recording Log. |
| 4 | Code review | - Completely review the source code.<br>- Follow the code review script and checklist.<br>- Fix and record every defect found.<br>- Record review time in the Time Recording Log. |
| 5 | Compile | - Compile the program.<br>- Fix and record all defects found.<br>- Record compile time in the Time Recording Log. |
| 6 | Test | - Test the program.<br>- Fix and record all defects found.<br>- Record testing time in the Time Recording Log. |
| 7 | Postmortem | - Complete the Project Plan Summary form with actual time, size, and defect data.<br>- Review the defect data and update the code review checklist.<br>- Record postmortem time in the Time Recording Log. |
| | Exit Criteria | - A thoroughly tested program<br>- A properly documented design<br>- A completed Code Review Checklist<br>- A complete program listing<br>- A completed Project Plan Summary<br>- Completed time and defect logs |

**Figure 3: A sample process script.**

**Forms**. Forms are used to guide thorough, complete data collection. Forms are used when the amount of data you collect is fixed. Three fundamental forms are used in the PSP:

Defect recording—An important activity of the PSP is collecting data about the defects that are injected and removed from the project. A form such as the one shown in Figure 4 is used to collect that data; this form is used by students learning the PSP. Each defect is assigned a unique defect number and is classified according to the type of defect using a defect classification scheme developed by IBM Research. (The defect classification scheme is the Orthogonal Defect Classification scheme or ODC [2].) The engineer records the development phase in which she believes the defect was injected, the phase in which the defect was found/removed, and how long it took to fix the defect. Finally, if it is believed this defect was injected while fixing another defect, the number of that initial defect is recorded.

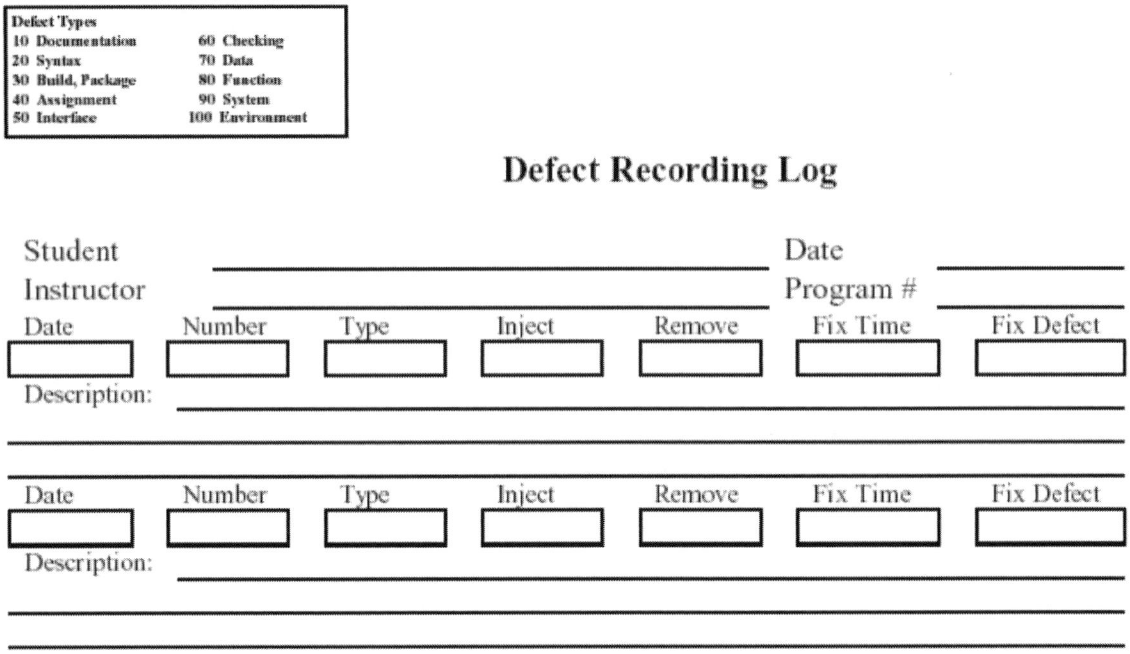

| Defect Types | |
|---|---|
| 10 Documentation | 60 Checking |
| 20 Syntax | 70 Data |
| 30 Build, Package | 80 Function |
| 40 Assignment | 90 System |
| 50 Interface | 100 Environment |

## Defect Recording Log

Student _____ Date _____

Instructor _____ Program # _____

| Date | Number | Type | Inject | Remove | Fix Time | Fix Defect |
|---|---|---|---|---|---|---|
| | | | | | | |

Description: _____

_____

| Date | Number | Type | Inject | Remove | Fix Time | Fix Defect |
|---|---|---|---|---|---|---|
| | | | | | | |

Description: _____

_____

_____

**Figure 4: PSP defect recording log.**

Time recording log—another important PSP activity is recording how much time is spent on development activities. This data is recorded in a form like the one shown in Figure 5 which was also designed for students learning PSP. When a developer starts to work, he records the date, the start time, and the development phase. If the developer is interrupted during work, the number of elapsed minutes of the interruption is recorded. When activity is completed, the stop time and any comments are noted.

198

# Time Recording Log

Student _____  Date _____

Instructor _____  Class _____

| Date | Start | Stop | Interruption Time | Delta Time | Activity | Comments | C | U |
|------|-------|------|-------------------|------------|----------|----------|---|---|
|      |       |      |                   |            |          |          |   |   |
|      |       |      |                   |            |          |          |   |   |
|      |       |      |                   |            |          |          |   |   |
|      |       |      |                   |            |          |          |   |   |
|      |       |      |                   |            |          |          |   |   |
|      |       |      |                   |            |          |          |   |   |
|      |       |      |                   |            |          |          |   |   |
|      |       |      |                   |            |          |          |   |   |
|      |       |      |                   |            |          |          |   |   |
|      |       |      |                   |            |          |          |   |   |
|      |       |      |                   |            |          |          |   |   |
|      |       |      |                   |            |          |          |   |   |
|      |       |      |                   |            |          |          |   |   |

**Figure 5: PSP time recording log.**

Project plan—a summary form that is used for the summarization, analysis, and utilization of the data that has been entered, as shown in Figure 30.5. Often, the time and data logging and the completion of the project plan form can be automated via available PSP tools.[13]

**PSP Project Plan Summary**

| Student | _____ | Date | _____ |
|---|---|---|---|
| Program | _____ | Program # | _____ |
| Instructor | _____ | Language | _____ |

| Summary | Plan | Actual | To Date |
|---|---|---|---|
| Minutes/LOC | ____ | ____ | ____ |
| LOC/Hour | ____ | ____ | ____ |
| *Defects/KLOC* | ____ | ____ | ____ |
| *Yield* | ____ | ____ | ____ |
| *A/FR* | ____ | ____ | ____ |

| Program Size (LOC): | Plan | Actual | To Date |
|---|---|---|---|
| Total New & Changed | ____ | ____ | ____ |
| Maximum Size | ____ | | |
| Minimum Size | | | |

| Time in Phase (min.) | Plan | Actual | To Date | To Date % |
|---|---|---|---|---|
| Planning | ____ | ____ | ____ | ____ |
| Design | ____ | ____ | ____ | ____ |
| Code | ____ | ____ | ____ | ____ |
| Code Review | ____ | ____ | ____ | ____ |
| Compile | ____ | ____ | ____ | ____ |
| Test | ____ | ____ | ____ | ____ |
| Postmortem | ____ | ____ | ____ | ____ |
| Total | ____ | ____ | ____ | ____ |
| Maximum Time | ____ | | | |
| Minimum Time | ____ | | | |

| Defects Injected | Plan | Actual | To Date | To Date % | Def./hour |
|---|---|---|---|---|---|
| Planning | | ____ | ____ | ____ | |
| Design | | ____ | ____ | ____ | |
| Code | | ____ | ____ | ____ | |
| Code Review | | ____ | ____ | ____ | |
| Compile | | ____ | ____ | ____ | |
| Test | | ____ | ____ | ____ | |
| Total | | ____ | ____ | ____ | |

| Defects Removed | Plan | Actual | To Date | To Date % | Def./hour |
|---|---|---|---|---|---|
| Planning | | ____ | ____ | ____ | |
| Design | | ____ | ____ | ____ | |
| Code | | ____ | ____ | ____ | |
| Code Review | | ____ | ____ | ____ | |
| Compile | | ____ | ____ | ____ | |
| Test | | ____ | ____ | ____ | |
| Total | | ____ | ____ | ____ | |

**Figure 6: Project plan template.**

**Templates.** Templates are important tools for being complete in development activities. The PSP has defined templates for test reporting, size estimating, task planning, schedule planning, issue tracking log, and for creating operational scenarios and functional, state, and logic specifications.

**Checklists.** Checklists help you to completely follow a procedure. PSP suggests an initial version of design and a code review checklist. The intent is that the developer learn about the kinds of defects he typically injects and continually adapts these checklists to surface those "typical" defects. Here are some examples of code review checklist items for a program written in C:

- o Verify that the code covers all the design
- o Verify that includes are complete
- o Verify the proper use of ==, =, ||, and so on.

## 1.3 Roles

PSP has only one role, the individual software engineer.

## 1.4 Process

PSP training is based on four levels of personal process: PSP Levels 0 through 3, as shown in Figure 2. Skills at one level are mastered before the engineer moves to the next level of personal process improvement.

**Level 0 (Personal Measurement):** The input to PSP is the requirements; requirements elicitation is assumed to have been completed and a requirements document delivered to the engineer. The PSP0 has three waterfall-like phases: planning, development (including design, code, compile, and test), and a postmortem. In the postmortem, the engineer ensures all data for the projects has been properly recorded and analyzed.

The software engineer begins by establishing a personal baseline of her current development process by basic measurements, such as the time spent on a program (using the form shown in Figure 5), the defects injected and removed in each development phase (using the form shown in Figure 4), and the size of the program (in lines of code), and creating some initial reports. This level is then improved by adding a coding standard, a size measurement, and the development of a personal process improvement plan (PIP). In the PIP, the engineer records ideas for improving her own process. The improvements constitute PSP0.1.

**Level 1 (Personal Planning):** Based upon the baseline data collected in PSP Level 0, the engineer estimates how large a new program will be and prepares a test report (PSP1). Accumulated data from previous projects is used to estimate the total time. Each new project will record the actual time spent. This information is used for task and schedule planning and estimation (PSP1.1).

**Level 2 (Personal Quality):** Defect prevention and removal are the focus at the PSP Level 2. Engineers construct and use checklists for design and code reviews (PSP2). PSP2.1 introduces design specification and analysis techniques. Engineers learn to evaluate and improve their process by measuring how long tasks take and the number of defects they inject and remove in each phase of development.

**Level 3 (Scaling Up):** In the final level, the programmer employs an incremental model of development for larger projects by dividing the problem into smaller sections, and then iteratively applies the PSP principles as each section is implemented.

## 1.5    Discussion

The main advantages of PSP have been demonstrated by several studies, including [3, 4, 12]:

Improved size estimation and time estimation

Improved productivity

Reduced testing time

Improved quality

The possible drawbacks of PSP are as follows:

Some people are not receptive to the detailed data recording.

The longevity of the PSP requires discipline. Several studies, including [19], have noted that engineers stop using the PSP over time unless they work on TSP teams (discussed in the next section) that are competently coached and managed.

# 2    Team Software Process<sup>SM</sup> (TSP<sup>SM</sup>)

The PSP, discussed in Section 1, is used to help an individual software engineer. Rarely, though, do engineers work alone. Most often, software engineers work as part of a team. The TSP [5, 10] provides a structure for self-directed teams to plan and track their work, to establish goals, and to create and own their processes and plans. It also provides guidance to individual software engineers on how to perform as an effective team member. To make a distinction, there is an industrial TSP for professional teams of up to 150 engineers who work on large, possibly multi-year projects. The material in this chapter comes from the Introductory Team Software Process (TSPi), a defined framework specifically developed for graduate or upper level undergraduate students. The process described here is the academic TSPi version of the TSP. The industrial strength TSP follows the same general principles described here, but it has many important differences. An overview description of industrial TSP principles can be found in *Winning with Software: An Executive Summary*. [11]

## 2.1    Overview

Watts Humphrey, the author of the PSP, also created the TSP and the TSPi. The TSP supports the development of industrial strength software through the use of team building, planning, and control. The overall structure of the TSPi is shown in Figure 7. The project starts with a product needed by a customer. A software development project to address this need is divided into overlapping, iterative development cycles. The team produces part of the product each cycle until the need is fulfilled with a finished product. Each of the cycles is a "mini waterfall" consisting of a cycle launch, strategy, planning, requirements, design, implementation, test, and postmortem. To some extent, the TSPi relies upon all the individual engineers using the PSP. However, TSPi is flexible enough that you could apply many of the principles and techniques if the individual engineers are not using PSP.

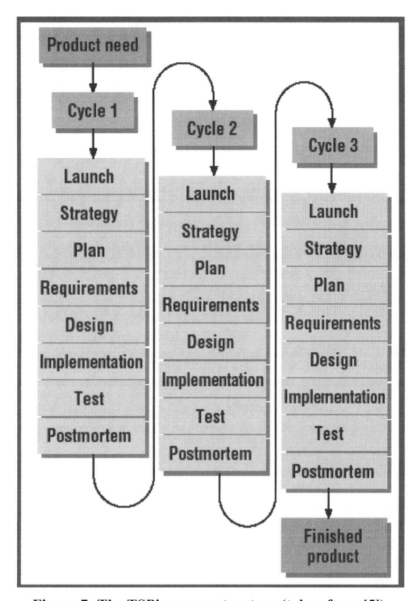

**Figure 7: The TSPi process structure (taken from [5]).**

## 2.2    *Documents and Artifacts*

The structure of the TSPi is similar to that of the PSP; TSPi is also a structured framework of scripts, forms, and standards. Specifically, there are 21 process scripts and 10 role scripts (role scripts are discussed in the next section), 21 forms, and 3 standards. As stated above, TSP works best when the individual engineers on the team are using the PSP for their own personal development. As such, the scripts, forms, and standards of the PSP of the PSP guide the work and process improvement of each engineer on the team. The scripts, forms, and standards of the TSP guide the structure, organization, and measurement of the team as a whole.

**Scripts.** The scripts lay out detailed steps to guide the teams through launching and running their projects so that each engineer can see how to do what she needs to do. A sample of a partial TSPi process script is shown in Figure 8. This is a script for updating requirements in the cycles after the first cycle. Each script shows the entry criteria, some general information, detail process steps, and finally exit criteria. There are scripts for design, development, implementation, team launch, development plan, postmortem, requirements development, configuration management, development strategy, integration and system test, unit test, and the weekly meeting.

# Requirements Development Script

| Purpose | To guide a team though developing and inspecting the requirements for a second or subsequent development cycle. |
|---|---|
| Entry Criteria | • The team has an updated development strategy and plan. |
| General | Update the software requirements specification to reflect<br>• Requirements problems with the prior cycles<br>• Previously specified SRS functions that were not developed<br>• Previously unspecified SRS functions that are now required<br><br>The team should also be cautious about expanding the requirements.<br><br>• Without experience with similar applications, seemingly simple functions can take substantially more work than expected.<br>• It is generally wise to add functions in small increments.<br>• If more time remains, add further increments.<br><br>The updated SRS defines the new product functions, including added use-case descriptions for each normal and abnormal user action. |

| Step | Activities | Description |
|---|---|---|
| 1 | Requirements Process Considerations | The instructor describes any problems with the prior requirements process that should be corrected for this cycle. |
| 2 | Need Statement Review | The development manager leads the team in reexamining the product need statement and formulating any new questions about<br>• The functions to be performed by this product version<br>• How these functions are to be used |
| 3 | Need Statement Cl | The development manager provides consolidated questions to the instructor, who discuss the answers with the te |
| 4 | | The d eads |

**Figure 8: TSPi process script (requirements).**

**Forms.** As with the PSP, the TSPi provides forms to guide in thorough, complete data collection. Some of the forms, such as the Defect Recording Log and the Time Recording Log, are identical to the PSP. Many of the forms, however, are for higher level data collection and analysis where the plans and data from the whole team are summarized. An example of a form is shown in Figure 9. This form is for student evaluation of their team member peers. When students work in a team, some team members might contribute less than their fair share of the work while others go above and beyond what is expected (sometimes to make up for the students who are not doing their share). The form shown in Figure 9 is used to provide feedback to the instructor on the contributions of team members. Other forms included in the TSPi collect necessary team information, such as configuration change and status, inspections, issues, and testing. Still others provide the format for team summary information, such as planning, weekly status, and task planning.

**Peer Evaluation**

Name _____    Team _____    Instructor _____

Date _____    Cycle No. _____    Week No. _____

| For each role, enter the student's name, a percentage of the total team effort (out of 100%), and the relative difficulty of their tasks – 1 (very low) to 5 (very high) | | | |
|---|---|---|---|
| **Role** | **Student Name** | **Contribution** | **Role Difficulty** |
| Team Leader | | | |
| Development Manager | | | |
| Planning Manager | | | |
| Quality/Process Manager | | | |
| Support Manager | | | |
| Total Contribution | | 100% | |

| Rate the overall team against each criterion. Circle one number from 1 (inadequate) to 5 (superior). | | | | |
|---|---|---|---|---|
| Team spirit | 1 | 2 | 3 | 4 | 5 |
| Overall effectiveness | 1 | 2 | 3 | 4 | 5 |
| Rewarding experience | 1 | 2 | 3 | 4 | 5 |
| Team productivity | 1 | 2 | 3 | 4 | 5 |
| Process quality | 1 | 2 | 3 | 4 | 5 |
| Product quality | 1 | 2 | 3 | 4 | 5 |

| Rate each student for their overall contribution to the project. Circle one number from 1 (inadequate) to 5 (superior). | | | | |
|---|---|---|---|---|
| Team Leader | 1 | 2 | 3 | 4 | 5 |
| Development Manager | 1 | 2 | 3 | 4 | 5 |
| Planning Manager | 1 | 2 | 3 | 4 | 5 |
| Quality/Process Manager | 1 | 2 | 3 | 4 | 5 |
| Support Manager | 1 | 2 | 3 | 4 | 5 |

| Rate the student in each role for helpfulness and support. Circle one number from 1 (inadequate) to 5 (superior). | | | | |
|---|---|---|---|---|
| Team Leader | 1 | 2 | 3 | 4 | 5 |
| Development Manager | 1 | 2 | 3 | 4 | 5 |
| Planning Manager | 1 | 2 | 3 | 4 | 5 |
| Quality/Process Manager | 1 | 2 | 3 | 4 | 5 |
| Support Manager | 1 | 2 | 3 | 4 | 5 |

| Rate each role for how well it was performed. Circle one number from 1 (inadequate) to 5 (superior). | | | | |
|---|---|---|---|---|
| Team Leader | 1 | 2 | 3 | 4 | 5 |
| Development Manager | 1 | 2 | 3 | 4 | 5 |
| Planning Manager | 1 | 2 | 3 | 4 | 5 |
| Quality/Process Manager | 1 | 2 | 3 | 4 | 5 |
| Support Manager | 1 | 2 | 3 | 4 | 5 |

**Figure 9: TSPi peer evaluation form.**

**Standards.** The TSPi includes standards for defects types, the project notebook, and quality criteria. The defect type standards provide the defect classification that is used on the defect recording log, as discussed in Section 1.2 and appear in the upper left corner of Figure 4. The project notebook standard provides useful guidance on what should be included in a project notebook. Official project information, such as copies of work products, weekly team status reports and test plans, is archived in the team's project notebook, which is maintained by the team leader. Finally, the quality criteria provide helpful standards that can be used to establish team quality goals. Some examples of these standards are having fewer than 10 unit test defects/ KLOC or inspecting fewer than two pages of requirements/hour.

## *2.3*     *Roles*

A very important factor for effective team building is defining clear team roles for each team member. Then, each engineer has clearly identified responsibilities and understands what she is expected to do in terms of planning, tracking, quality, support, and leadership tasks. The TSPi defines five team roles and provides a very thorough guide for each role. When possible, the assignment of the person to the role should be based upon the person's interest in that role. In addition to the responsibilities outlined in these roles, each software engineer on the team would have technical responsibilities for product development. Via these roles, each engineer shares in the essential "overhead" of product development in addition to making a technical contribution to the working product.

In the TSPi, each role has its own chapter, complete with the role's goals, helpful skills and abilities, principle activities, and project activities. The main responsibilities and goals of each of these is briefly described here [5]:

> *Team leader*: leads the team and ensures that engineers report their progress data and complete their work as planned.
> - o *Goal 1*: Build and maintain an effective team.
> - o *Goal 2*: Motivate all team members to work aggressively on the project.
> - o *Goal 3*: Resolve all the issues team members bring to you.
> - o *Goal 4*: Keep the instructor fully informed about the team's progress.
> - o *Goal 5*: Perform effectively as the team's meeting facilitator.
>
> *Development manager*: leads and guides the team in product design, development, and testing.
> - o *Goal 1*: Produce a superior product (documented and meeting all functional and operational objectives and quality criteria).
> - o *Goal 2*: Fully utilize the team members' skills and abilities.
>
> *Planning manager*: supports and guides the team in planning and tracking its work.
> - o *Goal 1*: Produce a complete, precise, and accurate plan for the team and for every team member.
> - o *Goal 2*: Accurately report team status every week.
>
> *Quality/process manager*: supports the team in defining the process needs and establishing and managing the quality plan.
> - o *Goal 1*: Ensure that all team members accurately report and properly use TSPi process data.
> - o *Goal 2*: Make certain that the team faithfully follows the TSPi quality plan and

produces a quality product.
- o *Goal 3*: Make all team inspections properly moderated and reported.
- o *Goal 4*: Make sure that all team meetings are accurately reported, and the reports put in the project notebook.

*Support manager*: supports the team in determining, obtaining, and managing the tools needed to meet its technology and administrative support needs.
- o *Goal 1*: Provide the team with suitable tools and methods to support its work.
- o *Goal 2*: Prevent unauthorized changes to baseline products.
- o *Goal 3*: Keep the risk-tracking system functional to keep the team's risks and issues recorded and reported each week.
- o *Goal 4*: Ensure that the team meets its reuse goals for the development cycle.

An important TSP role that is not in the TSPi (and is not in the preceding list) is the *team coach*. In the industrial form of the TSP, the team coach role is assumed by someone who is trained and qualified by the SEI and generally launches and coaches multiple projects. The team coach is not involved in the technical details of the project itself, as is even the team leader. In the industrial form of TSP, this role is assumed by the manager the team reports to or by some other person who is very knowledgeable on software process and might coach multiple projects. In academia, the teaching staff assumes this role. The job of this person is to motivate the team and to maintain a relentless focus on quality and excellence. This requires daily interaction with the team and an unceasing requirement that the process be followed, the data be gathered, and the results be analyzed. The team coach and the team meet regularly to review their performance and to ensure that the work meets the standards.

## 2.4 *Process*

Figure 7 lays out the process structure of the TSPi. TSPi uses multiple development cycles. Each cycle starts with a launch followed by seven iterative process steps: development strategy, development plan, requirements, design, implementation, test, and postmortem. The cycles can and should overlap. Each cycle should produce a *testable* version that is a subset of the final product.

The launch and the seven process steps are now briefly described. The TSP has a detailed script for the tasks of the launch and each of the seven process steps.

**Launch**. The customer (or instructor) describes the overall product objectives. Teams are formed and team structure is established (the engineers assume the roles as just described). The team establishes a meeting schedule and reporting structure. The team sets measurable goals and measurements. An example of a team goal and measurements is as follows [5]:

Team Goal: Produce a quality product
- Measure 1: More than 80 percent of the defects will be found before the first compile.
- Measure 2: No defects will be found during system test.
- Measure 3: At project completion, all product requirements will be correctly implemented.

**Strategy**. The development strategy specifies the order in which product functions are defined, designed, implemented, and tested. A high level conceptual design of the product is developed. Preliminary, high level size and time estimates are developed. Risks are assessed. Finally, a strategy is established for how the product will be enhanced in each cycle.

**Plan.** The team develops a comprehensive plan that includes the following:

> A list of the products to be produced with their estimated sizes;
>
> A list of tasks to be completed, each assigned a responsible team member and each complete with an estimation of how long it will take to complete the task, balancing team workload;
>
> A week-by-week schedule of tasks and available work hours;
>
> A quality plan that estimates the quantity of defects injected and removed by development phase; and
>
> A template summarizing the product's estimated and actual size, effort, and defect data.

These plans are often documented and updated via a TSPi spreadsheet tool.

**Requirements.** The team produces a clear and unambiguous description of what the product is to be. This is documented in Software Requirements Specifications (SRS) such as those described in Chapter 5 *Requirements Engineering and Elicitation*. Each cycle the SRS is re-examined and evolved.

**Design.** The principle objective of the design process step is to produce a precise, complete, high quality specification of how the product is to be built.

**Implementation**. The code is implemented utilizing standards, such as coding standards (which ensures the team's code looks the same person-to-person) or a defect classification standard, as previously discussed. All code is unit tested and is reviewed via formal inspections during the implementation phase.

**Test.** The product is integrated and tested. The purpose of this testing is to assess the product, not to fix it. If the assessment determines the product is not of high quality, testing should cease and the product should repeat any necessary requirements/design/implementation steps. Integration testing is done to verify that the product is properly built, all the parts are present, and that they function together. System testing is done to validate that the product does what the system requirements call for.

**Postmortem**. Similar to the postmortem in the PSP, the teamwork is reviewed to make sure all the tasks are complete and all the required data are recorded. The team also carefully reviews how the cycle went—to learn what went right and wrong and to brainstorm how they can do a better job in the next cycle or on the next project.

## 2.5    *Discussion*

In general, the advantages and disadvantages of the TSPi are similar to those of the PSP. It should be noted, however that the principal benefit of both the TSP and the academic TSPi is that it shows teams of students or engineers how to produce quality products for planned costs and on aggressive schedules. They do this by showing teams how to manage their work and by making them owners of their plans and processes. [9]

## 3    Rational Unified Process (RUP)

The RUP [16, 17] is very different from the prescribed PSP and TSP from two perspectives. First, the RUP specifically embeds object-oriented techniques and uses UML as its principle notation. Secondly, the RUP is a customizable process framework. Depending upon the project characteristics, such as team size, project size, and so on, the RUP can be tailored or extended to match the needs of an adopting organization.

## 3.1    *Overview*

The RUP combines the expertise from many sources and three decades of development and active use. Development started in Sweden by Dr. Ivar Jacobson [15] in the late 1980s. Jacobson was first at Ericsson, and then he started his own company, Objectory AB. Jacobson's process was called Objectory, which is an abbreviation of "Object Factory." Objectory AB was acquired by Rational, Inc. in the fall of 1995. Objectory was integrated with Rational's process (into the Rational Objectory Process or ROP) and became an iterative process, focused on software architecture spanning the whole development lifecycle; ROP 4.0 was launched in the fall of 1996. Finally, the Rational Unified Process was released in 1998 [17] as a unification of development approaches and the work of many methodologists. The RUP integrated a wide range of seemingly independent tools developed by Rational. In 2003, Rational—with RUP and its associate tools—was acquired by IBM. Similar to the TSP/TSPi, there is both a professional and a student version of RUP. [17, 18] The student version is called the Unified Process for Education, abbreviated UPEDU and pronounced *yoopeedoo*. Only the most important features of the RUP process are retained to enable students to focus on the essential components of learning to use the disciplined process.

The idea behind the creation of the RUP was to capture many of the best practices in modern software development and to put them into a form from which they could easily be composed into a suitable process for a wide range of projects and organizations. The overall process structure of RUP is shown in Figure 10. The horizontal axis represents the timeline of a project lifecycle as it unfolds. The core process disciplines that logically group software engineering activities that are often performed simultaneously are shown on the vertical axis. The height of the area indicates how much work is spent on a discipline at a given point in time. The figure indicates that the disciplines need work simultaneously throughout various phases of development and that the software product is designed and built in a succession of incremental iterations.

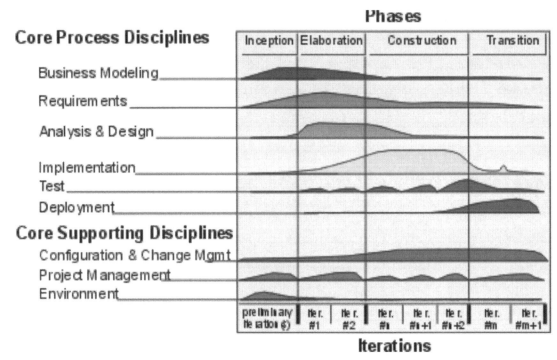

**Figure 10: RUP process structure (from [17]).**

Before describing the RUP, some basic definitions are needed so that you can understand the underlying structure. A *role* defines the responsibilities of team members who carry out their activities in their software process. The role of a team member evolves over time and is driven by the activities that are being performed at any given time. An *activity* is a piece of work (or "operation") that can be executed by one role. The granularity of an activity is usually a few hours to a few person-days. An activity is assigned to a particular role and must have a clear purpose, which is usually expressed in terms of creating or updating artifacts. An *artifact* is any piece of information or physical entity produced, modified, or used by the activities of the software engineering process. Artifacts are used as input to workers to perform an activity and are also the results of such activities.

RUP considers the software process as a collaboration among roles that perform activities on concrete, tangible artifacts. This association is shown as a class diagram in Figure 11.

**Figure 11: Association between roles, artifacts, and activities (from [18]).**

## 3.2    *Documents and Artifacts*

RUP is not just a defined, static process document. While there are published books on RUP [14, 16, 17], most utilize the RUP as a compilation of modular, electronic resources including a versioned process definition (that is updated approximately twice per year) and a multitude of

212

integrated support software. The RUP contains the activities, artifacts, guidelines, and examples necessary for modification and configuration by the adopting organization.

Each of the nine disciplines shown in Figure 10 is comprised of a set of specified activities. For example, in the UPEDU (the RUP for students) the requirements management discipline consists of five activities:

> Elicit stakeholder requests
> Find actors and use cases
> Structure the use-case model
> Detail a use-case model
> Review requirements

Each discipline has its own set of artifacts. The RUP defines about 30 top level artifacts. One role is responsible for each of these artifacts. For example, the UPEDU requirements management workflow has the following artifacts associated with it.

> Vision (provides stakeholders with a high level description of the product to be developed)
> Glossary (defines terms in the application domain that are needed to understand the requirements)
> Software requirements specification (functional requirements)
> Supplementary specification (nonfunctional requirements)
> Use case (describes the interactions between a user and a system)
> Use case model (all the actors and all the use cases, the totality of the functional behavior of the system)

Most often in RUP, artifacts are not paper documents. Instead, artifacts are contained within the tool that is used to create them, maintain them, and to help the developer make progress on the product. For example, a project requirements database in Rational RequisitePro is an example of an artifact.

Artifacts typically have associated guidelines and checkpoints, which present information on how to develop, evaluate, and use the artifacts. Some artifacts have concept pages associated with them. Additionally, templates (e.g. blank forms) are often associated with artifacts. Activities (or tasks) to accomplish process steps are defined in the RUP. The concept page for each artifact links the activities of the RUP by listing the activities that lead into the artifact and the activities to which the artifact contributes.

## 3.3    Roles

RUP defines the roles necessary to complete the disciplines. Roles have responsibility for particular activities and associated artifacts. A role in RUP may be performed by an individual or by a group of people. Equally, an individual or a group may perform several roles, even in the course of one day.

The recommended roles for a particular product are dependent upon the project characteristics (the bigger the project, the more roles are necessary). Some example roles are given here:

Analyst, who is responsible for eliciting the needs from the stakeholders, and communicating the needs to the development team.

Designer, who identifies and defines the design and makes sure it is consistent with the system architecture.

Implementer, who is responsible for developing and testing software components.

Reviewer, who reviews the software product or development activities.

Test Designer, who defines the test approach to make sure the test is successfully implemented.

Tester, who implements and runs the test suites.

Integrator, who is responsible for planning and performing integration tasks.

Project manager, who manages the resource and activities of the project to ensure the success of the outcome.

Technical writer, who composes the communications from the developer for the product stakeholder.

Software architect, who is responsible for the system architecture.

User interface designer, who works with the developers to produce desired user interface.

## *3.4    Process*

The RUP process is based upon six best practices:

1. Develop software iteratively.
2. Manage requirements.
3. Use component-based architectures.
4. Visually model software.
5. Continuously verify software.
6. Control changes to software.

In the RUP, the work is broken into nine workflows, as denoted in the vertical axis in Figure 10. These nine disciplines are briefly explained:

**Business modeling**: Describing the business processes of a company for which the software is to be developed.

**Requirements management**. Eliciting, organizing, and documenting requirements.

**Analysis and design.** Creating the architecture and the design of the software system.

**Implementation.** Writing, debugging, building and unit testing source code.

**Test.** Testing via integration, system, and acceptance testing.

**Deployment.** Packaging the software, creating installation scripts, writing end user documentation, and other tasks necessary for delivering the software to customers.

**Project Management.** Project planning and monitoring.

**Configuration and Change Management.** Planning and utilizing version and release management and change request management.

**Environment.** Adapting the RUP process to the needs of the environment and selecting, introducing, and supporting development tools.

The product cycle is divided into four types of phases; each phase may be run in one or more iterations. The iterations are show in Figure 10 as Elab #1, Elab #2, and so on. Each iteration builds upon the results of the previous iteration(s).

**Inception.** Defining the objectives of the project, including the business case. This involves risk analysis, initial project plans, and resource requirements.

**Elaboration.** Creating and validating the architecture of the software system, capturing the most important and critical requirements, and planning and estimating the rest of the project. The use cases developed in the inception phase are done in detail.

**Construction.** Implementing the system based on the executable architecture created in the elaboration phase.

**Transition.** Beta testing the system with some customers and preparing release candidates.

## 3.5    Discussion

RUP is a "generic" process framework that can be specialized for a large class of software systems, for different application areas, different types of organizations, different competence levels, and different project sizes. Organizations can modify, adjust, and expand the RUP to accommodate their specific needs, characteristics, constraints, culture, and domain. In doing so, the organizations can benefit from the years of experience of the many people who have contributed to its development.

The initial intent of the RUP was an organization that would be able to compose a set of best practices to meet the needs of a particular project—large or small. However, many still view the RUP as impractical for small, fast-paced projects. Some have worked to dispel this perception. Object Mentor has created RUP-XP and others, such as Hirsch [6], have surfaced the adaptable, agile aspects of the process. Hirsch emphasizes the need to carefully select the proper subset of artifacts and to keep the artifacts concise and free from unnecessary formalism.

Many plan-driven methods suffer from the difficulty in "tailoring down" just discussed. [1] The experts who develop the methods provide guidance for most situations and make the methods "tailor down-able." However, the users of the process don't have the experience the expert-authors have and often "take it all" in terms of the full set of plan, specification, and standards and cannot confidently tailor down to their own projects. [1] This must be taken into consideration when adopting a plan driven method.

## 4    Summary

Several practical tips for using plan-driven methodologies were presented throughout this chapter.  The keys for successful use of choosing and using plan-driven methodologies are summarized in Table 4.

| | |
|---|---|
| | The PSP can be used by an individual software engineering to improve his or her ability to consistently produce a high-quality software product on time. |
| | If a software engineer tracks the time he or she spends on their tasks, they can make better predictions for future commitments. Software engineers are often pressured to produce software according to an imposed schedule based upon a business objective date. By making sound commitments based on historical data, engineers can astutely and defensively fend off pressure to make unrealistic commitments. When an engineer makes an unrealistic commitment, often his or her personal life is impacted in an attempt to make the commitment. |
| | Using team roles outlined in the TSP, a team can produce their product in an organized fashion. |
| | In TSP, the Launch meeting provides the customer with the opportunity to state and/or re-state their product objectives. Additionally, the software engineers can devise realistic commitments for meeting these objectives. |
| | The RUP was specifically designed to use the UML diagrams taught throughout this book. |
| | The RUP can be customized to meet the needs of the team and the product. |

**Table 4: Key Ideas for Plan-Driven Methodologies**

In this chapter, we provided an overview of three prominent plan-driven methodologies, PSP, TSP, and RUP. We emphasized that each of these methodologies also has agile aspects to it and/ or can be adapted for a situation in which agility would be beneficial or for smaller projects. The PSP is a structured framework of forms, guidelines, and procedures that guides an engineer in using a defined, measured, planned, and quality controlled process. Additionally, the PSP helps engineers understand their own skills so they can modify the process to meet their personal needs and preferences and to improve their own personal performance. The TSP provides a structure for self-directed teams to plan and track their work, to establish goals, and to create and own their processes and plans. It also provides guidance to individual software engineers on how to perform as an effective team member. Finally, the RUP is a methodology that specifically embeds object-oriented techniques and uses UML as its principle notation. Additionally, the RUP is a customizable process framework whereby, depending upon the project characteristics, the RUP can be tailored or extended to match the needs of an adopting organization.

## Acknowledgements

Many thanks to Watts Humphrey and Philippe Kruchten for reviewing this chapter.

### Glossary of Chapter Terms

| Word | Definition | Source |
|---|---|---|
| Software development practice (or technique) | a disciplined, uniform approach to the software development process | [13] |
| Software development process (or methodology) | The process by which user needs are translated into a software product. The process involves translating user needs into software requirements, transforming the software requirements into design, implementing the design in code, testing the code, and sometimes installing and checking out the software for operational use. Note: these activities might overlap or be performed iteratively. | [13] |
| Software process model | simplified, abstracted description of a software development process | |

## References

[1]    B. Boehm and R. Turner, *Balancing Agility and Discipline: A Guide for the Perplexed.* Boston, MA: Addison Wesley, 2003.

[2]    R. Chillarege, I. Bhandari, J. Chaar, M. Halliday, D. Moebus, B. Ray, and M. Wong, "Orthogonal Defect Classification -- A Concept for In-Process Measurements," *IEEE Transactions on Software Engineering*, vol. 18, no. 11, pp. 943-956, November 1992.

[3]    P. Ferguson, W. S. Humphrey, S. Khajenoori, S. Macke, and A. Matvya, "Results of Applying the Personal Software Process," *IEEE Computer*, vol. 30, no. 5, pp. 24-31, May 1997.

[4]    W. Hayes and J. W. Over, "The Personal Software Process: An Empirical Study of the Impact of PSP on Individual Engineers," Software Engineering Institute, Pittsburgh, PA, CMU/SEI-97-TR-001, December 1997, 1997.

[5]    T. B. Hilburn and W. S. Humphrey, "Teaching Teamwork," *IEEE Software*, vol. 19, no. 5, pp. 72-77, September/October 2002.

[6]    M. Hirsch, "Making RUP Agile," Conference on Object Oriented Programming Systems Languages and Applications, Seattle, WA, 2002, pp.

[7]    W. S. Humphrey, *A Discipline for Software Engineering.* Reading, MA: Addison Wesley,

1995.

[8]     W. S. Humphrey, *Introduction to the Personal Software Process*. Reading, Massachusetts: Addison-Wesley, 1997.

[9]     W. S. Humphrey, "Three Dimensions of Process Improvement, Part III: The Team Process," *Crosstalk*, vol. April, no. 4, 1998.

[10]    W. S. Humphrey, *Introduction to the Team Software Process*. Reading, Mass.: Addison Wesley, 2000.

[11]    W. S. Humphrey, "Winning with Software:  An Executive Strategy." Boston: Addison Wesley, 2002.

[12]    W. S. Humphrey, "Using a Defined and Measured Personal Software Process," *IEEE Software*, vol. 13, no. 3, pp. 77-88, May 1996.

[13]    IEEE, "IEEE Standard 610.12-1990, IEEE Standard Glossary of Software Engineering Terminology," 1990.

[14]    I. Jacobson, G. Booch, and J. Rumbaugh, *The Unified Software Development Process*. Reading, Massachusetts: Addison-Wesley, 1999.

[15]    I. Jacobson, M. Christerson, P. Jonsson, and G. Övergaard, *Object-Oriented Software Engineering:  A Use Case Driven Approach*. Wokingham, England: Addison-Wesley, 1992.

[16]    P. Kroll and P. Kruchten, *The Rational Unified Process Made Easy:  A Practitioner's Guide to the RUP*. Boston: Addison Wesley, 2003.

[17]    P. Kruchten, *The Rational Unified Process:  An Introduction*, Third ed. Boston: Addison Wesley, 2004.

[18]    P. N. Robillard and P. Kruchten, *Software Engineering Process with the UPEDU*. Boston: Addison Wesley, 2003.

[19]    D. Webb, Humphrey, Watts, "Using the TSP on the TaskView Project," *Crosstalk*, vol. February 1999, no. 2, 1999.

## Chapter Questions

1. Name at least five characteristics of plan-driven methodologies.

2. What are the factors that distinguish RUP from the PSP and TSP?

3. Explain the relationship between PSP and TSP.

4. Name and explain the team roles of the TSP and of RUP.

5. What is the purpose of having templates, scripts, and checklists in the TSP and the PSP?

6. List the phases in RUP.

7. Describe the process of TSPi.

8. What are the three levels of PSP?

9. In RUP, software engineering process is organized by nine disciplines. Describe the nine disciplines in RUP

# A Survey of Agile Development Methodologies

Agile development methodologies are emerging in the software industry. In this chapter, we provide an introduction to agile development methodologies and an overview of four specific methodologies:

> Extreme Programming
> Crystal Methods
> Scrum
> Feature Driven Development

*Plan-driven methods work best when developers can determine the requirements in advance . . . and when the requirements remain relatively stable, with change rates on the order of one percent per month.*

*-- Barry Boehm [11]*

Plan-driven methods are those that begin with the solicitation and documentation of a set of requirements that is as complete as possible. Based on these requirements, one can then formulate a plan of development. Usually, the more complete the requirements, the better the plan. Some examples of plan-driven methods are various waterfall approaches and others such as the Personal Software Process (PSP) [28] and the Rational Unified Process (RUP) [30, 31]. An underlying assumption in plan-driven processes is that the requirements are relatively static. On the other hand, iterative methods, such as spiral-model based approaches [12, 14], evolutionary processes described in [5, 22, 32, 33], and recently agile approaches [45] count on change and recognize that the only constant is change. The question is only of the degree and the impact of the change. Beginning in the mid-1990's, practitioners began finding the rate of change in software requirements increasing well beyond the capabilities of classical development methodologies [11, 27]. The software industry, software technology, and customers expectations were moving very quickly and the customers were becoming increasingly less able to fully state their needs up front. As a result, agile methodologies and practices emerged as an explicit attempt to more formally embrace higher rates of requirements change. .

In this chapter, we provide background information on agile principles, and we provide an overview of three agile methodologies. For each of these methodologies, we will present an overview, the main roles involved in the methodology, the documents and artifacts produced, and the development process.

## 1    What is Agility in Software Development?

In this section, we discuss the model underlying agile software development.

### 1.1    Agile Model
Agile methods are a subset of iterative and evolutionary methods [32, 33] and are based on

220

iterative enhancement [5] and opportunistic development processes [18]. In all iterative products, each iteration is a self-contained, mini-project with activities that span requirements analysis, design, implementation, and test [32]. Each iteration leads to an iteration release (which may be only an internal release) that integrates all software across the team and is a growing and evolving subset of the final system. The purpose of having short iterations is so that feedback from iterations N and earlier, and any other new information, can lead to refinement and requirements adaptation for iteration N + 1. The customer adaptively specifies his or her requirements for the next release based on observation of the evolving product, rather than speculation at the start of the project [12]. There is quantitative evidence that frequent deadlines reduce the variance of a software process and, thus, may increase its predictability and efficiency. [40]

The pre-determined iteration length serves as a timebox for the team. Scope is chosen for each iteration to fill the iteration length. Rather than increase the iteration length to fit the chosen scope, the scope is reduced to fit the iteration length. A key difference between agile methods and past iterative methods is the length of each iteration. In the past, iterations might have been three or six months long. With agile methods, iteration lengths vary between one to four weeks, and intentionally do not exceed 30 days. Research has shown that shorter iterations have lower complexity and risk, better feedback, and higher productivity and success rates [32].

A point of commonality for all agile methods is the recognition of software development as an empirical process. In engineering, processes are classified as defined (also known as prescriptive) or empirical (or exploration-based) [36]. A defined process is one that can be started and allowed to run to completion, producing results with little variation each time [41]. Assembling an automobile is such a process. Engineers can design an unambiguous process to assemble a car and specify an assembly order and actions on the part of the assembly-line workers, machines, and robots. Generally speaking, if the manufacturing process follows these predefined steps, a high-quality car can be produced provided that the software process is under control and tolerances are appropriate, i.e., process variance is low. Such defined manufacturing processes are suitable for building items with a low degree of novelty or change and with a highly repeatable process [32].

Software development often has too much change during the time that the team is developing the product to be considered a defined process. A set of predefined steps may not lead to a desirable, predictable outcome because software development is a decidedly human activity: requirements change, technology changes, people are added and taken off the team, and so on. In other words, the process variance is high. In an engineering context, empirical processes are used for research-oriented, high-change, possibly unstable, and intellectually-intensive domains [32] that require constant monitoring and exploratory work [18]. These conditions necessitate short "inspect-and-adapt" cycles and frequent, short feedback loops [22, 36]. The short inspect-and-adapt cycles prominent in agile methodologies can help development teams to better handle the conflicting and unpredictable demands of some projects.

Another area of commonality among all agile methodologies is the importance of the people performing the roles and the recognition that, more so than any process or tool, these people are the most influential factoring in any project. Brooks' acknowledges the same in *The Mythical Man Month* [15], "The quality of the people on a project, and their organization and management, are more important factors in success than are the tools they use or the technical approaches they take." Unfortunately, there are commonalities among some agile methods that may be less than positive. One is that, unlike more classical iterative methods, explicit quantitative quality measurements and process modeling and metrics are often subdued and sometimes completely avoided. Possible justifications for this lack of modeling and metrics range from lack of time, to lack of skills, to intrusiveness, to social reasons.

Another potential problem area for agile methods is the ability to cope with corrections or deficiencies introduced into the product. Ideally, even in "classical" development environments, the reaction to change information need be quick; the corrections are applied within the same life-cycle phase in which the information is collected. However, introduction of feedback loops into the software process will depend on the software engineering capabilities of the organization, and the reaction latency will depend on the accuracy of the feedback models. For example, it is unlikely that organizations below the third maturity level on the Software Engineering Institute (SEI) Capability Maturity Model (CMM) scale [38] would have processes that could react to the feedback information in less than one software release cycle. This needs to be taken into account when considering the level and the economics of the "agile" methods. For instance, only relatively small teams can self-organize (one of the agile principles) into something resembling a CMM Level 4 or 5 performance. Also, since personnel resources are not unlimited, there is also some part of the software that may go untested, or may be verified to a lesser degree. The basic, and most difficult, aspect of system verification is to decide what must be tested, and what can be left untested, or partially tested [43].

**1.2    Agile Development and Principles**

In February 2001, several software engineering consultants joined forces and began to classify a number of similar change-sensitive methodologies as *agile* (a term with a decade of use in flexible manufacturing practices [34] which began to be used for software development in the late 1990's [3]). The term promoted the professed ability for rapid and flexible response to change of the methodologies. The consultants formed the Agile Alliance and wrote The Manifesto for Agile Software Development and the Principles Behind the Agile Manifesto [9, 25]. The methodologies originally embraced by the Agile Alliance were Adaptive Software Development (ASD) [26], Crystal [17], Dynamic Systems Development Method (DSDM) [42], Extreme Programming (XP) [6], Feature Driven Development (FDD) [16, 37] and Scrum [41].

*1.2.1 Agile Software Development*

The Agile Alliance documented its value statement [9] as follows:.

*We are uncovering better ways of developing software by doing it and helping others do it. Through this work we have come to value:*

222

*Individuals and interactions   over   processes and tools*
*Working software                       over   comprehensive documentation*
*Customer collaboration                        over   contract negotiation*
*Responding to change            over   following a plan*

*That is, while there is value in the items on the right, we value the items on the left more.*

The implication is that formalization of the software process hinders the human and practical component of software development, and thus reduces the chance for success. While this is true when formalization is misused and misunderstood, one has to be very careful not to overemphasize and under-measure the items on the left hand side since this can lead to the same problem, poor quality software. The key is appropriate balance [13].

*1.2.2*   The Principles

The Agile Alliance also documented the principles they follow that underlie their manifesto [9]. As such the agile methods are principle-based, rather than rule-based [32]. Rather than have predefined rules regarding the roles, relationships, and activities, the team and manager are guided by these principles:

1. *Our highest priority is to satisfy the customer through early and continuous delivery of valuable software.*
2. *Welcome changing requirements, even late in development. Agile processes harness change for the customer's competitive advantage.*
3. *Deliver working software frequently, from a couple of weeks to a couple of months, with a preference to the shorter time scale.*
4. *Business people and developers must work together daily through the project.*
5. *Build projects around motivated individuals. Give them the environment and support they need, and trust them to get the job done.*
6. *The most efficient and effective method of conveying information to and within a development team is face-to-face conversation.*
7. *Working software is the primary measure of progress.*
8. *Agile processes promote sustainable development.*
9. *The sponsors, developers, and users should be able to maintain a constant pace indefinitely.*
10. *Continuous attention to technical excellence and good design enhances agility.*
11. *Simplicity – the art of maximizing the amount of work not done – is essential.*
12. *The best architectures, requirements, and designs emerge from self-organizing teams.*
13. *At regular intervals, the team reflects on how to become more effective, then tunes and adjusts its behavior accordingly.*

## 2   Examples of Agile Software Development Methodologies

This section provides a brief introduction to three agile methodologies. The three were chosen to demonstrate the range of applicability and specification of the agile methodologies. For each methodology we provide an overview, and then discuss documents and artifacts produced by the development team, the roles the members of the development team assume, and the process.

### 2.1 Extreme Programming (XP)

Extreme Programming (XP) [6] originators aimed at developing a methodology suitable for "object-oriented projects using teams of a dozen or fewer programmers in one location." [29]

The methodology is based upon five underlying values: communication, simplicity, feedback, courage, and respect.

- o **Communication**. XP has a culture of oral communication and its practices are designed to encourage interaction. The communication value is based on the observation that most project difficulties occur because someone *should have* spoken with someone else to clarify a question, collaborate, or obtain help. "Problems with projects can invariably be traced back to somebody not talking to somebody else about something important." [6]
- o **Simplicity**. Design the simplest product that meets the customer's needs. An important aspect of the value is to only design and code what is in the current requirements rather than to anticipate and plan for unstated requirements.
- o **Feedback**. The development team obtains feedback from the customers at the end of each iteration and external release. This feedback drives the next iteration. Additionally, there are very short design and implementation feedback loops built into the methodology via pair programming and test-driven development [44].
- o **Courage**. The other three values allow the team to have courage in its actions and decision making. For example, the development team might have the courage to resist pressure to make unrealistic commitments.
- o **Respect**. Team members need to care about each other and about the project.

### 2.1.1 Documents and Artifacts

In general, XP relies on "documentation" via oral communication, the code itself, and tacit knowledge transfer rather than written documents and artifacts. However, while oral communication may work for small groups, it is not a recommended procedure for large systems, high-risk systems, or systems that require audit-ability for legal or software reliability engineering reasons. In these cases, the following "tools" may need to be more formally managed, recorded/preserved and regularly re-visited as part of a more "formal" and traceable XP process.

- o **User story cards**, paper index cards which contain brief requirement (features, fixes, non-functional) descriptions. The user story cards are intentionally not a full requirement statement but are, instead, a commitment for further conversation between the developer and the customer. During this conversation, the two parties will come to an oral understanding of what is needed for the requirement to be fulfilled. Customer priority and developer resource estimate are added to the card. The resource estimate for a user story must not exceed the iteration duration.

o **Task list**, a listing of the tasks (one-half to three days in duration) for the user stories that are to be completed for an iteration. Tasks represent concrete aspects of a user story. Programmers volunteer for tasks rather than are assigned to tasks.

o **CRC cards [10] (optional)**, paper index card on which one records the responsibilities and collaborators of classes which can serve as a basis for software design. The classes, responsibilities, and collaborators are identified during a design brainstorming/role-playing session involving multiple developers. CRC stands for **C**lass-**R**esponsibility-**C**ollaboration.

o **Customer acceptance tests**, textual descriptions and automated test cases which are developed by the customer. The development team demonstrates the completion of a user story and the validation of customer requirements by passing these test cases.

o **Visible Wall Graphs**, to foster communication and accountability, progress graphs are usually posted in team work area. These progress graphs often involve how many stories are completed and/or how many acceptance test cases are passing.

### 2.1.2 Roles

o **Manager,** owns the team and its problems. He or she forms the team, obtain resources, manage people and problems, and interfaces with external groups.

o **Coach**, teaches team members about the XP process as necessary, intervenes in case of issues; monitors whether the XP process is being followed. The coach is typically a programmer and not a manager.

o **Tracker**, regularly collects user story and acceptance test case progress from the developers to create the visible wall graphs. The tracker is a programmer, not a manager or customer.

o **Programmer**, writes tests, design, and code; refactors; identifies and estimates tasks and stories (this person may also be a tester)

o **Tester**, helps customers write and develop tests (this person may also be a programmer)

o **Customer**, writes stories and acceptance tests; picks stories for a release and for an iteration. A common misconception is that the role of the customer must be played by one individual from the customer organization. Conversely, a group of customers can be involved or a customer representative can be chosen from within the development organization (but external to the development team).

### 2.1.3 Process

The initial version of the XP software methodology [6] published in 2000 had 12 programmer-centric, technical practices. These practices interact, counterbalance and reinforce each other [6, 27]. However, in a survey [20] of project managers, chief executive officers, developers, and vice-presidents of engineering for 21 software projects, it was found that none of the companies adopted XP in a "pure" form wherein all 12 practices were used without adaptation. In 2005, XP was changed to include 13 primary practices and 11 corollary practices [8]. The primary practices are intended to be [8] useful independent of each other and the other practices used, though the interactions between the practices may amplify their effect. The corollary practices are likely to be difficult without first mastering a core set of the primary practices.

Below the 13 primary technical practices of XP are briefly described:
- **Sit together,** the whole team develops in one open space.
- **Whole team,** utilize a cross-functional team of all those necessary for the product to succeed.
- **Informative workspace,** place visible wall graphs around the workspace so that team members (or other interested observers) can get a general idea of how the project is going.
- **Energized work**, XP teams do not work excessive overtime for long periods of time. The motivation behind this practice is to keep the code of high quality (tired programmers inject more defects) and the programmers happy (to reduce employee turnover). Tom DeMarco contends that, "Extended overtime is a productivity-reducing technique." [19]
- **Pair programming** [46], refers to the practice whereby two programmers work together at one computer, collaborating on the same design, algorithm, code, or test.
- **Stories**, the team write short statements of customer-visible functionality desired in the product. The developers estimate the story; the customer prioritizes the story.
- **Weekly cycle**, at the beginning of each week a meeting is held to review progress to date, have the customer pick a week's worth of stories to implement that week (based upon developer estimates and their own priority), and to break the stories into tasks to be completed that week. By the end of the week, acceptance test cases for the chosen stories should be running for demonstration to the customer to drive the next weekly cycle.
- **Quarterly cycle**, the whole team should pick a theme or themes of stories for a quarter's worth of stories. Themes help the team reflect on the bigger picture. At the end of the quarter, deliver this business value.
- **Slack,** in every iteration, plan some lower-priority tasks that can be dropped if the team gets behind such that the customer will still be delivered their most important functionality.
- **Ten-minute build,** structure the project and its associated tests such that the whole system can be built and all the tests can be run in ten minutes so that the system will be built and the tests will be run often.
- **Test-first programming,** all stories have at least one acceptance test, preferably automated. When the acceptance test(s) for a user story all pass, the story is considered to be fulfilled. Additionally, automated unit tests are incrementally written using the test-driven development (TDD) [7] practice in which code and automated unit tests are alternately and incrementally written on a minute-by-minute basis.
- **Continuous integration**, programmers check in to the code base completed code and its associated tests several times a day. Code may only be checked in if all its associated unit tests and all of unit tests of the entire code base pass.
- **Incremental design**, rather than develop an anticipatory detailed design prior to implementation, invest in the design of the system every day in light of the experience of the past. The viability and prudence of anticipatory design has changed dramatically in our volatile business environment [27]. Refactoring [24] to improve the design of previously-written code is essential. Teams with robust unit tests can safely experiment with

226

refactorings because a safety net is in place.

Below the 11 corollary technical practices of XP are briefly described:

- o **Real customer involvement**, the customer is available to clarify requirements questions, is a subject matter expert, and is empowered to make decisions about the requirements and their priority. Additionally, the customer writes the acceptance tests.
- o **Incremental deployment,** gradually deploy functionality in a live environment to reduce the risk of a big deployment.
- o **Team continuity,** keep effective teams together.
- o **Shrinking team,** as a team grows in capacity (due to experience), keep their workload constant but gradually reduce the size of the team.
- o **Root cause analysis,** examine the cause of a discovered defect by writing acceptance test(s) and unit test(s) to reveal the defect. Subsequently, examine why the defects was created but not caught in the development process.
- o **Shared code**, once code and its associated tests are checked into the code base, the code can be altered by any team member. This collective code ownership provides each team member with the feeling of owning the whole code base and prevents bottlenecks that might have been caused if the "owner" of a component was not available to make a necessary change.
- o **Code and tests,** maintain only the code and tests as permanent artifacts. Rely on social mechanisms to keep alive the important history of the project.
- o **Daily deployment,** put new code into production every night.
- o **Negotiated scope contract,** fix the time, cost, and required quality of a project but call for an on-going negotiation of the scope of the project.
- o **Pay-per-use,** charge the user every time the system is used to obtain their feedback by their usage patterns.

Though not one of the "official" XP practices, essentially all XP teams also have short **Stand-Up Meetings** daily [4]. In these meetings, the team stands in a circle (standing is intentional to motivate the team to keep the meeting short). In turn, each member of the team tells the group:

- o What he or she accomplished the prior day
- o What he or she plans to do today
- o Any obstacles or difficulties he or she is experiencing

Often the pair-programming pairs are dynamically formed during the daily meeting as the tasks for the day are discussed and the two programmers that are best equipped to handle the task join together.

A "courageous" XP manager will keep a record of such meetings in order to turn them into quantitative progress measures of the project [21, 35, 43]. The burden of this quantification may be eased and automated through appropriate tools.

## 2.2 Crystal

The Rational Unified Process (RUP) [30, 31] is a customizable process framework. Depending upon the project characteristics, such as team size and project size, the RUP can be tailored or extended to match the needs of an adopting organization. Similarly, the family of Crystal Methods [17] were developed to address the variability of the environment and the specific characteristics of the project. However, RUP generally starts with a plan-driven base methodology and tailors down for smaller, less critical projects. Conversely, Crystal author Alistair Cockburn feels that the base methodology should be "barely sufficient." He contends, "You need one less notch control than you expect, and less is better when it comes to delivering quickly." [27] Moreover, since the project and the people evolve over time, the methodology so too must be tuned and evolved during the course of the project.

Crystal is a family of methods because Cockburn believes that there is no "one-size-fits-all" development process. As such, the different methods are assigned colors arranged in ascending opacity; the most agile version is Crystal Clear, followed by Crystal Yellow, Crystal Orange, and Crystal Red. The graph in Figure 2 is used to aid the choice of a Crystal Method starting point (for later tailoring). Along the x-axis is the size of the team. As a team gets larger (moves to the right along the x-axis), the harder it is to manage the process via face-to-face communication and, thus, the greater the need for coordinating documentation, practices, and tools. The y-axis addresses the system's potential for causing damage. The lowest damage impact is loss of comfort, then loss of discretionary money, loss of essential money, and finally loss of life. Based on the team size and the criticality, the corresponding Crystal methodology is identified. Each methodology has a set of recommended practices, a core set of roles, work products, techniques, and notations.

Figure 1: The Family of Crystal Methods [adapted from [17]]

All the Crystal Methods emphasize the importance of people in developing software. "[Crystal] focuses on people, interaction, community, skills, talents, and communication as first order effects on performance. Process remains important, but secondary". [27] There are only two absolute rules of the Crystal family of methodologies. First, incremental cycles must not exceed four months. Second, reflection workshops must be held after every delivery so that the methodology is self-adapting. Currently, only Crystal Clear and Crystal Orange have been defined. Summaries of these two methodologies are provided below.

2.2.1   Crystal Clear
Crystal Clear [17] is targeted at a D6 project and could be applied to a C6 or a E6 project and possibly to a D10 project. Crystal Clear is an optimization of Crystal that can be applied when the team consists of three to eight people sitting in the same room or adjoining offices. The property of close communication is strengthened to "osmotic" communication meaning that people overhear each other discussing project priorities, status, requirements, and design on a daily basis. Crystal Clear's model elements are as follows:

o   **Documents and artifacts**:   release plan, schedule of reviews, informal/low-ceremony use cases, design sketches, running code, common object model, test cases, and user manual o **Roles**: project sponsor/customer, senior designer-programmer, designer-programmer, and user (part time at least)

o **Process**: incremental delivery, releases less than two to three months, some automated testing, direct user involvement, two user reviews per release, and methodology-tuning retrospectives. Progress is tracked by software delivered or major decisions reached, not by documents completed.

### 2.2.2 Crystal Orange

Crystal Orange is targeted at a D40 project. Crystal Orange is for 20-40 programmers, working together in one building on a project in which defects could cause the loss of discretionary money (i.e., medium risk). The project duration is between one and two years and time-to-market is important. Crystal Clear's model elements are as follows:

o **Documents and artifacts**: requirements document, release plan, schedule, status reports, UI design document, inter-team specs, running code, common object model, test cases, migration code, and user manual

o **Roles**: project sponsor, business expert, usage expert, technical facilitator, business analyst, project manager, architect, design mentor, lead designer-programmer, designer-programmer, UI designer, reuse point, writer, and tester

o **Process**: incremental delivery, releases less than three to four months, some automated testing, direct user involvement, two user reviews per release, and methodology-tuning retrospectives.

## 2.3 Scrum

### 2.3.1 Overview

The Scrum process [27, 41] puts a project management "wrapper" around a software development methodology. The methodology is flexible on how much/how little ceremony but the Scrum philosophy would guide a team towards as little ceremony as possible. Usually a Scrum teams works co-located. However, there have been Scrum teams that work geographically distributed whereby team members participate in daily meeting via speakerphone. Scrum teams are self-directed and self-organizing teams. The team commits to a defined goal for an iteration and is given the authority, autonomy, and responsibility to decide how best to meet it.

### 2.3.2 Documents and Artifacts

There are three main artifacts produced by Scrum teams, the Product Backlog, the Sprint Backlog, and the Sprint Burndown chart. All of these are openly accessible and intentionally visible to the Scrum Team.

o **Product Backlog**, an evolving, prioritized queue of business and technical functionality that needs to be developed into a system and defects that need to be fixed [41] during the release. For each requirement, the Product Backlog contains a unique identifier for the requirement, the category (feature, enhancement, defect), the status, the priority, and the estimate for the feature. It is kept in a spreadsheet-like format.

- o **Sprint Backlog**, a list of all business and technology features, enhancements, and defects that have been scheduled for the current iteration (called a Sprint). The Sprint Backlog is also maintained in a spreadsheet-like format. The requirements are broken down into tasks. For each task in the backlog, the spreadsheet contains a short task description, who originated the task, who owns the task, the status and the number of hours remaining to complete the task. The Sprint Backlog is updated each day by a daily tracker who visits the team members to obtain the latest estimates of the work remaining to complete the task. Estimates can increase when the team member realizes that the work was underestimated.
- o **Sprint Burndown chart**. The hours remaining to complete Sprint tasks are graphed and predominantly displayed for the team. A sample of a burndown chart is shown in Figure 3.

Figure 3: Sprint Burndown Chart

### 2.3.3 Roles

- o **Product Owner**, the person who is responsible for creating and prioritizing the Product Backlog, choosing what will be included in the next iteration/Sprint, and reviewing the system (with other stakeholders) at the end of the Sprint.
- o **Scrum Master,** knows and reinforces the product iteration and goals and the Scrum values and practices, conducts the daily meeting (the Scrum Meeting) and the iteration demonstration (the Sprint Review), listens to progress, removes impediments (blocks), and provides resources. The Scrum Master is also a Developer (see below) and participates in product development (is not just management).
- o **Developer,** member of the Scrum team. The Scrum Team is committed to achieving a Sprint Goal and has full authority to do whatever it takes to achieve the goal. The size of a Scrum team is seven, plus or minus two.

### 2.3.4 Process

An overview of the Scrum process is provided in Figure 4. Each of the elements of the process will be discussed in this section.

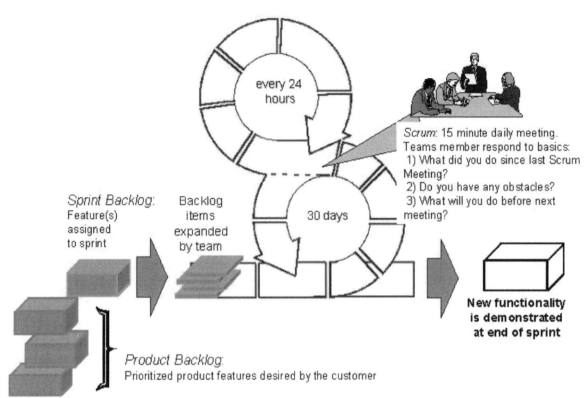

Figure 4: The Scrum Process (from [1])

The Scrum process is composed of the following:

- o A *Sprint Planning* meeting is held with the development team, management, and the Product Owner. The Product Owner is a representative of the customer or a contingent of customers. The Product Owner creates and prioritizes the Product Backlog. In the planning meeting, the Product Owner chooses which features are included in the next 30-day increment (called a Sprint) usually driven by highest business value and risk. Additionally a Sprint Goal is established which serves as a minimum, high-level success criteria for the Sprint and keep the Scrum Team focused on the big picture, rather than just on the chosen features. The development team figures out the tasks and resources required to deliver those features. Jointly, they determine a reasonable number of features to be included in the next Sprint. Once this set of features has been identified, no re-prioritization takes place during the ensuing 30-day Sprint in which features are designed, implemented and tested.

- o During a Sprint, code is integrated and regression tested daily.

- o Short, 15-minute *Scrum Meetings* are held daily. These meetings are similar to XP Stand Up Meetings described above because XP's meetings are based on the success Scrum had with its Scrum Meetings. The meeting is held in a room with a whiteboard so that tasks and blocks can be written down. While others (such as managers) may attend the Sprint Meeting, only the team members and the Scrum Master can speak. Each team member answers the following questions:

  - o What have you done since the last Scrum?

  o What will you do between now and the next Scrum?

  o What got in your way of doing work?

The Scrum Meeting is an essential component of the methodology. Social promises are made in the meeting which seems to increase responsibility and follow-through and to keep the project on course. However, these meetings can become unmanageable if they are run with too many people; it is recommended that each team has a maximum of seven members. For use with larger teams, the team subdivides into smaller groups, each having its own Scrum meeting. One representative from each of the smaller groups attends a "Scrum of Scrums" meeting. This representative answers the Scrum questions, highlighting the activities of his or her own sub-team. In this way, essential information is passed between sub-teams.

  o At the end of a Sprint, a *Sprint Review* takes place to review progress, demonstrate features to the customer, management, users and the Product Owner and review the project from a technical perspective. The meeting is conducted by the Scrum Master. The Product Owner and other interested stakeholders attend the meeting. The latest version of the product is demonstrated in which the functions, design, strength, weaknesses, and trouble spots are shared with the Product Owner. The focus is on showing the product itself; formal presentations (such as with PowerPoint slides) are forbidden.

  o The cycle continues with a Sprint Planning meeting taking place to choose the features for the next Sprint.

## 2.4  Feature-Driven Development (FDD)

Feature Driven Development (FDD) [16, 37] authors Peter Coad and Jeff de Luca characterize the methodology as having "just enough process to ensure scalability and repeatability and encourage creativity and innovation all along the way." [27] Throughout, FDD emphasizes the importance of having good people and strong domain experts. FDD is build around eight best practices:  domain object modeling; developing by feature; individual class ownership; feature teams; inspections; regular builds; configuration management; reporting/visibility of results. UML models [23] are used extensively in FDD.

2.4.1 Documents and Artifacts

  o **Feature lists**, consisting of a set of features whereby features are small, useful in the eyes of the client, results; a client-valued function that can be implemented in two weeks or less. If a feature would take more than two weeks to implement, it must be further decomposed.

  o **Design packages** consist of sequence diagrams and class diagrams and method design information

  o **Track by Feature**, a chart which enumerates the features that are to be built and the dates when each milestone has been completed.

  o **"Burn Up" Chart**, a chart that has dates (time) on the x axis. On the y axis is an increasing number of features that have been completed. As features are completed this chart indicates a positive slope over time.

2.4.2 Roles

o **Project manager**, is the administrative lead of the project responsible for reporting progress, managing budgets, and fighting for and managing resources including people, equipment, and space.

o **Chief architect**, is responsible for the overall design of the system including running workshop design sessions with the team.

o **Development manager**, is responsible for leading the day-to-day development activities including the resolution of resource conflicts.

o **Chief programmer**, as outlined by Brooks' ideas on surgical teams [15], is an experienced developer who acts as a team lead, mentor, and developer for a team of three to six developers. The chief programmer provides the breadth of knowledge about the skeletal model to a feature team, participates in high-level requirements analysis and design, and aids the team in low-level analysis, design, and development of new features.

o **Class owner**, is responsible for designing, coding, testing, and documenting new features in the classes that he or she owns.

o **Domain experts,** users, clients, sponsors, business analysts, etc. who have deep knowledge of the business for which the product is being developed.

o **Feature teams** are temporary groups of developers formed around the classes with which the features will be implemented. A feature team dynamically forms to implement a feature and disbands when the feature has been implemented (two weeks or less).

### 2.4.3 Process

The FDD process has five incremental, iterative processes, as shown in Figure 5. Guidelines are given for the amount of time that should be spent in each of these steps, constraining the amount of time spent in overall planning and architecture and emphasizing the amount of time designing and building features. Processes 1 through 3 are done at the start of a project and then updated throughout the development cycle. Processes 4 and 5 are done incrementally on two week cycles. Each of these processes has specific entry and exit criteria, whereby the entry criterion of Process N is the exit criteria of Process N-1.

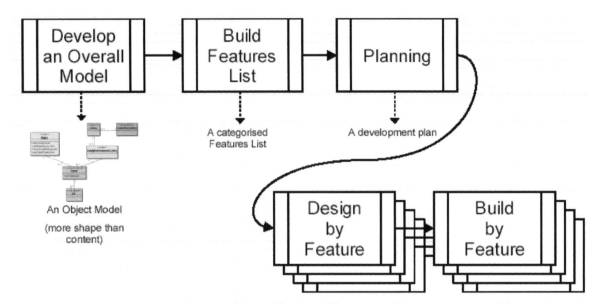

**Figure 5: Overview of Feature Driven Development**

o **Process 1: Develop an overall model** (time: 10 percent initially, 4 percent ongoing)
Domain and development team members work together to understand the scope of the system and its context. High-level object models/class diagrams are developed for each area of the problem domain. Model notes record information about the model's shape and why some alternatives were selected and others rejected.

o **Process 2: Build a features list** (time: 4 percent initially, 1 percent ongoing)
Complete list of all the features in the project; functional decomposition which breaks down a "business activity" requested by the customer to the features that need to be implemented in the software.

o **Process 3: Plan by feature** (time: 2 percent initially, 2 percent ongoing)
A planning team consisting of the project manager, development manager, and chief programmer plan the order in which features will be developed. Planning is based on dependencies, risk, complexity, workload balancing, client-required milestones, and checkpoints. Business activities are assigned month/year completion dates. Every class is assigned to a specific developer. Features are bundled according to technical reasons rather than business reasons.

o **Process 4: Design by feature** (time 34% ongoing in two-week iterations)
The chief programmer leads the development of design packages and refines object models with attributes. The sequence diagrams are often done as a group activity. The class diagrams and object models are done by the class owners. Domain experts interact with the team to refine the feature requirements. Designs are inspected.

o **Process 5: Build by feature** (time: 43% ongoing in two-week iterations)
The feature team implements the classes and methods outlined by the design. This code is inspected and unit tested. The code is promoted to the build.

Progress is tracked and made visible during the Design by feature/Build by feature phases. Each feature has six milestones, three from the Design by feature phase (domain walkthrough, design, and design inspection) and three from the Build by feature phase (code, code inspection, promote to build). When these milestones are complete, the date is placed on the Track by Feature chart which is prominently displayed for the team. When a feature has completed all six milestones, this completion is reflected on the "Burn Up" chart. All features are scoped to be completed within a maximum of two weeks, including all six milestones.

## 3 Summary

In this chapter we presented an overview of the agile software development model and the characteristics of the projects that may be suited for the use of this model. Additionally, we provided overviews of three representative methodologies, XP, Crystal, and FDD. A summary of the distinguishing factors of these three methodologies is presented in Table 1.

| Agile Methodology | Distinguishing Factor |
|---|---|
| **Extreme Programming** | Intended for 10-12 co-located, object-oriented programmers<br>Four values<br>12 highly-specified, disciplined development practices<br>Minimal archival documentation<br>Rapid customer and developer feedback loops |
| **Crystal** | Customizable family of development methodologies for small to very large teams<br>Methodology dependent on size of team and criticality of project<br>Emphasis of face-to-face communication<br>Consider people, interaction, community, skills, talents, and communication as first-order effects<br>Start with minimal process and build up as absolutely necessary |
| **Scrum** | Project management wrapper around methodology in which developer practices are defined<br>30-day Sprints in which priorities are not changed<br>Daily Scrum meeting of Scrum Team<br>Burndown chart to display progress |
| **Feature Driven Development** | Scalable to larger teams<br>Highly-specified development practices<br>Five sub-processes, each defined with entry and exit criteria<br>Development are architectural shape, object models and sequence diagrams (UML models used throughout)<br>Two-week features |

Table 1: A summary of three agile software development methodologies

Several key ideas about agile methodologies presented in this chapter. The keys for successful use of choosing and using agile methodologies are summarized in Table 2.

| | |
|---|---|
| | Agile methods are a subset of iterative and evolutionary methods. Iterations are short to provide for more timely feedback to the project team. |
| | The Agile Manifesto documents the priorities that underlie the principles and practices of agile software development methodologies. |
| | Extreme Programming is based upon four values and 12 specific software development practices. |
| | The Crystal family of methodologies is customizable based upon the characteristics of the project and the team. |
| | Scrum mainly deals with project management principles. The methodology allows the team freedom to choose its specific development practices. |
| | Of the four methodologies presented in the chapter, FDD has the most thorough analysis and design practices. |

**Table 2: Key Ideas for Agile Software Development Methodologies**

There are other defined agile software development methodologies as well. These includes Adaptive Software Development (ASD) [26], Agile Modeling [2], Dynamic Systems Development Method (DSDM) [42], Lean Development [39], and Scrum [27, 41]. Additionally, teams can configure an agile RUP methodology. All agile methodologies consider software development to be an empirical process that necessitates short "inspect and adapt" feedback loops throughout the project.

**References**

[1]     ADM Inc., *What is SCRUM*: http://controlchaos.com, 2004.
[2]     S. W. Ambler, *Agile Modeling*. New York, NY: John Wiley and Sons, 2002.
[3]     M. Aoyama, "Agile Software Process and its Experience," International Conference on Software Engineering, Kyoto, Japan, 1998, pp. 3-12.
[4]     K. Auer and R. Miller, *XP Applied*. Reading, Massachusetts: Addison Wesley, 2001.
[5]     V. R. Basili and A. J. Turner, "Iterative Enhancement: A Practical Technique for Software Development," *IEEE Transactions on Software Engineering*, vol. 1, no. 4, pp. 266 - 270, 1975.
[6]     K. Beck, *Extreme Programming Explained: Embrace Change*. Reading, Mass.: Addison-Wesley, 2000.
[7]     K. Beck, *Test Driven Development -- by Example*. Boston: Addison Wesley, 2003.
[8]     K. Beck, *Extreme Programming Explained: Embrace Change*, Second ed. Reading, Mass.:

Addison-Wesley, 2005.

[9]     K. Beck, M. Beedle, A. van Bennekum, A. Cockburn, W. Cunningham, M. Fowler, J. Grenning, J. Highsmith, A. Hunt, R. Jeffries, J. Kern, B. Marick, R. C. Martin, S. Mellor, K. Schwaber, J. Sutherland, and D. Thomas, "The Agile Manifesto," http://www.agileAlliance.org, 2001, 2001.

[10]    D. Bellin and S. S. Simone, *The CRC Card Book*. Reading, Massachusetts: Addison-Wesley, 1997.

[11]    B. Boehm, "Get Ready for Agile Methods, with Care," *IEEE Computer*, vol. 35, no. 1, pp. 64-69, 2002.

[12]    B. Boehm, "A Spiral Model for Software Development and Enhancement," *Computer*, vol. 21, no. 5, pp. 61-72, May 1988.

[13]    B. Boehm and R. Turner, "Using Risk to Balance Agile and Plan-Driven Methods," *IEEE Computer*, vol. 36, no. 6, pp. 57-66, June 2003.

[14]    B. W. Boehm, *Software Engineering Economics*. Englewood Cliffs, NJ: Prentice-Hall, Inc., 1981.

[15]    F. P. Brooks, *The Mythical Man-Month, Anniversary Edition*: Addison-Wesley Publishing Company, 1995.

[16]    P. Coad, E. LeFebvre, and J. DeLuca, *Java Modeling in Color with UML*: Prentice Hall, 1999.

[17]    A. Cockburn, *Agile Software Development*. Reading, Massachusetts: Addison Wesley Longman, 2001.

[18]    B. Curtis, "Three Problems Overcome with Behavioral Models of the Software Development Process (Panel)," International Conference on Software Engineering, Pittsburgh, PA, 1989, pp. 398-399.

[19]    T. DeMarco, *Slack: Getting Past Burnout, Busywork, and the Myth of Total Efficiency*: Broadway, 2002.

[20]    K. El Emam, "Finding Success in Small Software Projects," *Agile Project Management*, vol. 4, no. 11, 2003.

[21]    S. E. Elmaghraby, E. I. Baxter, and M. A. Vouk, "An Approach to the Modeling and Analysis of Software Production Processes," *Intl. Trans. Operational Res*, vol. 2, no. 1, pp. 117-135, 1995.

[22]    R. Fairley, *Software Engineering Concepts*. New York: McGraw-Hill, 1985.

[23]    M. Fowler, *UML Distilled*. Reading, Massachusetts: Addison Wesley, 2000.

[24]    M. Fowler, K. Beck, J. Brant, W. Opdyke, and D. Roberts, *Refactoring: Improving the Design of Existing Code*. Reading, Massachusetts: Addison Wesley, 1999.

[25]    M. Fowler and J. Highsmith, "The Agile Manifesto," in *Software Development*, August 2001, pp. 28-32.

[26]    J. Highsmith, *Adaptive Software Development*. New York, NY: Dorset House, 1999.

[27]    J. Highsmith, *Agile Software Development Ecosystems*. Boston, MA: Addison-Wesley, 2002.

[28]    W. S. Humphrey, *A Discipline for Software Engineering*. Reading, MA: Addison Wesley, 1995.

[29]    R. Jeffries, A. Anderson, and C. Hendrickson, *Extreme Programming Installed*. Upper Saddle River, NJ: Addison Wesley, 2001.

[30]    P. Kroll and P. Kruchten, *The Rational Unified Process Made Easy: A Practitioner's Guide to the RUP*. Boston: Addison Wesley, 2003.

[31]    P. Kruchten, *The Rational Unified Process: An Introduction*, Third ed. Boston: Addison Wesley, 2004.

[32]    C. Larman, *Agile and Iterative Development: A Manager's Guide*. Boston: Addison Wesley, 2004.

[33]    C. Larman and V. Basili, "A History of Iterative and Incremental Development," *IEEE Computer*, vol. 36, no. 6, pp. 47-56, June 2003.

[34]    Lehigh University, "Agile Competition is Spreading to the World," http://www.ie.lehigh.edu/, 1991, 1991.

[35]    N. Nagappan, L. Williams, and M. A. Vouk, "Towards a Metric Suite for Early Software Reliability Assessment," International Symposium on Software Reliability Engineering Fast Abstract, Denver, CO, 2003, pp.

[36]    B. A. Ogunnaike and W. H. Ray, *Process Dynamics, Modeling, and Control*. New York: Oxford University Press, 1994.

[37]    S. R. Palmer and J. M. Felsing, *A Practical Guide to Feature-Driven Development*. Upper Saddle River, NJ: Prentice Hall PTR, 2002.

[38]    M. C. Paulk, B. Curtis, and M. B. Chrisis, "Capability Maturity Model for Software Version 1.1," Software Engineering Institute CMU/SEI-93-TR, February 24, 1993, 1993.

[39]    M. Poppendieck and T. Poppendieck, *Lean Software Development*. Boston: Addison Wesley, 2003.

[40]    T. Potok and M. Vouk, "The Effects of the Business Model on the Object-Oriented Software Development Productivity," *IBM Systems Journal*, vol. 36, no. 1, pp. 140-161, 1997.

[41]    K. Schwaber and M. Beedle, *Agile Software Development with SCRUM*. Upper Saddle River, NJ: Prentice-Hall, 2002.

[42]    J. Stapleton, *DSDM: The Method in Practice*, Second ed: Addison Wesley Longman, 2003.

[43]    M. Vouk and A. T. Rivers, "Construction of Reliable Software in Resource-Constrained Environments," in *Case Studies in Reliability and Maintenance*, W. R. Blischke and D. N. P. Murthy, Eds. Hoboken, NJ: Wiley-Interscience, John Wiley and Sons, 2003, pp. 205-231.

[44]    L. Williams, "The XP Programmer: The Few Minutes Programmer," *IEEE Software*, vol. 20, no. 3, pp. 16-20, May/June 2003.

[45]    L. Williams and A. Cockburn, "Special Issue on Agile Methods," *IEEE Computer*, vol. 36, no. 3, June 2003.

[46]    L. Williams and R. Kessler, *Pair Programming Illuminated*. Reading, Massachusetts: Addison Wesley, 2003.

# Maintenance

Software maintenance is typically the single biggest consumer of the time and effort of a software organization.  In this chapter, we will explain the following:

   principles of software maintenance and evolution

   the different types of software maintenance

   aspects of the software maintenance process

   strategies and metrics that can be used to monitor and control maintenance costs

## 1   An Introduction to Software Maintenance

*All successful software gets changed. Two processes are at work. First, as a software product is found to be useful, people try it in new cases at the edge of or beyond the original domain. The pressures for extended function come chiefly from users who like the basic function and invent new uses for it.*

*Second, successful software survives beyond the normal life of the machine vehicle for which it is first written. If not new computers, than at least new disks, new displays, new printers come along; and the software must be conformed to its new vehicles of opportunity.*        —Fred Brooks, *No Silver Bullet* [8]

*Software maintenance* is defined as *the process of modifying a software system or component after delivery to correct faults, improve performance or other attributes, or adapt to a changed environment* [17].  Software maintenance can consume as much as 90 percent of all the total effort expended on a system in its lifetime [6].  Some computer scientists prefer to use the term *evolution* rather than maintenance to indicate that a product normally and naturally evolves over time.

People—including software engineers—make mistakes.[14] They particularly make mistakes when working at the edge of their competence, and software projects present a challenge that often skirts that edge [15]. As a result, failures[15] continue to be discovered in the software, even after the software has been successfully maintained for many years.

## 2   Why Software Must be Maintained

Schach [30] summarizes the reasons why useful software has to undergo change:

1. Software is a model of reality. As the reality changes, the software must adapt or die.
2. If software is found to be useful, there are pressures, chiefly from satisfied users, to extend the functionality of the product.
3. Software is much easier to change than hardware. As a result, changes are made to the

software whenever possible.

4. Successful software survives well beyond the lifetime of the hardware for which it was written. In part, this is because hardware wears down and over time. But, more significant is the fact that technology changes so rapidly that improved hardware components, such as larger disks, faster CPUs, more powerful monitors, or new versions of the operating system become available while the software still is viable. In general, the software has to be modified to run on the new hardware and operating system.

A considerable amount of valuable software development resources are expended on maintenance (or evolutionary) activities. Studies show that between 40 percent [9, 11] and 90 percent of total software product effort is spent on maintenance. So, while most of your education is spent developing new programs starting from requirements (called *greenfield development*), most of your professional life will be spent fixing, adapting, and enhancing existing programs. Maintenance is the most difficult of all aspects of software production because, as you will see, it involves all phases of the software process. Unfortunately, this difficulty and relentless change has a harmful effect on the quality of software. The processes and practices for managing this change and for curtailing the deleterious effects on the quality of the product are the subjects of this chapter.

## 3 Lehman's Laws of Software Evolution

Professor Manny Lehman of Imperial College in London has empirically studied the evolution of a number of systems, starting from the OS/360-70 from 1968-1985 and more recently the FEAST system from 1996-2001. Through these efforts, he formulated eight related laws of software evolution, "Lehman's Laws" [21-23], as shown in Table 1. In the table, an *E-type program* is software that is actively (and regularly) used to solve a problem or address an application in a **real-world** domain [22]. In such real-world programs, *functionality* and factors, such as *quality*, *behavior* in execution, *performance*, ease of use, and *changeability,* are all of concern [22].

Lehman has called these properties *laws* because they are *"...so powerful that they constantly break through all barriers erected for their suppression...."* [5] Lehman compares these Laws of Software Evolution to the laws of supply and demand found in economics.

Table 1:  Lehman's Laws of Software Evolution

| No. | Law | Description |
|-----|-----|-------------|
| I | Continuing change | An E-type system must be continually **adapted** or else it becomes progressively less satisfactory. |
| II | Increasing complexity | As an E-type system evolves, its complexity increases unless work is done to maintain or reduce it. |
| III | Self regulation | Program evolution is a self-regulating control process, often accomplished via feedback mechanisms. |

| IV | Conservation of organizational stability | Over an E-type system's lifetime, its activity rate (elements *handled* per release) is approximately constant. |
| V | Conservation of familiarity | Over the lifetime of an E-type system, the average incremental growth tends to decline due to factors such as decreasing interest in the product. |
| VI | Continuing growth | An E-type system must be continually **grown** to satisfactorily support new situations and circumstances. |
| VII | Declining quality | Unless rigorously adapted to take into account changes in the operational environment, the quality of an E-type system will appear to decline as it is evolved. |
| VIII | Feedback System | E-type evolution processes are multi-level, multi-loop, multi-agent feedback systems. |

The first and sixths laws state that system maintenance, via adaptation and growth, is an inevitable process. As the system's environment changes, new requirements emerge, and the system must be modified. In this chapter, we discuss *adaptive maintenance,* which is used to enable a program to be usable in a changed environment (first law). We also discuss *perfective maintenance,* which is used to extend the software beyond its original functional requirements (sixth law).

The second and seventh laws state that, as a system is changed, its structure is degraded. This degradation often occurs because maintenance teams make hasty patches to fix problems. To counter the degradation, the team must explicitly invest resources in *preventative maintenance* and spend time improving the structure of the program without adding to its functionality. We discuss preventative maintenance in this chapter as well.

## 4   Types of Software Maintenance

IEEE defines three types of software maintenance: corrective maintenance, adaptive maintenance, and perfective maintenance. Each of these is discussed in this section. Additionally, we explain one additional, proactive form of maintenance that has not been defined by IEEE, preventative maintenance.

### 4.1   *Corrective Maintenance*

The first form of maintenance we discuss is corrective maintenance (which can be considered to be "fixing mistakes"). *Corrective maintenance* is *maintenance performed to correct faults in hardware or software* [17]. A fault can result from design errors, logic error, algorithm errors and/or coding errors. Even with sound quality assurance, it is likely that the customer will uncover faults in the software. Corrective maintenance changes the software to correct these faults while leaving the specifications unchanged. Functionality is not added or changed in corrective maintenance.

Corrective maintenance is particularly complex. The maintenance programmer needs to have far above average debugging and interpersonal skills. The process starts when a fault report is filed by a user of the system. The user perceives that the product is not working as it should. The following steps are generally taken:

1. Attempt to reproduce the problem the customer has reported. If the failure can be reproduced, the steps in the reproduction are a key test case for testing the fix.
2. Perhaps the failure cannot be reproduced despite several attempts and conversations with the customer. Possibly nothing at all could be wrong. The user may have just misunderstood the user manual or is using the product incorrectly. In this situation, the user might just need some education, or the user manual might need to be clarified. The maintenance engineer must work patiently with the customer (who quite possibly might be irate) to obtain the necessary information and to try to get an acceptable workaround to get him back in operation.
3. Sometimes, the problem might be due to a change made to the hardware or to the upgrade of a software system component (such as the operating system) which were somehow incompatible with the system. These types of failures are very hard for the development team to reproduce in their own labs without the exact customer environment. In this case, the problem is of adaptive maintenance (see below), and the simplest temporary fix is to revert to the original hardware and software configuration.
4. Often, however, a fault lies somewhere in the code. If the programmer is fortunate, clues to the cause of the defect might lie in the specification or design documents.
5. Alas, often the documentation is nonexistent or obsolete. In this frequent case, the programmer must rely on the code for clues or may try to find the original programmer to glean at least a starting point for problem determination.
6. Once the maintenance programmer has located the fault, he or she must fix it without inadvertently introducing another fault elsewhere in the product. *Faults injected when fixing other problems* are called *regression faults*.
7. The maintenance programmer must now test that the modification works correctly and that no regression faults have been introduced.

The maintenance programmer primarily must be a superb diagnostician to determine whether there is a fault. If so, she must be an expert technician in order to find and fix it. Throughout this process, the programmer must be an engaged counselor to patiently work with the customer, obtaining information and offering help where possible.

## 4.2 *Adaptive Maintenance*

The second type of software maintenance, related to Lehman's first law of continuing change, is adaptive maintenance. *Adaptive maintenance is software maintenance performed to make a computer program usable in a changed environment* [17]. The term *environment* refers to the totality of all conditions and influences that act from outside upon the system, for example, business rules, government policies, work patterns, software platforms, compilers, and hardware upgrades [35]. An example of a government policy that had far-reaching ramifications on software systems has been the introduction of the Euro to replace many European currencies.

Adaptive maintenance is a reaction to changes in the environment to *preserve* existing functionality and performance. Adaptive maintenance is not explicitly requested by the customer. Instead, the need is externally imposed on the software provider.

## 4.3   *Perfective Maintenance*

The third type of software maintenance, related to Lehman's sixth law of continuing growth, is perfective maintenance. *Perfective maintenance is software maintenance performed to improve the performance, maintainability, or other attributes of a computer program.* [17] [Note: we consider the maintainability aspect of maintenance in the next section on preventative maintenance.] As opposed to adaptive maintenance, which is necessary to preserve functionality, perfective maintenance extends the software beyond its original functional or non-functional requirements. A successful piece of software tends to be subjected to a succession of changes to build upon its initial requirements. The need to build upon the system is based on the premise that as the software becomes useful, the users tend to experiment with new cases beyond the scope for which it was initially developed. [35]

## 4.4   *Preventative Maintenance*

Computer software deteriorates due to changes from the three previously discussed types of maintenance. The final type of maintenance, reflected in Lehman's second and seventh laws, is preventative maintenance. *Preventative maintenance is maintenance performed for the purpose of preventing problems before they occur* [17]. Preventative maintenance is undertaken to prevent programming aging and malfunctions or to improve the maintainability of the software by making it more easily corrected, adapted, and enhanced. The change is usually explicitly initiated from within the maintenance organization. Preventative change does not increase the baseline functionality, yet it costs a significant amount of money and absorbs resources that might otherwise be occupied on revenue-generating adaptations. Therefore, it can sometimes be hard for programmers and managers to dedicate valuable time towards essential, rebuilding, preventative maintenance.

Preventative maintenance is often called software reengineering. Software reengineering is concerned with re-implementing legacy systems to make them more maintainable. On a large scale, reengineering may involve re-documenting the system, organizing and restructuring the system, translating the system to a more modern programming language, and modifying and updating the structure and values of the system's data. [29]

Arnold [2] defines a number of benefits that can be achieved when software is restructured:
> Programs have higher quality, better documentation, and less complexity, and conform to modern software engineering practices and standards.
> Frustration among software engineers who must work on the program is reduced, improving their productivity and making learning easier.

Effort required to perform maintenance activities is reduced.
Software is easier to test and debug.

Through software restructuring, source code and/or data is modified to make it amenable to future changes. The restructuring focuses on the design details of individual modules and on local data structures defined within modules. *Data restructuring* aims to improve the weak data architecture of a program. For many applications, the data architecture has more to do with the long-term viability of a program than does the source code. *Code restructuring* is performed to yield a design that produces the same function but with higher quality (in terms of latent faults and of design quality) than the original program.

Additionally, "mini-reengineering activities," often called refactorings, are implemented to improve the understandability and to simplify larger reengineering activities. [31] With a similar goal to all reengineering activities, *refactoring* is *the process of changing a software system in such a way that it does not alter the external behavior of the code yet it improves its internal structure* [14]. Refactoring makes the code easier to understand and cheaper to modify without changing its observable behavior. Without such refactoring, the design of the program will decay. [14] As people maintain, the code loses its structure, and the loss of the structure of code has a cumulative effect. The harder it is to see the design in the code, the harder it is to preserve it, and the more rapidly it decays. Regular refactoring helps code retain its shape. [14] After completing the refactoring, the developer must validate the functional equivalence of the code before and after refactoring. [19]

Ideally, the reengineering process should run concurrently with the general maintenance process. The organization should periodically monitor "system health" and prevent "system illness" by monitoring maintenance and maintainability metrics, as is discussed in Section 8. The frequency of applying the reengineering process should be linked to these metrics. Each time the cost of changes becomes intolerable and the reliability decreases under an acceptable threshold, an iteration of reengineering should be initiated. [20]

## 4.5 *The Frequency of Each Type of Maintenance*

There is a common misconception that software maintenance is all about fixing defects. This may be because, as software consumers, we might longingly wish the software would have added functionality, or we might choose one product over another due to functionality. But when our software fails or "hangs," we can get very emotional and this stands out prominently in our minds. This is especially true of industrial applications where a store full of shoppers might have to wait while the cash registers reboot, or we hear of a safety-critical flaw causing tragedy in a medical application. In fact, several sources [1, 25, 26, 29, 34] indicate that approximately only 20 percent of software maintenance resources is spent on corrective maintenance. Lientz et al. [25] compiled a study that broke down the resources expended towards the IEEE maintenance activities (corrective, adaptive and perfective, and not preventative). Their results are shown in Figure 1.

244

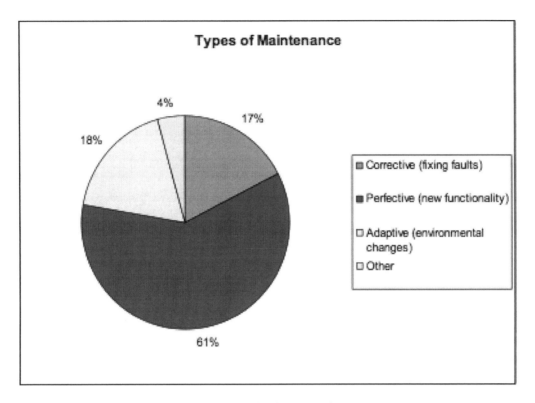

**Figure 1: Types of software maintenance.**

One more thing that's important to understand is that maintenance cost is strongly affected by the number of users. More users find more bugs [9] because each user uses the software in at least a slightly different way.

## 5 The Maintenance Process

So far, you might have the impression that all proposed (or "needed") fixes are implemented. Actually, each proposed fix is analyzed both in terms of the resources it would take to implement and in terms of its impact (i.e. how much of the system is affected by the change). Information about the proposed change, as shown in Figure 2, is documented on a *change request form*. [35] Often, an organization has a change control board to analyze these change request forms and to decide which will be implemented. A *change control board* is a *group of people responsible for evaluating and approving or disapproving proposed changes to configuration items, and for ensuring implementation of approved changes* [17]. The change control board considers the effect of the change from a strategic and organizational viewpoint, rather than a technical one and decides whether or not the change would be cost effective. [35] If the proposed change is for a critical customer situation (which would happen less than 20 percent of the time because no more than 20 percent of maintenance is spent on correcting faults), the change control board would likely act quickly to authorize the change so that the customer's normal operations can continue. Alternately, emergency fixes might bypass the change control board altogether.

```
┌─────────────────────────────────────────────────────┐
│                Change Request Form                  │
│                                                     │
│  System:                                            │
│  Version:                                           │
│  Date:                                              │
│  Requested by:                                      │
│  Summary of Change:                                 │
│                                                     │
│                                                     │
│  Reasons for Change:                                │
│                                                     │
│                                                     │
│  Software components needing change:                │
│                                                     │
│                                                     │
│  Documents needing change:                          │
│                                                     │
│                                                     │
│  Estimated cost:                                    │
│                                                     │
│                                                     │
│  Estimated time:                                    │
│                                                     │
└─────────────────────────────────────────────────────┘
```

**Figure 2: Sample software change request form.**

In non-emergency situations, proposed changes are systematically reviewed. All proposed changes (corrective, adaptive, perfective, and preventative) are considered. A decision is then made on which changes to implement in the next version of the system. Those that are accepted are planned into a new release of the system. It is cheaper and more controlled to collect and implement a number of changes, test them all, change the documentation, and ask customers to install the new version, than it is to repeat the entire cycle for each change. As a result, organizations accumulate noncritical maintenance tasks and implement the changes as a group.

The selected changes are implemented using one of the three known maintenance processes that will now be discussed, or a variant of one of these.

## 5.1  Quick Fix

The quick fix process of software maintenance is akin to the code-and-fix new development process. With quick fix, there is a quick cycle through finding a problem and fixing it, such as is shown in Figure 3. This process is basically an ad hoc, "fire fighting" approach to maintaining software where the team waits for a problem to occur and then fixes it as quickly as possible.

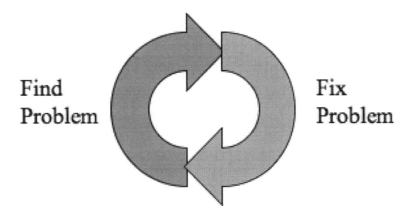

**Figure 3: Quick-fix process for software maintenance.**

Quick fix is often used in emergency, corrective maintenance. *Emergency maintenance is unscheduled corrective maintenance performed to keep a system operational* [18]. (These emergency fixes are often called "patches.") The requirements, software design, and code gradually become inconsistent when quick fix is used often. A workable solution, rather than the best solution, is often implemented. These factors accelerate the process of software aging so that future changes become progressively more difficult, and maintenance costs increase. The ad hoc nature of this approach can cause a range of problems that include unforeseen ripple effects. With unforeseen ripple effects, a change to one part of a program affects other sections in an unpredictable fashion. [35]

If customers are demanding the correction of an error, they may not be willing to wait for the organization to go through detailed and time-consuming analysis. In cases such as these, the customer's emergency should be handled as expediently as possible. When the panic subsides, the fix should be reanalyzed via a more systematic process, such as the iterative enhancement or the reuse-based processes, discussed in the following sections. There is evidence that small code changes, on a defects-per-changed-LOC basis, are nearly 40 times as error-prone as new development. [16] Leaving these quick fixes in without further review could cause more harm than good in the long run—increasing maintenance costs and reducing system reliability and customer satisfaction.

## 5.2   Iterative Enhancement

The iterative enhancement process is more systematic than the quick fix process. This process is based on the tenet that the implementation of changes to a software system throughout its lifetime is an iterative process (such as the planned releases that are comprised of approved changes) and involves enhancing a system in an iterative way. Iterative enhancement is similar to the evolutionary development paradigm. [35]

However, iterative enhancement assumes that complete documentation is available because it relies on modification of this documentation as the starting point for each iteration. Iterative enhancement involves a three-staged cycle. [35]

Analysis

Characterization of proposed modifications

Redesign and implementation

The existing documentation for each stage (requirements, design, coding, testing, and analysis) is modified starting with the highest-level document affected by the proposed changes. These modifications are propagated through the rest of the documents, and the system is redesigned.

## 5.3   Reuse-Based

The reuse-oriented model [4] is based on the principle that maintenance could be viewed as an activity involving the reuse of existing program components. The reuse model has four main steps:

Identifying the parts of the old system that are candidates for reuse

Understanding these system parts

Modifying the old system parts appropriate to the new requirements

Integrating the modified parts into the new system.

A 1998 study revealed that the great majority of organizations (84 percent) still use the quick-fix model. Fifty-seven percent of organizations use quick fix without documentation change, and 27 percent use quick fix with documentation change. The remaining 16 percent of organizations use iterative enhancement or reuse-based models. [34] This phenomenon only perpetuates the vast amount of resources that are dedicated towards maintenance in the software industry.

## 5.4   Documentation

It is essential in the maintenance phase to record all the changes made and the reason for each change. For corrective maintenance, this documentation can start as a *fault report,* which is filed by a user. These fault reports are compiled into a bug-tracking database.

The fault report must include enough information to enable the maintenance programmer to re-create the problem. If what the user reports appears to be a new fault, then the maintenance programmer should quickly study the problem and attempt to find its cause and a way to fix it. In addition, an attempt should be made to find a work-around for the problem. With the release planning process described at the start of this section, it may take six months or more before resources can be dedicated to make the necessary changes to the software if the user's problem is non-critical. The maintenance programmer's conclusions should then be added to the fault report. Any supporting documentation, such as listings, designs, and references to the manuals used to arrive at those conclusions, should also be added to the fault report.

Eventually, the fault report must be updated to reflect a detailed description of what was changed, why it was changed, by whom, and when. This information should also be added to the prologue comments of any changed module. Ideally, design or specification documents are also changed.

These fault reports in the bug-tracking database are also effective for supporting communication across groups (software engineers, managers, customer support, and so on). Bug-tracking databases are likely to be kept current, resulting in more complete and accurate textual representation of the state of system changes.

## 5.5   Configuration Management

Configuration management is critical for maintenance/enhancement releases [18]. It might be necessary to reproduce an older version of a system if a new one has serious problems, or we might want to re-create a specific configuration that a customer with a problem is using.

## 5.6   Maintenance Testing

There are two aspects to testing fixes and maintenance changes to a product. The first is to check that the required changes have been implemented correctly—essentially the same as is done with new development. Appropriate white- and black-box test cases should be written to verify the change. When a user identifies a fault, many advocate that the developer first write test case(s) that reveal the fault and variations of the fault. After the fix is made, the test case(s) can be used to demonstrate the properly implemented program. This new test case (including its expected results) is added to the test repository. One added benefit from the test-before-fix practice is that the developer learns about the types of testing he or she should have done to reveal the fault before delivery to a user.

The second aspect of maintenance testing is regression testing. *Regression testing* is *selective retesting of a system or component to verify that modifications have not caused unintended effects and that the system or component still complies with its specified requirements* [17]. Once the programmer has determined that the desired changes have been properly implemented (as discussed in the prior paragraph), the product must be tested again using a repository of existing test cases. To assist in regression testing, it is necessary that all previous test cases and the results of running those test cases be retained. The regression test cases are a central form of documentation for the maintenance phase. As possible and affordable, regression test cases should be automated for ease of re-running them often.

# 6   Why Maintenance Is So Expensive (and Can Be Destructive)

The three major cost drivers of software maintenance are (1) documentation; (2) communication and coordination; and (3) testing [18].  Sommerville [33] lists four key factors that distinguish new development from maintenance and which lead to such high maintenance costs:

1. **Team stability**. In many organizations, software engineers can be considered to be either "new project developers" or "maintenance engineers." Therefore, after a system has been delivered, it is normal for the development team to be reassigned to new projects. The maintenance team that inherits the product does not understand the system or the

background of system design decisions. Especially in the beginning, much effort is spent learning the system before the maintenance engineers are able to implement changes to it.

2. **Contractual responsibility**. The contract to maintain a system is often separate from the system development contract. This factor, along with the lack of team stability just discussed, means that there is no incentive for a development team to write the software so that it is maintainable. With this "throw it over the wall" philosophy (where the developers throw the product over the wall to the maintainers and then disappear), a development team can be highly motivated to cut corners to save effort during development.

3. **Staff skills**. The maintenance staff is often relatively inexperienced and unfamiliar with the application domain when compared with new project developers. Unfortunately, maintenance has a poor image among software engineers even though effective maintainers need to be highly skilled detectives, debuggers, and coders. Maintenance is often allocated to the most junior staff. Furthermore, old systems may be written in obsolete programming languages. The maintenance staff may not have much, if any, experience with these languages.

4. **Program age and structure**. As programs age, their structure tends to be degraded by change, and so they become harder to understand and change. Furthermore, many legacy systems have been developed without modern software engineering techniques. They were never well structured and were often optimized for efficiency rather than understandability, as was the focus years ago when memory and speed were more important issues. The documentation for old systems is often lost or inconsistent with the reality of the code. Old systems may not have been subject to configuration management, so time is often wasted finding the right versions of system components to change.

## 7 Strategies for Managing Maintenance Expense

Often software engineers approach development as if it is the only or final release of the software. Instead, we need to realize that we are developing the first release of many follow-up releases. There are several strategies that can be used to proactively manage maintenance expense.

Good programming style that can be guided by an accepted coding standard can reduce the impact of change and thereby reduce maintenance costs. [24]

Code reuse can save about 18 percent of maintenance costs. [30] A reusable component need not necessarily be code. It could also be design, a part of a document, or test cases/ test data. There are two different types of reuse: accidental reuse and deliberate reuse: [30]

- o *Accidental reuse* occurs if *the developers of a new product "accidentally" realize that a previously developed product can be reused in the new product.*
- o *Deliberate reuse* occurs *when a software component is constructed specifically for possible reuse.*

One advantage of deliberate reuse is that components specially constructed for use in future products are more likely to be easy and safe to reuse. Such components are generally robust, well documented, and thoroughly tested. In addition, they usually display a uniformity of style that makes maintenance easier. [30] However, deliberate reuse can be very expensive. It takes additional time to specify, design, implement, test, and document a software component to be reused, and there is no guarantee that such a component will ever actually be reused.

Developers can focus on maintainability throughout code development and maintenance. *Maintainability* is *the ease with which a software system or component can be modified to correct faults, improve performance or other attributes, or adapt to changed environment.* [17] Maintainability is not only a coding consideration. Products are more maintainable if they are accompanied by up-to-date and consistent specification and design documents, and test plan documents. Maintainability is dependent not only on the product but also on the person performing the maintenance, the supporting documentation and tools, and the proposed usage of the software. [12]

Pair programming can be used to aid in problem determination. One maintenance team that used pair programming [27, 28] saw a measurable peak in productivity over and above the previous several months when pair programming was not used. They also felt that the increased use of pair programming improved their lack of cross-training among the code base's many modules. Another psychology-based study indicated that the pair was better able to solve perfective maintenance problems and to devise solutions. [13]

Software developers can facilitate problem determination by providing clues to where failures occurred. This can be accomplished via a structured use of exceptions with informative messages, usually recorded on a log file

## 8  Maintenance and Maintainability Metrics

Software metrics can be used to signal when maintenance costs are becoming excessive, when it is time for some preventative maintenance, and when maintainability levels are dropping. Some possible metrics are discussed in this section.

**Mean-time-to-repair (MTTR).** This metric can also be referred to as mean-time-to change (MTTC) or downtime. *Mean-time-to-repair* is the *expected or observed time required to repair a system or component and return it to normal operation.* [17]  This is the time it takes to analyze the change request, design an appropriate modification, implement the change, test it, and distribute the change to all users. On average, programs that are maintainable have a lower MTTR than programs that are not maintainable. [29] If a team sees their MTTR rising, it can be a signal for some preventative maintenance.

**Number of requests for corrective maintenance.** If the number of failure reports is increasing, this may indicate that more errors are being introduced into the program than are being repaired during the maintenance process or may indicate a decline in maintainability.[33] An increase in maintenance requests may also be an indication that more users are adopting the system and using it in different ways.

**Average time required for impact analysis.** *Impact analysis* is the *identification of all systems and system products affected by a change request and the development of an estimate of the resources needed to accomplish the change* [3].  If the time to assess the impact of a change increases, it implies that more and more components are affected by the changes. Potentially, this is a signal that maintainability is decreasing.[33]

**Number of outstanding change requests.** If this number increases with time, it may imply a decline in maintainability, [33] resulting in the maintenance engineers having greater difficulty implementing changes.

**Complexity.** The more complex a system or component, the more expensive it is to maintain. Established complexity metrics, such as the CK metrics suite [10] or the MOOD metric suite [7] for object-oriented code, can be used to identify overly complex components that are candidates for preventative maintenance.

## 9   The Four Truths

Ten corporate groups were interviewed about their work practices. [32] Four "truths" about software maintenance stood out across most organizations:

1. **Source code is king.** The source code is the primary source of information about the system. (This finding is also supported by [34].) Secondary to source code, maintainers find another person, preferably the author of that part of the code, for help. This "truth" supports the agile principles that code is the main source of documentation and that interpersonal communication is the most efficient and effective method of conveying information.

2. **Documentation is untrustworthy.** The biggest problem with having up-to-date, consistent documentation was ongoing maintenance. During maintenance activities, documentation sometimes gets updated, but sometimes it does not. It can also be hard to find the document you want/need and can be a navigation nightmare at least as great as searching the source code. In-line commentary was believed to be much more accurate than documents generated as attachments to the source.

3. **The bug-tracking database stores knowledge.** The bug-tracking database is seen as an important repository for historical information about the system and is seen as very useful for finding similar problems and/or fixes. The database is also effective for supporting communication across groups (software engineers, managers, customer support, and so on). Bug-tracking databases are likely to be kept current, resulting in more complete and accurate textual representation of the system.

4. **Reproduction is essential to obtaining a solution.** Software engineers felt that if a problem could be reproduced, it could be solved. This was because reproducing the problem scenario leads to a) a better understanding of the problem, b) a better understanding of what the code is supposed to be doing, and c) the place in the code where the problem is located. Reproducing the problem often necessitates getting the same setup in the office that was used when the problem appeared (hardware and software). Reproducing is also important to ensure that the problem was a real problem and not a perceived one or caused by external sources such as software interactions.

## 10 Summary

Several practical tips for software maintenance were presented throughout this chapter. The keys for successful maintenance are summarized in Table 3.

**Table 2: Key Ideas for Software Maintenance**

| | |
|---|---|
| 🔑 | Use detective-like skills to identify the cause of a customer-reported problem, understanding that the cause could lie in a user manual, could be user error or could be due to a change in the hardware or operating system. |
| 🔑 | Use a mini-development iterative enhancement cycle (analysis, design, code, test) when making and verifying any code changes. Maintenance is an error-prone process which can cause the injection of new faults – new faults which might cause more problems than the original problem – if the maintenance engineer is not careful and thorough. |
| 🔑 | Avoid the quick-fix process for software maintenance to avoid the introduction of increased program complexity and unforeseen ripple effects. If you cannot avoid it, reanalyze the fix via a more systematic process once the crisis is over. |
| 🔑 | In organizations that have change control boards, complete a software change request form and submit to this board for approval of proposed adaptive, perfective, and preventative maintenance. |
| 🔑 | Complete a fault report for all needed corrective maintenance to describe a reported problem. Update this form with a detailed description of what was changed and why. |
| 🔑 | First, create white- and black-box test cases to reveal customer-reported faults. Make code changes to correct the problem. Finally, run the test cases to ensure the changes correct the problem. |
| 🔑 | Perform a thorough set of regression tests with a set of existing test cases to check that any changes do not break existing, working functionality. |
| 🔑 | Prevent excessive maintenance costs by using good programming style, reusing code when possible, focusing on maintainability in all development activities including writing clear and detailed exceptions messages, and using pair programming for problem determination. |
| 🔑 | Use maintainability metrics to signal when maintenance costs are becoming excessive and when it is time for some preventative maintenance. |

In this chapter, we learned about four different types of maintenance: corrective, adaptive, perfective, and preventative which can consume the majority of the time and effort of a software organization. Corrective maintenance is performed to correct faults in the software. Adaptive and preventative maintenance improve the software without increasing its functionality. Adaptive maintenance is performed to react to changes in the environment (such as software platforms and government policies) so that the original functionality still works. Preventative maintenance prevents aging and improves maintainability considering the high degree of change in the software over time. Perfective maintenance is done to extend the software beyond its original functional or non-functional requirements.

**Glossary of Chapter Terms**

| Word | Definition | Source |
|---|---|---|
| adaptive maintenance | software maintenance performed to make a computer program usable in a changed environment | [17] |
| accidental reuse | the developers of a new product "accidentally" realize that a previously developed product can be reused in the new product | [30] |
| change control board (also called configuration control board) | group of people responsible for evaluating and approving or disapproving proposed changes to configuration items, and for ensuring implementation of approved changes | [17] |
| corrective maintenance | maintenance performed to correct faults in hardware or software | [17] |
| deliberate reuse | when a software component is constructed specifically for possible reuse | [30] |
| emergency maintenance | unscheduled corrective maintenance performed to keep a system operational | [18] |
| failure | the inability of a system or component to perform its required function within specified performance requirements | [17] |
| impact analysis | identification of all systems and system products affected by a change request and the development of an estimate of the resources needed to accomplish the change | [3] |
| maintainability | the ease with which a software system or component can be modified to correct faults, improve performance or other attributes, or adapt to changed environment | [17] |
| mean-time-to-repair (or downtime) | expected or observed time required to repair a system or component and return it to normal operation | [17] |
| mistake | human action that produces an incorrect result | [17] |
| perfective maintenance | software maintenance performed to improve the performance, maintainability, or other attributes of a computer program | [17] |
| preventative maintenance | maintenance preformed for the purpose of preventing problems before they occur | [17] |
| refactoring | the process of changing a software system in such a way that it does not alter the external behavior of the code yet it improves its internal structure | [14] |
| regression fault | faults injected when fixing other problems | |

| regression testing | selective retesting of a system or component to verify that modifications have not caused unintended effects and that the system or component still complies with its specified requirements | [17] |
|---|---|---|
| software maintenance | the process of modifying a software system or component after delivery to correct faults, improve performance or other attributes, or adapt to a changed environment | [17] |

**References:**

[1]     A. Abran and H. Nguyenkim, "Measurement of the Maintenance Process from a Demand-Based Perspective," *Journal of Software Maintenance:  Research and Practice*, vol. 5, no. 2, pp. 63-90, 1993.

[2]     R. S. Arnold, "Software Restructuring," *Proceedings of the IEEE*, vol. 77, no. 4, pp. 607-617, 1989.

[3]     L. J. Arthur, *Software Evolution:  The Software Maintenance Challenge*: John Wiley & Sons, 1988.

[4]     V. Basili, "Viewing Software Maintenance as Reuse-Oriented Software Development," *IEEE Software*, vol. 7, no. 1, pp. 19-25, January 1990.

[5]     W. J. Baumol, "Macro-Economics of Unbalanced Growth – The Anatomy of Urban Cities," in *American Economics Review*, vol. 62, 1967, pp. 415-426.

[6]     K. Bennett, "Software evolution: past, present and future," *Information and Software Technology*, vol. 38, no. 11, pp. 673-680, November 1996.

[7]     F. Brito e Abreu, "The MOOD Metrics Set," ECOOP '95 Workshop on Metrics, 1995, pp.

[8]     F. P. Brooks, "No Silver Bullet," *IEEE Computer*, vol. 20, no. 4, pp. 10-19, 1987.

[9]     F. P. Brooks, *The Mythical Man-Month, Anniversary Edition*: Addison-Wesley Publishing Company, 1995.

[10]    S. R. Chidamber and C. F. Kemerer, "A Metrics Suite for Object Oriented Design," *IEEE Transactions on Software Engineering*, vol. 20, no. 6, 1994.

[11]    D. Coleman, D. Ash, B. Lowther, and P. Oman, "Using Metrics to Evaluate Software System Maintainability," *IEEE Computer*, vol. 27, no. 8, pp. 44-49, August 1994.

[12]    N. E. Fenton and S. L. Pfleeger, *Software Metrics: A Rigorous and Practical Approach*: Brooks/Cole, 1998.

[13]    N. V. Flor and E. L. Hutchins, "Analyzing Distributed Cognition in Software Teams:  A Case Study of Team Programming During Perfective Software Maintenance," Empirical Studies of Programmers:  Fourth Workshop, 1991, pp. 36-63.

[14]    M. Fowler, K. Beck, J. Brant, W. Opdyke, and D. Roberts, *Refactoring:  Improving the Design of Existing Code*. Reading, Massachusetts: Addison Wesley, 1999.

[15]    D. Hamlet and J. Maybee, *The Engineering of Software*. Boston: Addison Wesley, 2001.

[16]    W. S. Humphrey, *A Discipline for Software Engineering*. Reading, Mass.: Addison

Wesley Longman, 1995.

[17]   IEEE, "IEEE Standard 610.12-1990, IEEE Standard Glossary of Software Engineering Terminology," 1990.

[18]   IEEE, "IEEE Standard for Software Maintenance 1219-1998," no., 1998.

[19]   Y. Kataoka, T. Imai, H. Andou, and T. Fukaya, "A Quantitative Evaluation of Maintainability Enhancement by Refactoring," International Conference on Software Maintenance (ICSM 2002), Montreal, Quebec, Canada, 2002, pp. 576-585.

[20]   F. Lanubile and F. Visaggio, "Iterative Reengineering to Compensate for Quck-Fix Maintenance," International Conference of Software Maintenance, Opio (Nice), France, 1994, pp. 140-146.

[21]   M. M. Lehman and L. Belady, "Program Evolution: Processes of Software Change." London: Academic Press, 1985.

[22]   M. M. Lehman and J. F. Ramil, "Rules and Tools for Software Evolution Planning and Management," *Annals of Software Engineering*, vol. 11, no. 1, pp. 15-44, 2001.

[23]   M. M. Lehman, J. F. Ramil, P. D. Wernick, D. E. Perry, and W. M. Turski, "Metrics and Laws of Software Evolution -- The Nineties View," 4th International Software Metrics Symposium (METRICS '97), Albuquerque, NM, 1997, pp. 20-32.

[24]   K. J. Lieberherr and I. M. Holland, "Tools for preventative software maintenance," International Conference on Software Maintenance (ICSM 1989), 1989, pp. 2-13.

[25]   B. P. Lientz, E. B. Swanson, and G. E. Tompkins, "Characteristics of Application Software Maintenance," *Communications of the ACM*, vol. 21, no. 6, pp. 466-471, June 1978.

[26]   T. M. Pigoski, *Practical Software Maintenance: Best Practices for Managing your Software Investment*: John Wiley & Sons, 1997.

[27]   C. Poole and J. W. Huisman, "Using Extreme Programming in a Maintenance Environment," *IEEE Software*, vol. 18, no. 6, pp. 42-50, 2001.

[28]   C. J. Poole, T. Murphy, J. W. Huisman, and A. Higgins, "Extreme Maintenance," International Conference on Software Maintenance (ICSM 2001), Florence, Italy, 2001, pp. 301-309.

[29]   R. Pressman, *Software Engineering: A Practitioner's Approach*. Boston: McGraw Hill, 2001.

[30]   S. R. Schach, *Object-Oriented and Classical Software Engineering*, Fifth ed. Boston: McGraw-Hill, 2002.

[31]   F. Simon, F. Steinbrückner, and C. Lewerentz, "Metrics Based Refactoring," Fifth Conference on Software Maintenance and Reengineering (CSMR 2001), Lisbon, Portugal, 2001, pp. 30-38.

[32]   J. Singer, "Practices of Software Maintenance," International Conference on Software Maintenance, Bethesda, Maryland, 1998, pp. 139-145.

[33]   I. Sommerville, *Software Engineering*, Sixth ed. Harlow, England: Addison-Wesley, 2001.

[34]   M. J. Sousa and H. M. Moreira, "A Survey on the Software Maintenance Process," International Conference on Software Maintenance, Bethesda, Maryland, 1998, pp. 265-274.

[35]  A. A. Takang and P. A. Grubb, *Software Maintenance:  Concepts and Practice.* London: International Thomson Computer Press, 1996.

## Chapter Questions

1. Lehman's Laws of Software Evolution describe what Lehman feels are inevitable phenomenon in software maintenance. Which of these laws (if any) apply to corrective maintenance? adaptive maintenance? perfective maintenance? preventative maintenance. Name and provide the description of the law.

2. What type of maintenance incorporates refactoring? Why can it be hard to justify time for refactoring?

3. What is the most common type of maintenance? Why is this so?

4. What is the most common software maintenance process? Why is its use so popular? What are the potential problems with this process?

5. Why is software maintenance so expensive?

6. Sometimes organizations need to maintain two different versions of a code base of the same project at the same time. This situation is called "dual maintenance." You can imagine that dual maintenance requires more resource, cost, and effort. List some conditions when dual maintenance might be necessary.

7. Give three examples of software maintainability metrics.

8. List the four key factors that distinguish new development from maintenance.

9. The reuse-based maintenance process model considers maintenance as an activity involving the reuse of existing program components. What are the four main steps of the reuse-based model?

10. Documentation is an important part of software maintenance. However, in agile methods, there are no explicit requirements for documentation. If a project is developed with an agile method, it is likely that the development team does not have detailed document for requirements, analysis, and design. Does it mean that software maintenance will be difficult with agile methods?

# Risk Management

The proactive management of risks throughout the software development lifecycle is important for project success. In this chapter, we will explain the following:

the risk management practice, which involves risk identification, analysis, prioritization, planning, mitigation, monitoring, and communication

software development risks that seem to reoccur in educational and industrial projects

a risk-driven process for selecting a software development model

> *Risk in itself is not bad; risk is essential to progress, and failure is often a key part of learning. But we must learn to balance the possible negative consequences of risk against the potential benefits of its associated opportunity.* (Van Scoy 1992)

A *risk* is a *potential future harm that may arise from some present action* (Wikipedia 2004), such as, a schedule slip or a cost overrun. The loss is often considered in terms of direct financial loss, but also can be a loss in terms of credibility, future business, and loss of property or life.

This chapter is about doing proactive planning for your software projects via risk management. *Risk management* is a *series of steps whose objectives are to identify, address, and eliminate software risk items before they become either threats to successful software operation or a major source of expensive rework.* (Boehm 1989) The software industry is fraught with failed and delayed projects, most of which far exceed their original budget. The Standish Group reported that only 28 percent of software projects are completed on time and on budget. Over 23 percent of software projects are cancelled before they ever get completed, and 49 percent of projects cost 145 percent of their original estimates. (Standish 1995) In hindsight, many of these companies indicated that their problems could have been avoided or strongly reduced if there had been an explicit early warning of the high-risk elements of the project. Many projects fail either because simple problems were reported too late or because the wrong problem was addressed. (Bruegge and Dutoit 2000)

Problems happen. Teams can choose to be reactive or proactive about these problems. *Reactive* teams fly into action to correct the problem rapidly in a crisis-driven, fire-fighting mode. Without proper planning, problems often occur late in the schedule. At this point, resolving any serious problems can require extensive modification, leading to big delays. *Proactive* teams begin thinking about risks even before technical work is initiated. Their objective is to be able to avoid risk whenever possible, to solve problems before they manifest themselves and to respond to problems that do happen in a controlled and effective manner. This chapter is about being proactive.

## 1  The Risk Management Practice

The risk management process can be broken down into two interrelated phases, risk assessment and risk control, as outlined in Figure 1. These phases are further broken down. Risk assessment involves risk identification, risk analysis, and risk prioritization. Risk control involves risk planning, risk mitigation, and risk monitoring. (Boehm 1989) Each of these will be discussed in this section. It is essential that risk management be done iteratively, throughout the project, as a part of the team's project management routine.

Figure 1: The Risk Management Cycle.

## 1.1 Risk Identification

In the risk identification step, the team systematically enumerates as many project risks as possible to make them explicit before they become problems. There are several ways to look at the kinds of software project risks, as shown in Table 1. It is helpful to understand the different types of risk so that a team can explore the possibilities of each of them. Each of these types of risk is described below.

Table 1: General Categories of Risk

| Generic Risks | | Product-Specific Risks | |
|---|---|---|---|
| Project Risks | Product Risks | Business Risks | |
| Factors to consider: People, size, process, technology, tools, organizational, managerial, customer, estimation, sales, support | | | |

*Generic risks* are potential threats to *every* software project. Some examples of generic risks are changing requirements, losing key personnel, or bankruptcy of the software company or of the customer. It is advisable for a development organization to keep a checklist of these types of risks. Teams can then assess the extent to which these risks are a factor for their project based upon the known set of programmers, managers, customers, and policies. *Product-specific risks* can be distinguished from generic risks because they can only be identified by those with a clear understanding of the technology, the people, and the environment of the specific product. An example of a product-specific risk is the availability of a complex network necessary for testing.

Generic and product-specific risks can be further divided into project, product, and business risks. *Project risks* are those that affect the project schedule or the resources (personnel or budgets) dedicated to the project. *Product risks* are those that affect the quality or performance of the software being developed. Finally, *business risks* are those that threaten the viability of the software, such as building an excellent product no one wants or building a product that no longer fits into the overall business strategy of the company.

There are some specific factors to consider when examining project, product, and business risks. Some examples of these factors are listed here, although this list is meant to stimulate your thinking rather than to be an all-inclusive list.

*People risks* are associated with the availability, skill level, and retention of the people on the

260

development team.

*Size risks* are associated with the magnitude of the product and the product team. Larger products are generally more complex with more interactions. Larger teams are harder to coordinate.

*Process risks* are related to whether the team uses a defined, appropriate software development process and to whether the team members actually follow the process.

*Technology risks* are derived from the software or hardware technologies that are being used as part of the system being developed. Using new or emerging or complex technology increases the overall risk.

*Tools risks*, similar to technology risks, relate to the use, availability, and reliability of support software used by the development team, such as development environments and other Computer-Aided Software Engineering (CASE) tools.

*Organizational and managerial risks* are derived from the environment where the software is being developed. Some examples are the financial stability of the company and threats of company reorganization and the potential of the resultant loss of support by management due to a change in focus or a change in people.

*Customer risks* are derived from changes to the customer requirements, customers' lack of understanding of the impact of these changes, the process of managing these requirements changes, and the ability of the customer to communicate effectively with the team and to accurately convey the attributes of the desired product.

*Estimation risks* are derived from inaccuracies in estimating the resources and the time required to build the product properly.

*Sales and support risks* involve the chances that the team builds a product that the sales force does not understand how to sell or that is difficult to correct, adapt, or enhance.

Spontaneous and sporadic risk identification is usually not sufficient. There are various risk elicitation techniques the team can use to systematically and proactively surface risks:

*Meeting*. The team, including the development team and the marketing and customer representatives if possible, gathers together. The group brainstorms; each participant spontaneously contributes as many risks as they can possibly think of.

*Checklists/Taxonomy*. The risk elicitors are aided in their risk identification by the use of checklists and/or taxonomies (in other words, a defined, orderly classification of potential risks) that focuses on some subset of known and predictable risks. Checklists and taxonomies based upon past projects are especially beneficial. These artifacts should be used to interview project participants, such as the client, the developers, and the manager.

*Comparison with past projects*. The risk elicitors examine the risk management artifacts of previous projects. They consider whether these same risks are present in the new project.

*Decomposition*. Large, unwieldy, unmanageable risks that are identified are further broken down into small risks that are more likely to be managed. Additionally, by decomposing the development process into small pieces, you may be able to identify other potential problems.

Project participants can be reluctant to communicate potential failures or shortcomings and can be too optimistic about the future. It is essential that all participants are encouraged to report

261

risks so they can be monitored and managed. Participants should be rewarded for identifying risks and problems as early as possible.

It is recommended that risks should be stated using the condition-transition-consequence (CTC) format (Gluch 1994):

***Given that \<condition\> then there is a concern that (possibly) \<transition\> \<consequence\>.***

> Condition is a description of the current conditions prompting concern.
> Transition is the part that involves change (time).
> Consequence is a description of the potential outcome.

For example, *given that no one in our team has ever developed a product in Prolog, then there is a concern that (possibly) the project will take two months longer than has been estimated.*

## 1.2 Analyze

After risks have been identified and enumerated, the next step is risk analysis. Through *risk analysis,* we transform the risks that were identified into decision-making information. In turn, each risk is considered and a judgment made about the probability and the seriousness of the risk. For each risk, the team must do the following:

> Assess the *probability* of a loss occurring. Some risks are very likely to occur. Others are very unlikely. Establish and utilize a scale that reflects the perceived likelihood of a risk. Depending upon the degree of detail desired and/or possible, the scale can be numeric, based on a percentage scale, such as "10 percent likely to lose a key team member" or based on categories, such as: very improbable, improbable, probable, or frequent. In the case that a categorical assignment is used, the team should establish a set numerical probability for each qualitative value (e.g. very improbable= 10 percent, improbable = 25 percent).
> Assess the *impact* of the loss if the loss were to occur. Delineate the consequences of the risk, and estimate the impact of the risk on the project and the product. Similar to the probability discussion above, the team can choose to assign numerical monetary values to the magnitude of loss, such as $10,000 for a two-week delay in schedule. Alternately, categories may be used and assigned values, such as 1=negligible, 2=marginal, 3=critical, or 4=catastrophic.

Determining the probability and the magnitude of the risk can be difficult and can seem to be arbitrarily chosen. One means of determining the risk probability is for each team member to estimate each of these values individually. Then, the input of individual team members is collected in a round robin fashion and reported to the group. Sometimes the collection and reporting is done anonymously. Team members debate the logic behind the submitted estimates. The individuals then re-estimate and iterate on the estimate until assessment of risk probability and impact begins to converge. This means of converging on the probability and estimate is called the Delphi Technique (Gupta and Clarke 1996). The Delphi Technique is a group consensus method that is often used when the factors under consideration are subjective.

The analyzed risks are organized into a risk table. The template for a risk table is shown in Table 2. In Sections 2 and 3, we show you some completed sample risk tables. The information that is to be provided in each of the columns is now explained.

*Rank* will be discussed in section 1.3.

*Risk* is the description of the risk itself, preferably stated in CTC format.

*Probability* is the likelihood of the risk occurring, using either a numeric or categorical scale, as discussed in the last section.

*Impact* is the magnitude of the loss if the risk were to occur, using either a numeric or a categorical scale.

*Rank last week* and the number of *weeks on list* are documented so the team can monitor changes in priority, to determine if actions are being taken that cause changes in the stature of the risk.

*Action* documents what the team is doing to manage the risk, as will be discussed in sections 1.4-1.5. The action field is often not completed until the risks have been prioritized, as will be discussed in the next section.

Table 2: Risk Table Template

| Rank | Risk | Probability | Impact | Rank Last Week/ Weeks on list | Action |
|------|------|-------------|--------|-------------------------------|--------|
|      |      |             |        |                               |        |
|      |      |             |        |                               |        |

## 1.3  Prioritize

After the risks have been organized into a risk table, such as Table 4.2, the team prioritizes the risks by ranking them. It is too costly and perhaps even unnecessary to take action on *every* identified risk. Some of them have a very low impact or a very low probability of occurring – or both. Through the prioritization process, the team determines which risks it will take action on.

The team sorts the list so that the high probability, high impact risks percolate to the top of the table and the low-probability, low impact risks drop to the bottom. If the team used categorical values for probability (e.g. very improbable, improbable, probable, or frequent) and/or impact (e.g. negligible, marginal, critical, or catastrophic), group consensus techniques may need to be used to produce the risk ranking. We will show you an example of this type of ranking in Section 2.

If numerical values were given for probability (percentage) and impact (monetary), the risk exposure can be calculated. Risk exposure is calculated as follows (Boehm 1989):

$$Risk\ Exposure\ (RE) = P \boxed{\times} C$$

where $P$ = probability of occurrence for a risk and $C$ is the impact of the loss to the product should the risk occur. For example, if the probability of a risk is 10 percent and the impact of the risk is \$10,000, the risk exposure = (0.1)(\$10,000) = \$1,000. If RE is calculated for each risk, the prioritization is based upon a numerical ranking of the risk exposures. We will show you an example of this type of ranking in Section 3.

After the risks are prioritized, the team, led by the project manager, defines a cut off line so that only the risks above the line are given further attention. The activities of this "further attention" are to plan, mitigate, monitor, and communicate – as is discussed in the following sections. The lower ranked risks stay on the table for the time being with no action other than monitoring.

## 1.4   Plan

Risk management plans should be developed for each of the "above the line" prioritized risks so that proactive action can take place. These actions are documented in the Action column of the Risk Table (Table 2). Following are some examples of the kinds of risk planning actions that can take place:

*Information buying*. Perceived risk can be reduced by obtaining more information through investigation. For example, in a project in which the use of a new technology has created risk, the team can invest some money to learn about the technology. Throw-away prototypes can be developed using the new technology to educate some of the staff on the new technology and to assess the fit of the new technology for the product.

*Contingency plans*. A contingency plan is a plan that describes what to do if certain risks materialize. By planning ahead with such a plan, you are prepared and have a strategy in place do deal with the issue.

*Risk reduction*. For example, if the team is concerned that the use of a new programming language may cause a schedule delay, the budget might contain a line item entitled "potential schedule" to cover a potential schedule slip. Because the budget already covers the potential slip, the financial risk to the organization is reduced. Alternately, the team can plan to employ inspections to reduce the risk of quality problems.

*Risk acceptance*. Sometimes the organization consciously chooses to live with the consequences of the risk (Hall 1998) and the results of the potential loss. In this case, no action is planned.

## 1.5   Mitigate

Related to risk planning, through risk mitigation, the team develops strategies to reduce the possibility or the loss impact of a risk. Risk mitigation produces a situation in which the risk items are eliminated or otherwise resolved. These actions are documented in the Action column of the Risk Table (Table 2). Some examples of risk mitigation strategies follow:

*Risk avoidance*. When a lose-lose strategy is likely (Hall 1998),[16] the team can opt to eliminate the risk An example of a risk avoidance strategy is the team opting not to develop a product or a particularly risky feature.

*Risk protection*. The organization can buy insurance to cover any financial loss should the risk become a reality. Alternately, a team can employ fault-tolerance strategies, such as parallel processors, to provide reliability insurance.

Risk planning and risk mitigation actions often come with an associated cost. The team must do a cost/benefit analysis to decide whether the benefits accrued by the risk management steps outweigh the costs associated with implementing them. This calculation can involve the calculation of risk leverage (Pfleeger 1998).

*Risk Leverage =*
*(risk exposure before reduction – risk exposure after reduction)/cost of risk reduction*

If risk leverage value, *rl*, is ▣ 1, clearly the benefit of applying risk reduction is not worth its cost. If *rl* is only slightly > 1, still the benefit is very questionable, because these computations are based on probabilistic estimates and not on actual data. Therefore, *rl* is usually multiplied by a *risk discount factor* $\rho$ < 1. If $\rho$ *rl* > 1, then the benefit of applying risk reduction is considered worth its cost. If the discounted leveraged valued is not high enough to justify the action, the team should look for other, less costly or more effective, reduction techniques.

## 1.6   Monitor

After risks are identified, analyzed, and prioritized, and actions are established, it is essential that the team regularly monitor the progress of the product and the resolution of the risk items, taking corrective action when necessary. This monitoring can be done as part of the team project management activities or via explicit risk management activities. Often teams regularly monitor their "Top 10 risks."

Risks need to be revisited at regular intervals for the team to reevaluate each risk to determine when new circumstances caused its probability and/or impact to change. At each interval, some risks may be added to the list and others taken away. Risks need to be reprioritized to see which are moved "above the line" and need to have action plans and which move "below the line" and no longer need action plans. A key to successful risk management is that proactive actions are owned by individuals and are monitored. (Larman 2004)

As time passes and more is learned about the project, the information gained over time may alter the risk profile considerably. Additionally, time may make it possible to refine the risk into a set of more detailed risks. These refined risks may be easier to mitigate, monitor, and manage.

## 1.7   Communicate

On-going and effective communication between management, the development team, marketing, and customer representatives about project risks is essential for effective risk management. This communication enables the sharing of all information and is the cornerstone of effective risk management.

## 2   Risk Management in Educational Projects

Sometimes the need for risk management can seem far off for students. After all, you don't do anything close to buying insurance to reduce the risk for your class projects! However, consider that your success (your grade) in the class is at risk. In beginning computer science classes, your assignments were probably small, the requirements of these assignments crisp and defined, and you worked alone. Your chances of being successful were well within your own control. As you advance in your academic career, course projects will likely become quite a bit longer, you will be working with at least one other person, and the requirements will be more ambiguous and even changeable. All of a sudden, things aren't nearly as under control. What can you do to improve your odds of getting a good grade? Employing risk management can help.

Table 3 shows the ranked "Top 10" risk items based upon the frequency with which they were identified during the six weeks of risk management by 24 student teams in an undergraduate software engineering class. The students worked in teams of four or five students on a project that lasted seven weeks. All project teams completed the same project. A graduate student performed the role of customer for the students. You should consider whether your own projects could encounter these same risks.

Table 3: Student Top 10 Risk Items

| Risk Item | Risk Management Technique |
|---|---|
| Overriding other people's work, not having the latest versions of code | Use a configuration management tool effectively. |
| Lack of exposure to and/or experience with technologies | Take time to learn tools and technologies, seek help from teaching staff. |
| Being overwhelmed by work in other classes | Have a project management plan with deadlines and ownership, update the project management plan frequently. |
| Common meeting times | In the beginning of the project, determine all possible common times to meet based on class schedules and other commitments. |
| Requirements understanding | Meet with, e-mail, or phone customer. |
| Lack of communication | Set up a group Web page, group e-mail accounts, trade instant messaging IDs, meet regularly. |
| Project organization | Assign each team member a role, break down work in project management plan. |
| Loss of a team member | Assure files are uploaded and integrated consistently, use knowledge management strategies such as pair programming to understand each other's work. |
| Difficulty integrating work | Increase communication, integrate often. |

| Planning taking up too much time, not enough time to work on | Don't get more detailed than necessary with the planning. |
|---|---|
| product | |

A sample student team risk management table from the class described above is shown below in Table 4; the team is in the fifth week of the project. Both the probability and the impact use categorical values, which is typical of a student project. Because of this, the student teams must use a group consensus technique to rank their risks. The method of using categories for risk analysis and group consensus for risk prioritization is also used in industry.

Table 4: Sample Student Risk Table

| Rank | Risk | Probability | Impact | Rank Last Week/ Weeks on list | Action |
|---|---|---|---|---|---|
| 1 | None of us knows how to use the technology. | frequent | critical | 1/5 | Read. Do tutorials. |
| 2 | Integration problems. | frequent | critical | 2/5 | Integrate all work Sunday nights. |
| 3 | Someone drops the class. | improb | critical | 4/5 | Pair programming for all work. |
| 4 | Team members missing important team meetings. | improb. | marginal | 5/4 | Person who misses meeting has to supply Sunday night pizza the next week. |

| 5 | Overriding each other's work | improb | marginal | 3/5 | Continue using CVS. |
|---|---|---|---|---|---|

## 3   Risk Management in Industrial Projects

Industrial projects have many different types of risks than you would experience as a student. Some of the risks, such as changing requirements and losing team members are similar. Boehm developed a top 10 risk item for industrial projects by surveying several experienced managers. This list is shown below in Table 5.

Table 5: Industry Top 10 Software Risk Items, adapted from (Boehm 1989; Boehm January 1991)

| Risk Item | Risk Management Technique |
|---|---|
| Personnel shortfall | Staffing with top talent, job matching, team building, key personnel agreements, cross training |
| Unrealistic schedules and budgets | Detailed milestone cost and schedule estimation, design to cost, incremental development, software reuse, requirements scrubbing |
| Developing the wrong functions and properties | Organizational analysis, mission analysis, operations-concept formulation, user surveys and user participation, prototyping, early users' manuals |
| Developing the wrong user interface | Prototyping, scenarios, task analysis, user participation |
| Gold-plating (e.g. implementing "neat features" not asked for by customer) | Requirements scrubbing, prototyping, cost-benefit analysis, designing to cost |

| Continuing stream of requirements changes | High change threshold information hiding, incremental development (deferring changes to later increments) |
|---|---|
| Shortfalls in externally-furnished components (e.g. component reuse) | Benchmarking, inspections, reference checking, compatibility analysis |
| Shortfalls in externally performed tasks (e.g. worked performed by a contractor) | Reference checking, pre-award audits, award-fee contracts, competitive design or prototyping, team building |
| Real-time performance shortfalls | Simulation, benchmarking, modeling, prototyping, instrumentation, tuning |
| Straining computer science capabilities | Technical analysis, cost-benefit analysis, prototyping, reference checking |

Table 6 shows a sample risk table for an industrial team. The kinds of risk that rise to the top are different than in the student risk table. Additionally, while the student example used categories for probability and impact, the industrial team uses their best estimate of numerical probability and impact. As discussed earlier, using these numerical values, the risk exposure can be calculated (risk exposure = probability * impact). Risk exposure can then be used for ranking the risks.

Table 6 Sample Industrial Risk Table

| Rank | Risk | Prob. | Impact | Risk Exp. | Rank Last Week/ Weeks on list | Action |
|---|---|---|---|---|---|---|
| 1 | Delay by Raleigh team to deliver toolkit | 50% | $10,000 | $5,000 | 3/10 | Weekly status meeting, Possibility of interim releases. |
| 2 | Requirements changes | 40% | $7,000 | $2,800 | 1/12 | Bi-weekly deliverables. |

| 3 | Aggressive performance requirements | 30% | $9,000 | $2,700 | 4/5 | Prototyping, performance testing. |
|---|---|---|---|---|---|---|
| 4 | Lose team member | 5% | $50,000 | $2,500 | 8/12 | Pair programming. |
| 5 | Unsure of desired graphical user interface | 5% | $1,000 | $50 | 6/12 | Design with the Model-View-Controller pattern. |

It can be difficult, even for an industrial team, to estimate numerical values for probability and loss. To overcome this, you can assess these two values on a relative scale of 0 to 10 rather than trying to estimate numerical values.

## 4 Risk Management for Software Development Model Selection

(with credit to Barry Boehm and Richard Turner)

One large and potentially risky decision for a software development team is the selection of the software development methodology and associated practices. We have introduced the plan-driven software development model and the agile software development model. Depending upon the type of project and team, one of these models or a hybrid of the two is best. This section of the chapter is very important for you to understand. As you proceed through the rest of the book, you will be presented with alternatives for many development practices (such as plan-driven requirements, agile requirements, plan-driven design, and agile design). It is important for you to understand that you need to choose the alternative that is appropriate for the project you are working on.

In this section, we explain a risk-driven approach to making the selection between an agile, a plan-driven, or a hybrid software development model. The five-step method was developed by Barry Boehm and Richard Turner (Boehm and Turner 2003; Boehm and Turner June 2003). Boehm and Turner developed the method so that software developers can enjoy the benefits of both agile and plan-driven methods, while mitigating many of their drawbacks. The guidance given by their method is important because every development practice has its situation-dependent shortcomings and its home ground (the situations for which each is best suited). Agile methodologies promise increased customer satisfaction, lower defect rates, faster development times, and a solution to rapidly changing requirements. Agile methods are highly iterative in nature – meaning that partial working product is delivered to customers often. Iteration is a prudent risk mitigation strategy because the partial deliverables uncover risks while there is still time to alleviate them. Plan-driven approaches promise predictability, stability, and high assurance. It's all about picking the right model for the job depending upon the most important consideration of the project.

### *4.1 Personal Characteristics of Team*

270

Some background is necessary before describing Boehm and Turner's method. To start, Boehm and Turner believe the personal characteristics of the people who make up the software development team are a key factor in determining whether to use an agile or plan-driven approach. Think about it. A team made up of very experienced team members is very different from a team that consists of all new people to the technology and the domain. The technology is the programming language, hardware platform, and so forth. The domain is the subject area of the program (for example, medical software or networking software). To classify individual skill level, Boehm and Turner adopted and then adapted the classification scheme of Alistair Cockburn (Cockburn 2001), as shown in Table 7. In the table, the term *method* refers to a single (or set of) software development practice (such as eliciting requirements or automating tests).

Table 7: Levels of Software Method Understanding and Use (adapted from (Boehm and Turner June 2003))

| Level | Characteristics | Applicability |
|---|---|---|
| 3 | Able to revise a method, breaking its rules to fit an <u>un</u>precedented new situation. | Can function well on any team. |
| 2 | Able to tailor a method to fit a precedented situation. With training, some can become Level 3. | Can function well in managing a small, precedented agile or plan-driven project but need the guidance of level 3s in unprecedented situations. |
| 1A | With training, able to perform discretionary method steps such as providing resource estimates to decide which requirements should be included each release. With experience, can become Level 2. | Can function well on both agile and plan-driven teams that have enough Level 2 people to guide them. |
| 1B | With training, able to perform procedural method steps such as coding a simple program, following coding standards, or running tests. With experience can master some Level 1A skills. | Function well in performing straightforward development in a stable situation. Would likely slow an agile team, particularly if a large percentage of the team was made up of 1B people. |
| -1 | May have technical skills, but unable or unwilling to collaborate or follow shared methods. | Transfer to other work. |

It is important to consider both technology and domain expertise when considering a person's skill level. A Level 3 expert in an object-oriented language such as Java developing software for the retail industry might temporarily revert back to being a Level 1B if moved to an assignment like developing a compiler in a functional language such as Haskell. This person's prior expertise enables him to fairly rapidly advance through the skill levels, most likely to the old Level 3. However, it is important to consider the person's current (not potential) skill level when considering the make up of the team relative to agile and plan-driven methods.

## 4.2 Agile and Plan-Driven Home Grounds

Boehm and Turner have observed projects succeed that have used purely an agile approach, they have observed projects succeed with purely plan-driven methods, and they have observed projects succeed with hybrid methods. Based on these experiences, they share the project characteristics of agile "home grounds" and plan-driven "home grounds" where home ground is defined as the situation for which each is best suited. These home grounds are summarized in Table 8.

Table 8: Agile and Plan-driven Home Grounds (adapted from (Boehm and Turner June 2003))

| Project Characteristics | Agile Home Ground | Plan-Driven Home Ground |
|---|---|---|
| Application | | |
| **Primary goals** | Rapid value, responding to change. | Predictability, stability, high assurance. |
| **Size** | Smaller teams and projects. | Larger teams and projects. |
| **Environment** | Turbulent, high change, project focused. | Stable, low change, project and organization focused. |
| Management | | |
| **Customer relations** | Dedicated on-site customer, focused on prioritized product releases (increments). | As-needed customer interactions, focused on fulfilling a contract. |
| **Planning and control** | Team has an understanding of plans and monitors to this plan. | Documented plans and explicit monitoring to plans. |
| **Communications** | Passed from person to person (tacit, interpersonal). | Knowledge documented in team artifacts (explicit). |
| Technical | | |
| **Requirements** | Prioritized, informal stories and test cases. Requirements are likely to change in unpredictable ways. | Formalized requirements. Requirements may change in predictable ways. |
| **Development** | Simple design, short increments | Extensive design, longer increments. |
| **Test** | Automated, executable test cases are used to further define the specifics of the requirements. | Documented test plans and procedures. |
| Personnel | | |
| **Customers** | Dedicated, co-located CRACK* performers. | CRACK performers, not always co-located. |
| **Developers** (See Section 4.1) | At least 30% Level 2 and 3 experts; no level 1B or Level -1 personnel. | 50% Level 3s early; 10% throughout; 30% Level 1B's workable; no Level -1s. |
| **Culture** | Team enjoys being empowered and having freedom (thriving on chaos). | Team is empowered via freedom embodied in policies and procedures (thriving on order). |

*CRACK = Collaborative, Representative, Authorized, Committed, and Knowledgeable

## 4.3   Critical Factors and the Polar Chart

The analysis of the home grounds in Table 8 and the general characteristics of agile and plan-driven methods led Boehm and Turner to define five critical factors that can be used to describe a project environment and can be used to help determine the appropriate balance between agile and plan-driven methods. These five factors, intended to guide the choice of the right balance between flexibility and structure, are shown in Table 9.

Table 9: The Five Critical Agility and Plan-Driven Factors
(adapted from (Boehm and Turner June 2003))

| Factor | Agility discriminators | Plan-driven discriminators |
|---|---|---|
| Size (Number of people on team) | Well matched to small products and teams; reliance on person-to-person knowledge transfer and retention limits scalability. | Methods evolved to handle large projects and teams; hard to tailor down to small projects. |
| Criticality (The potential impact of a software defect in terms of comfort, money, and/or lives) | Untested on safety-critical products; potential difficulties with simple design and lack of documentation. | Methods evolved to handle highly critical products; hard to tailor down efficiently to low-criticality products. |
| Dynamism (The degree of requirements and technology change) | Simple design and continuous restructuring is excellent for highly dynamic environments, but present a source of potentially expensive rework for highly stable environments. | Detailed plans and "big design up front" excellent for highly stable environments, but a source of expensive rework for highly dynamic environments. |
| Personnel (Skill level of team) | Require continuous presence of a critical mass of scarce Level 2 or 3 experts; risky to use non-agile Level 1B people. | Need a critical mass of Level 2 and 3 experts during project definition, but can work with fewer later in the project. Can usually accommodate some Level 1B people. |
| Culture (Whether the individuals on the team prefer predictability/order or change) | Thrive in a culture where people feel comfortable and empowered by having many degrees of freedom; thrive on chaos. | Thrive in a culture where people feel comfortable and empowered by having their roles defined by clear policies and procedures; thrive on order. |

Boehm and Turner have created a polar chart as a means for visually displaying a team's values for each of these criticality factors. An example of such a polar chart can be found in Figure 2. Each of the five factors has an axis. Each of the axes is labeled with carefully chosen values

274

based on the authors' history. For each axis, the further from the graph's center, the more conducive the method is toward plan-driven methods. Conversely, the more points lie toward the center of the chart, the more a project would likely benefit from agile methods.

Consider the black line joining the points of a sample project in Figure 4.2. Starting at the top of the chart, this team is comprised of a large number of novices and a small number of experts. Additionally, the requirements are not expected to change much throughout the project. The team members have a fairly strong preference for order and predictability. There are about 15 people on the team. The impact of a software defect is in essential funds. To clarify, an impact of "essential funds" indicates that a business could lose a large amount of money if there was a defect in the software. For example, an auction application could cause a loss of a large amount of money due to a software defect, as could software that ran a grocery store. Based on the shape of the polar chart for this particular application, the team would be best served by a plan-driven software development methodology.

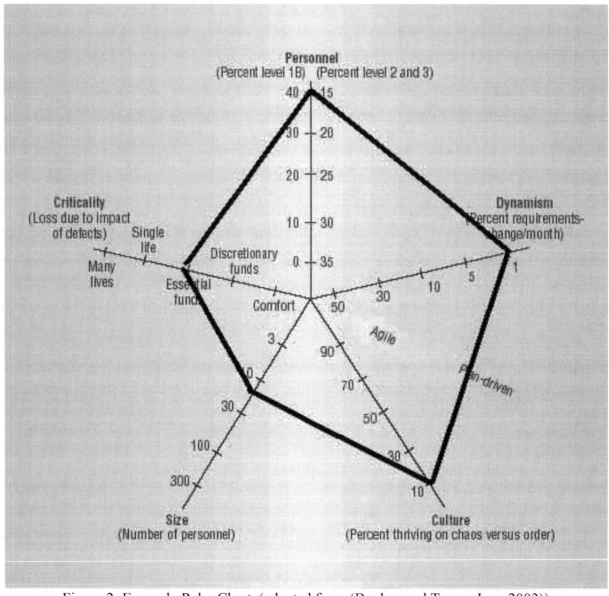

Figure 2: Example Polar Chart. (adapted from (Boehm and Turner June 2003))

## 4.4   Risk-Driven Method for Balancing Agile and Plan-Driven Methods

With this background, you can now understand Boehm and Turner's five-step, risk-driven method for balancing agile and plan-driven methods. Each of the five steps will now be explained. The interactions between the steps are displayed in Figure 3.

**Step One: Risk Analysis**

Three different areas of risk are analyzed: environmental, agile, and plan-driven. Each of these areas is now defined.

*Environmental risks* – risks that result from the project's general environment, as discussed in the earlier sections of this chapter and enumerated in Table 1.

*Agile risks* – risks that are specific to the use of agile methods. Some of these are issues related to the ability of agile methods to scale to larger teams and projects and to handle the reliability needs of critical projects. Additionally, there are agile risks associated with not thoroughly documenting prior to coding, with the potential of personnel turnover/ churn, and with having enough skilled people.

*Plan-driven risks* – risks that are specific to the use of plan-driven methods. Some of these issue relate to the ability of plan-driven methods to handle rapid technology and/or requirements change, the need to deliver rapid results, and/or having enough team members skilled in plan-driven methods.

If not enough information is known about any of these risks, some resources can be spent to obtain some information about the project's aspects until the team feels more confident about the project risks.

## Step Two: Risk Comparison

After the risks are identified, the team assesses and compares them. If the plan-driven risks outweigh the agile risks (meaning the issues related to using a plan-driven methodology are more concerning), then the team should adopt an agile method and proceed to Step Four. If the agile risks outweigh the plan-driven risks, then the team should adopt a plan-driven method and proceed to Step Four. If neither dominates – and the project characteristics do not clearly lie in the agile or plan-driven home ground – then the team should proceed to Step Three.

## Step Three: Architecture Analysis

The optional Step Three is done when the project characteristics do not clearly lie in either the agile or plan-driven home ground or when parts of the system lie in an agile home ground and other parts of the system lie in the plan-driven home ground. If possible, the team develops a system architecture so that the team is able to use agile methods on the parts of the system where their strengths can be best applied. The remainder of the system is developed via plan-driven methods.

## Step Four: Tailor Life Cycle

A project strategy is developed to address the risks identified in Step One, as was discussed earlier in the chapter. The life-cycle process is tailored around the identified risk patterns.

## Step Five: Execute and Monitor

Consistent with the need to consistently monitor risk items, as discussed earlier in the chapter – the team must consistently reassess the risks related to agile and plan-driven methods. If the risk profile changes, the team should consider their choice of process model.

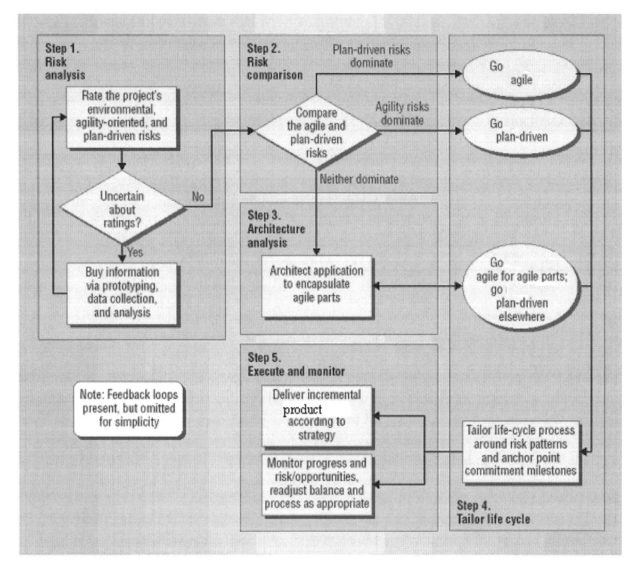

Figure 3: Boehm and Turner's Five Step Risk-Based method for balancing Agile and Plan-Driven methods. (adapted from (Boehm and Turner 2003; Boehm and Turner June 2003))

## 5 Summary

Several practical tips for risk management were presented throughout this chapter. The keys for successful risk management are summarized in Table 10.

Table 10 Key Ideas for Risk Management

| | |
|---|---|
| 🔑 | Be proactive about managing risk or you'll constantly be in crisis-driven, fire-fighting mode. |
| 🔑 | Systematically surface risks by meeting with marketing and the customer, by using checklists and taxonomies, by comparing with past projects, and by decomposing large, unwieldy risks into smaller, more manageable risks. |
| 🔑 | All the stakeholders must communicate about risks throughout the entire development cycle. Communication is at the center of the risk management process. |
| 🔑 | Prioritize risks by computing the risk exposure of each risk. Sort the list of risks based upon the risk exposure and proactively manage those on the top of the list. |
| 🔑 | Develop a "Top 10" risk list for your projects. It is likely that this "Top 10" list will contain risks that will appear on your next projects as well. |
| 🔑 | Utilize a risk-driven process for choosing between an agile and a plan-driven process, or a hybrid of the two. |

In the risk management cycle, product and project risks are identified, analyzed, and prioritized. The top-ranking risks are planned and mitigated. All risks are monitored. It is important for a project to focus on its critical success factors while keeping an eye on its risk factors. Risk management practices enable the team to find the opportunity in the risk items. Be proactive!

## Glossary of Chapter Terms

| Word | Definition | Source |
|---|---|---|
| Risk | potential future harm that may arise from some present action | (Wikipedia 2004) |
| Risk Exposure | the product of the probability of a risk occurring multiplied by the magnitude of the loss if the risk did occur | (Boehm 1989) |
| Risk Leverage | the quotient of the difference of the risk exposure before risk reduction minus the risk exposure after risk reduction, divided by the cost of risk reduction | (Pfleeger 1998) |
| Risk Management | series of steps whose objectives are to identify, address, and eliminate software risk items before they become either threats to successful software operation or a major source of expensive rework | (Boehm 1989) |

## References

Boehm, B. (1989). Software Risk Management. Washington, DC, IEEE Computer Society Press.
Boehm, B. (January 1991). "Software Risk Management: Principles and Practices." IEEE Software: 32-41.

Boehm, B. and R. Turner (2003). <u>Balancing Agility and Discipline: A Guide for the Perplexed</u>. Boston, MA, Addison Wesley.

Boehm, B. and R. Turner (June 2003). "Using Risk to Balance Agile and Plan-Driven Methods." <u>IEEE Computer</u> **36**(6): 57-66.

Bruegge, B. and A. H. Dutoit (2000). <u>Object-Oriented Software Engineering: Conquering Complex and Changing Systems</u>. Upper Saddle River, NJ, Prentice Hall.

Cockburn, A. (2001). <u>Agile Software Development</u>. Reading, Massachusetts, Addison Wesley Longman.

Gluch, D. P. (1994). A Construct for Describing Software Development Risks. Pittsburgh, PA, Software Engineering Institute.

Gupta, U. G. and R. E. Clarke (1996). "Theory and Applications of the Delphi Technique: A bibliography (1975-1994)." <u>Technological Forecasting and Social Change</u> **53**: 185-211.

Hall, E. M. (1998). <u>Managing Risk: Methods for Software Systems Development</u>, Addison Wesley.

Larman, C. (2004). <u>Agile and Iterative Development: A Manager's Guide</u>. Boston, Addison Wesley.

Pfleeger, S. L. (1998). <u>Software Engineering: Theory and Practice</u>. Upper Saddle River, NJ, Prentice Hall.

Standish (1995). "The Chaos Report."

Van Scoy, R. L. (1992). Software Development Risk: Opportunity, Not Problem. Pittsburgh, PA, Software Engineering Institute.

Wikipedia (2004). Wikipedia, The Free Encyclopedia. <u>http://www.wikipedia.org</u>.

## Chapter Questions

1.  The Jones family has just moved in a new house. Mr. Jones did some research of this area and found out that the probability for a house to be flooded once in a six-month period is 0.5% and no house has flooded twice in a six-month period. Additionally, Mr. Jones evaluated that, in case a flood would happen, the property damage would be $4,000, on average. If Mr. Jones wants to buy flood insurance, what should he pay for a six-month policy based upon his research?

2.  (Continued from Question 1) It is not possible for an insurance company to provide a rate quote as low as Mr. Jones likes it to be (or the insurance company wouldn't make any money!) After contacting several insurance companies, Mr. Jones found out that the lowest rate is $50 every six months. Compute the risk leverage if Mr. Jones buys the insurance. (Assume that the insurance company would pay $4,000 dollars if the flood occurs.)

3.  Believe it or not, buying music CD can be a risky business. One day, your friend tells you that your favorite band has just released a new CD, and it is awesome (in her opinion, anyway). Complete a risk table for buying a new CD in order to minimize your risk.

4.  A college student often has several assignments due each week. What are some of the factors a college student should think about in doing risk management for his or her assignments?

5.  Explain the five critical agile and plan-driven factors.

# An Introduction to the Unified Modeling Language

*A picture is worth a thousand words.*

Most people refer to the Unified Modeling Language as UML. The UML is an international industry standard graphical notation for describing software analysis and designs. When a standardized notation is used, there is little room for misinterpretation and ambiguity. Therefore, standardization provides for efficient communication (a.k.a. "a picture is worth a thousand words") and leads to fewer errors caused by misunderstanding.

The U in UML stands for unified because the UML is a unification and standardization of earlier modeling notations of Booch, Rumbaugh, Jacobson, Mellor, Shlaer, Coad, and Wirf-Brock, among others. The UML most closely reflects the combined work of Rumbaugh, Jacobson, and Booch – sometimes called *the three amigos*. The UML has been accepted as a standard by the Object Management Group[17] (OMG). The OMG is a non-profit organization with about 700 members that sets standards for distributed object-oriented computing.

In this appendix, we bring together for ease of reference five fundamental UML models: use case, class, sequence, state, and activity diagrams. The intent is not for this to be your only UML reference, but to succinctly provide you with the essential 20% of the UML that will provide you with the 80% of the capability you will use often.

## 1. Use Case Diagrams

Use case diagrams are used during ***requirements elicitation and analysis*** as a graphical means of representing the functional requirements of the system. Use cases are developed during requirements elicitation and are further refined and corrected as they are reviewed (by stakeholders) during analysis. Use cases are also very helpful for ***writing acceptance test cases***. The test planner can extract scenarios from the use cases for test cases. Note: The use case diagram is accompanied by a textual use case flow of events. The flow of events is not explained in this document.

A *use case,* a concept invented by Ivar Jocbson [4], is a sequence of transactions performed by a system that yields an outwardly visible, measurable result of value for a particular actor. A use case typically represents a major piece of functionality that is complete from beginning to end [1].

In UML, a use case is represented as an ellipse, as shown in Figure 1. In a Monopoly game, some use cases are: Enter Player Info, Buy House, and Draw Card. Give your use case a unique name expressed in a few words (generally no more than five words). These few words must begin with <u>a present-tense</u> <u>verb phrase in active voice</u>, stating the action that must take place (notice: **Enter** Player Info, **Buy** House, **Draw** Card, and **Switch** Turn).

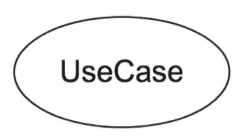

**Figure 1: The UML symbol for a use case**

An *actor* represents whoever or whatever (person, machine, or other) interacts with the system. The actor is <u>not</u> part of the system itself and represents anyone or anything that must interact with the system to:

Input information to the system;
Receive information from the system; or
Both input information to and receive information from the system.

The total set of actors in a use case model reflects everything that needs to exchange information with the system [6]. In UML, an actor is represented as a stickman, shown below in Figure 2. In a Monopoly game, some actors are the player and a bad player (who has the audacity to want to take two turns in a row!). As you see, actors can be people or they can be other systems. The name of an actor is always a <u>noun</u>. However, the name should not be that of a particular person. Instead, the name should identify the <u>role</u> or set of roles the actor plays relative to one or more use cases.

**Figure 2: The UML symbol for an actor**

A *use case diagram* is a visual representation of the relationships between actors and use cases together that documents the system's intended behavior. A simple use case diagram is shown in

Figure 3.

Arrows and lines are draw between actors and use cases and between use cases to show their relationships. We discuss these relationships more detail later in this appendix. The default relationship between an actor and a use case is the «communicates» relationship, denoted by a line. For example, in Figure 3, the actor is communicating with the use case.

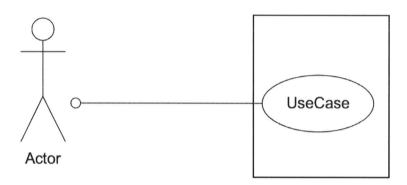

**Figure 3: A UML use case diagram**

There are several different kinds of relationships between actors and use cases. Earlier, we said that the default relationship is the «communicates» relationship. The «communicates» relationship indicates that one of these entities initiated invoked a request of the other. An actor communicates with use cases because actors want measurable results. It might not be quite as obvious that use cases can communicate with other use cases. This happens if a case needs information from or to initiate action of another use case. When a line or an arrow is drawn on a diagram and there is no label on the arrow, it is, by default, a «communicates» relationship.

There are two other kinds of relationships between use cases (not between actors and use cases) that you might find useful. These are «include» and «extend». You use the «include» relationship when a chunk of behavior is similar across more than one use case, and you don't want to keep copying the description of that behavior [1]. This is similar to breaking out re-used functionality in a program into its own methods that other methods invoke for the functionality. For example, suppose many actions of a system require the user to login to the system before the functionality can be performed. These use cases would *include* the login use case.

The «include» relationship is not the default relationship. Therefore in a use case diagram, the arrow is labeled with «include» when one use case makes full use of another use case, as shown in Figure 4. The Draw Card and the Buy House both use the View Information functionality.

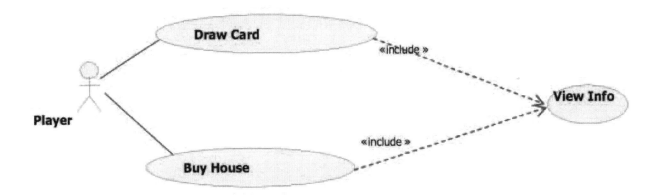

**Figure 4: Includes Use Case**

You use the «extend» relationship when you are describing a variation on normal behavior or behavior that is only executed under certain, stated conditions. The extend relationship is used when the alternative flow is fairly complex and/or multi-stepped, possibly with its own sub-flows and alternative flows. For example, consider the players moving on a Monopoly board.

   *A player moves on the board because he or she has to go to jail.*
   *A player moves on the board because he or she has to go to Free Parking.*

This scenario involves a player moving. However, sometimes a player has to deal with "exceptional" situations – rather than just moving to a new property cell. Therefore, we can extend the Move use case with the Go to Jail and the Go to Free Parking use case (and some others) as shown in Figure 5.

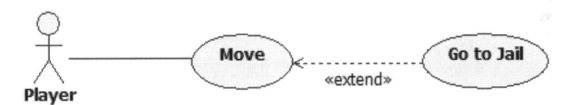

**Figure 5: Extends Use Case**

It is common to be confused as to whether to use the include relationship or the extend relationship. Consider the following distinctions between the two:

   Use Case X includes Use Case Y:
   X has a multi-step subtask Y. In the course of doing X or a subtask of X, Y will **always** be completed.

   Use Case X extends Use Case Y:
   Y performs a sub-task and X is a similar but more specialized way of accomplishing that subtask (e.g. closing the door is a sub-task of Y; X provides a means for closing a blocked

door with a few extra steps). X **only happens in an exception situation**. Y can complete without X ever happening.

In general, extend relationship makes the use cases difficult to understand. It is suggested that developers use this relationship sparingly.

## 2.  Class Diagrams

Class diagrams are used in both the **analysis** and the **design** phases. During the analysis phase, a very high-level conceptual design is created. At this time, a class diagram might be created with only the class names shown or possibly some pseudo code-like phrases may be added to describe the responsibilities of the class. The class diagram created during the analysis phase is used to describe the classes and relationships in the problem domain, but it does not suggest how the system is implemented. By the end of the design phase, class diagrams that describe how the system to be implemented should be developed. The class diagram created after the design phase has detailed implementation information, including the class names, the methods and attributes of the classes, and the relationships among classes.

The class diagram describes the types of objects in a system and the various kinds of static relationships that exist among them [1]. In UML, a class is represented by a rectangle with one or more horizontal compartments. The upper compartment holds the name of the class. The name of the class is the only required field in a class diagram. By convention, the class name starts with a capital letter. The (optional) center compartment of the class rectangle holds the list of the class attributes/data members, and the (optional) lower compartment holds the list of operations/ methods.

The complete UML notation for a class is shown in Figure 6. Attribute1 and Operation1 are private (denoted by the – sign); Attribute2 and Operation2 are protected (denoted by the # sign); Attribute3 and Operation3 are public (denoted by the + sign). The -, #, and + signs are optional, depending upon the level of detail of the design.

| **ClassName** |
| --- |
| -Attribute1<br>#Attribute2<br>+Attribute3 |
| -Operation1()<br>#Operation2()<br>+Operation3() |

**Figure 6: UML notation for a class**

## 2.1 Static Relationships

There are two principle types of static relationships between classes: inheritance and association. The relationships between classes are drawn on class diagram by various lines and arrows.

Inheritance (termed "*generalization*" for class diagrams) is represented with an empty arrow, pointing from the subclass to the superclass, as shown in Figure 7. In this figure, UtilityCell inherits from Cell (a.k.a UtilityCell "is-a" specialized version of a Cell). The subclass (UtilityCell) inherits all the methods and attributes of the superclass (Cell) and may override inherited methods.

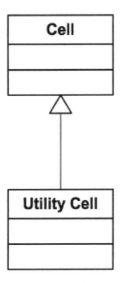

**Figure 7: Generalization**

An association represents a relationship between two instances of classes. An association between two classes is shown by a line joining the two classes. Association indicates that one class utilizes an attribute or methods of another class. If there is no arrow on the line, the association is taken to be bi-directional, that is, both classes hold information about the other class. A unidirectional association is indicated by an arrow pointing from the object which holds to the object that is held. There are two different specialized types of association relationships: aggregation, and composition.

If the association conveys the information that one object is part of another object, but their lifetimes are independent (they could exist independently), this relationship is called *aggregation*. For example, we may say that "a Department contains a set of Employees," or that "a Faculty contains a set of Teachers." Where generalization can be though of as an "is-a" relationship, aggregation is often thought of as a "has-a" relationship – "a Department 'has-a' Employee." Aggregation is implemented by means of one class having an attribute whose type is in included class (the Department class has an attribute whose type is Employee).

Aggregation is stronger than association due to the special nature of the "has-a" relationship. Aggregation is unidirectional: there is a container and one or more contained objects. An aggregation relationship is indicated by placing a white diamond at the end of the association next to the aggregate class, as shown in Figure 8.

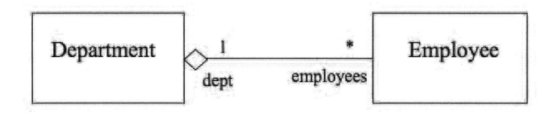

**Figure 8: Aggregation**

Even stronger than aggregation is *composition*. There is composition when an object is contained in another object, and it can exist only as long as the container exists and it only exists for the benefit of the container. Examples of composition are the relationship Invoice-InvoiceLine, and Drawing-Figure. An invoice line can exist only inside an invoice, and a specific geometric figure only inside a drawing (in the context of a graphic editor). Any deletion of the whole (Invoice) is considered to cascade to all the parts (the InvoiceLine's are deleted).

Composition is shown by a black diamond on the end of association next to the composite class, as shown in Figure 9. In this figure, we show also the fact that the relationship between a Gameboard and its Cells can be navigated only from Gameboard to Cell (an arrow points from Gameboard to Cell). Therefore, this relationship is a composition, and not an aggregation.

**Figure 9: Composition**

To summarize – aggregation is a special form of association; composition is a stronger form of aggregation. Both aggregation and composition are a part-whole hierarchy.

## 2.2 Attributes and Operations

Attributes or data members are shown in the middle box of the class diagram. It is optional to show the attributes. When an attribute is included, it is possible to only specify the name of the attribute. UML notation also allows showing their type (the class of the data type of the attribute), their default value, and their visibility with respect to access from outside the class. Public attributes are denoted with a + sign, protected with a # sign, and private with a -, as shown in Figure 10. The UML syntax for an attribute is:

*visibility name : type = defaultValue*

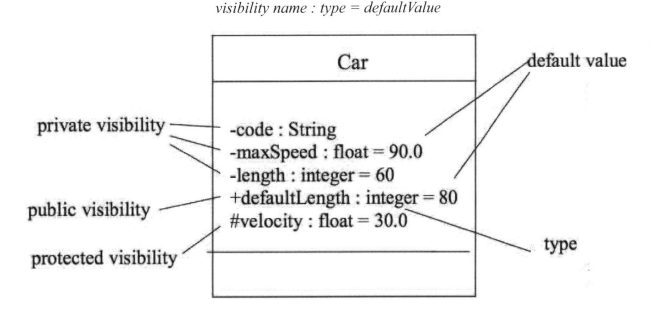

**Figure 10: Notation for attributes**

The third and bottom compartment of class symbol in UML notation holds a list of class operations or methods. The operations are the services that a class is responsible for carrying out. They may be specified giving their signature (the names and types of their arguments/ parameters), the return type, and their visibility (private, protected, public) may be shown. An optional property string indicates property values that apply to the operation. UML notation for operations/methods is shown in Figure 11. The UML syntax for an operation is:

*visibility name(parameter-list) : return-type{property string}*

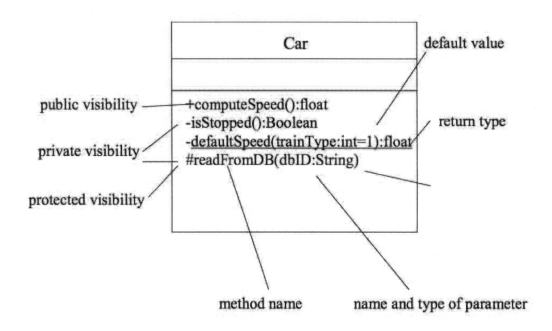

**Figure 11: UML notation for operations/methods**

## 2.3 Multiplicity

Associations have a multiplicity (sometimes called cardinality) that indicates how many objects of each class can legitimately be involved in a given relationship. Multiplicity is expressed by the "$n..m$" symbol put near to the association line, close to the class whose multiplicity in the association we want to show. Here "$n$" refers to the minimum number of class instances that may be involved in the association, and "$m$" to the maximum number of such instances. If $n = m$, only an "$n$" is shown. An optional relationship is expressed by writing "0" as the minimum number. Table 1 shows the most common cases of multiplicity.

**Table 1: Multiplicity notation**

| Cardinality and modality | UML symbol |
|---|---|
| One-to-one and mandatory | 1 |
| One-to-one and optional | 0..1 |
| One-to-many and mandatory | 1..* |
| One-to-many and optional | * |
| With lower bound $l$ and upper bound $u$ | l..u |
| With lower bound $l$ and no upper bound | 1..* |

We demonstrate several of the aspects of association and multiplicity in Figure 12 .

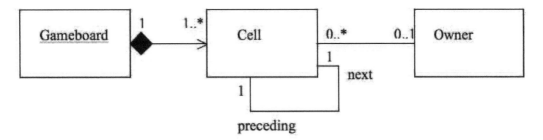

**Figure 12: An UML class diagram with three classes, their associations, and multiplicity**

Table 2 summarizes the associations between these three classes. Notice the "next" and "preceding" labels on the Cells association. These are called "roles." Labeling the end of associations with role names allows us to distinguish multiple associations originated from a class and clarify the purpose of the association. [1]

**Table 2: Details about the associations of Figure 12**

| Classes of association | Kind | Information held |
|---|---|---|
| Gameboard, Cell | Composition | A gameboard contains one or more cells. A cell is contained in one and only one gameboard. The gameboard can access its sections but the cells do not need to access their gameboard. The cells cannot exist in isolation, but only if contained by a gameboard. |
| Cell, Cell | Association | Every Cell is associated with, and must be able to access, its *next* Cell and its *preceding* Cell, along the Gameboard. |
| Cell, Player | Association | A Cell is owned by zero or more Owners. An Owner owns zero or more Cells. The Cell can access its Owner, and the Owner can access the Cells it owns. |

## 2.4 *More Advanced Class Diagram Concepts*

The prior sections on class diagram provided you with most of the information you will need to create complete diagrams. There are a few more aspects that you might find helpful for some more advanced diagrams.

### 2.4.1 Abstract Classes

If you have an abstract class or method, the UML convention is to italicize the name of the abstract item. You can also label the item with {abstract}.

### 2.4.2 Packages

If a system is big, it should be partitioned in smaller sub-systems, each with its own class diagram. In UML notation, the partitions/sub-systems are called *packages*. A package is a grouping of model elements, and as such it is a UML construct used also in other UML diagrams. Packages themselves may be nested within other packages. A package may contain both subordinate packages and ordinary elements of the class diagram, although it is not usually a good idea to mix in the same diagram packages and classes.

The symbol of two collapsed packages is shown in Figure 13. The name of the package is placed within the large rectangle. A collapsed package does not show its contents (which classes are contained in the package) and are used in a higher-level system diagram that shows all packages composing the system and their dependencies. A package depends on another package if at least one of its classes depends on the classes of the latter package.

**Figure 13:  UML notation for two collapsed packages with a dependency relationship**

A package may also be drawn showing its contents. In this case, its name is placed in the small rectangle on the upper-left side, while a UML class diagram, showing the classes or the packages contained in it is shown in Figure 14.

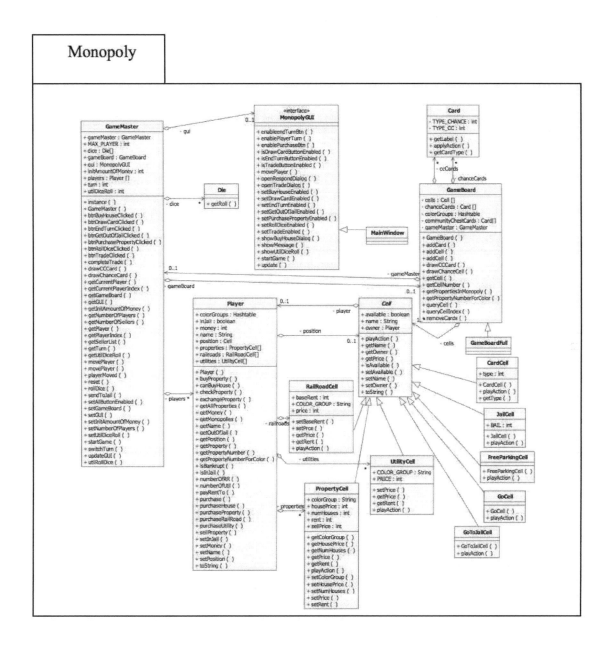

**Figure 14: A (non-collapsed) package diagram**

### 2.4.3 Stereotypes

Stereotypes are a high-level classification of an object that gives you some indication of the kind of object it is. Classes can be grouped under *stereotypes*, whose name is written between matched guillemots (« »), over the class name. Stereotypes can also be shown with specific icons. All model elements can have stereotypes. For example, common class stereotypes are:

«control», a class, an object of which denotes an entity that controls interactions between a collection of objects;

«entity», a class that represents a domain-specific situation or a real-world object and that

does not initiate interactions; and
«boundary», a class that lies on the periphery of a system but within it.

Other stereotypes can be defined by the team within the context of the system to be developed.

### 2.4.4 Notes
The class diagram may also include a *note* which is represented as a rectangle with a "bent corner" in the upper right corner. Notes are used to "attach" comments and constraints to the model elements. Notes may appear on any UML diagram and may be attached to zero or more modeling elements by dashed lines. Notes have no impact on the model.

### 2.5 Object Diagrams
UML class diagrams show the classes of the system, their data structure, their relationships and their interfaces. Ideally, a full UML class diagram show all system classes, although for practical reasons they are usually partitioned in many class diagrams, referring to various packages. A UML object diagram, on the other hand, shows a snapshot of the detailed state of a system at a point in time. A UML object diagram shows some specific instance of the classes of the system. While there is only class diagram of the system, there may be hundreds of different object diagrams. In an object diagram, many different instances of the same class, and no instance of other classes, may be shown.

Figure 15 shows UML notation for an object. The notation is similar to the class notation, with three key differences:

The name of the object is underlined, and is followed by its class name, separated by a colon. Often, there is no need to explicitly name a class. In this case, only the colon and the object name are written in the rectangle.
The attribute compartment may hold a list with the values of relevant attributes of the object.
There is no operation compartment.

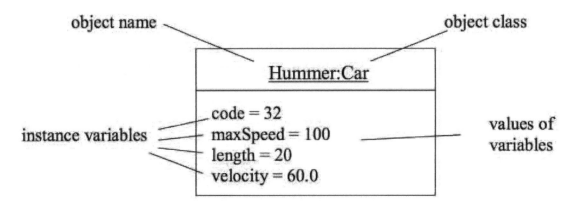

**Figure 15:  UML notation for an object**

294

In object diagrams, the associations among objects are shown as *links*. A binary link is shown as a path between two objects. In the case of a reflexive association, it may involve a loop with a single object.

A role name may be shown at each end of the link. An association name may be shown near the path; if present, it is underlined to indicate an instance. Multiplicity is not shown for links because they are instances. Other association adornments (aggregation, composition, navigation) may be shown on the link roles. A sample object diagram is shown in Figure 16.

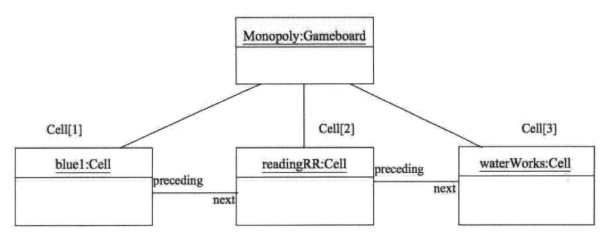

**Figure 16: Object diagram with a Monopoly Gameboard and some specific Cells**

## 3   Sequence Diagrams

Sequence diagrams are used in the **analysis** and **design** phases. Sequence diagrams are often used to depict the chronologically-structured event flow (e.g. a scenario) through a use case. A scenario is a sequence of actions that illustrates behavior. A scenario may be used to illustrate an interaction or the execution of a use case instance. [7]

*As with other UML diagrams, there is no one correct sequence diagram.* By creating a sequence diagram, the objects that participate in the use case are identified. Additionally, pieces of the use case behavior are assigned to objects in the form of services. The process of creating a sequence diagram often results in the refinement of the use case, potentially identifying missing but desired behaviors.

Sequence diagrams represent a system behavior based upon the needed interactions among a set of objects in terms of the messages that exchange among them to produce the desired result. Sequence diagrams highlight the sequence of messages through time. However, they do not show how objects are linked and may send messages to each other.

In a sequence diagram, objects are shown in columns, with their object symbol on the top of the line. Similar to the class diagram, the object name appears in a rectangle. If a class name is specified, it appears before the colon. The object name always appears after a colon (even if no class name is specified). If an external actor (see the preceding Use Case Diagram section above) initiates any interaction, the stick figure can be used rather than a rectangle.

A sequence diagram has two dimensions: the vertical dimension represents time; the horizontal dimension represents different objects. Initiation of the sequence starts in the top-left corner, and time proceeds down the page (from top to bottom). The vertical line is called the object's lifeline. There is no significance to the horizontal ordering of the objects.

A message sent from one object to another is shown as an arrow from the line of the sender to the line of the receiver. Each message is labeled at a minimum with message name. You can optionally include the arguments containing information that needs to be passed with the message. The reception of a message triggers a corresponding operation to execute. During this execution, other messages may be sent to other objects, and eventually the methods end. An object may send a message to itself. This is shown by an arrow from the object line to the same line. The method execution is represented in the sequence diagram by a thickening of the object line.

You begin to create a sequence diagram by writing a scenario highlighting all the nouns in the scenario. The nouns generally become the objects. For example, consider the following scenario. The unique nouns have been underlined. Each of these nouns is likely to become an object (though not all do, as you will see with the noun "turn").

*A player rolls the dice and gets a 6. The player moves 6 cells. The player lands on a cell that is an un-owned property. The player's turn is over.*

Figure 17 shows a possible sequence diagram for this scenario.

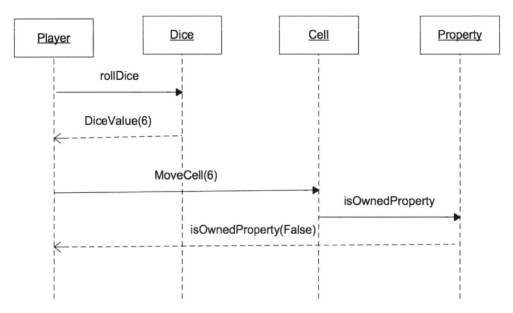

**Figure 17:  A sequence diagram representing a player taking a turn**

Conditional logic may also be expressed in a sequence diagram a guard.  In this way, a sequence diagram can express a set of scenarios in a more general way.

*A <u>player</u> rolls the <u>dice</u> and moves the number of cells indicated on the dice. If the player lands on a cell that is an un-owned <u>property</u>, the player's <u>turn</u> is over. If the player lands on a cell that is owned, the player must pay <u>rent</u> to the <u>owner</u> of the property.  Then, the player's turn is over.*

Figure 17 shows a possible sequence diagram for this set of scenario.

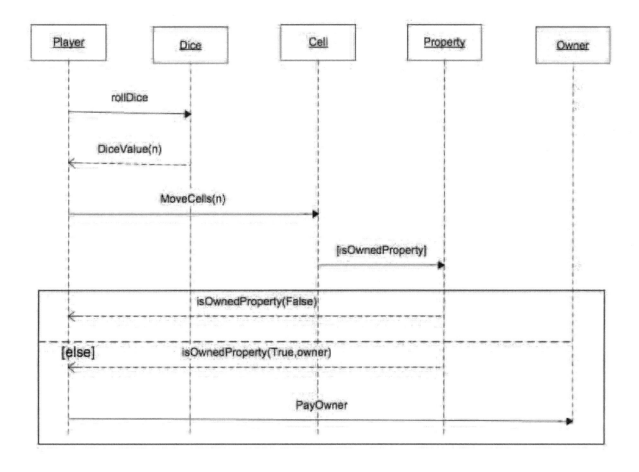

**Figure 18:  A sequence diagram representing a player taking a turn**

# 4   State Diagrams

State diagrams are created during the **analysis** and **design** phase to describe the behavior of nontrivial objects. State diagrams are good for describing the behavior of one object across several use cases and are used to identify object attributes and to refine the behavior description of an object. State diagrams are typically only used for complex objects.

A state is a condition in which an object can be at some point during its lifetime, for some finite period of time [8]. State diagrams describe all the possible states a particular object can get into and how the objects state changes as a result of external events that reach the object. [2] In this section, we'll present instead the notation for state diagrams that was first introduced by Harel [3], and then adopted by UML. In a state diagram:

A state is represented by a rounded rectangle.
A start state is represented by a solid circle.
A final state is represented by a solid circle with another open circle around it.
A transition is a change of an object from one state (the source state) to another (the target state) triggered by events, conditions, or time. Transitions are represented by an arrow connecting two states.

Each transition has a label that comes in three parts. All the parts are optional.

```
trigger-signature [guard]/activity
```

The trigger-signature is usually a single event that triggers a potential change of state. A missing trigger-signature, which happens rarely, indicates that you take the transition immediately.

The guard, if present, is a Boolean condition that must be true for the transition to be taken. A guarded transition occurs only if the guard resolves to true. Only one transition can be taken out of a given state. If more than one guard condition is true, only one transition will fire. The choice of transition to fire is nondeterministic if no priority rule is given [7]. A missing guard indicates that you always take the transition once the trigger-signature has fired.

The activity is some behavior that's "executed" during the transition. A missing activity means that you don't do anything during the transition.

Figure 19 shows the state diagram for the following:

*When a home is for sale, and a buyer and seller agree to a contract, the home goes under contract in the MLS system. When a home is under contract, other potential buyers can see the house but will understand it is under contract. The buyer submits a mortgage application and receives feedback. If the buyer's mortgage application is not approved, the contract is void. If the buyer's mortgage application is approved, the home is considered sold and is not longer available for viewing by other potential buyers. Once the sale transaction takes place, the home is removed from the system.*

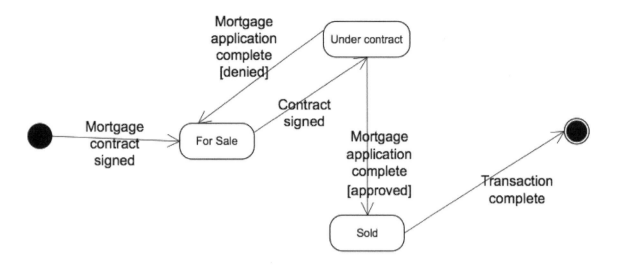

**Figure 19: UML State Diagram for a Turn in Monopoly**

## 5 Activity Diagrams

Activity diagrams are used during the **design** phase of complex methods. Alternately, the activity diagram can also be used during **analysis** to break down the complex flow of a use case. Through an activity diagram, the designer/analyst specifies the essential sequencing rules the method or use case has to follow.

UML activity diagrams are an updated and enhanced form of flowcharts; the main enhancement over flowcharts is the ability to handle parallelism, as will be discussed. An activity diagram is a variation of a state chart, discussed in the prior section, in which the states are activities representing the performance of operations and the transitions are triggered by the unconditional completion of the operations. An activity is a single step that needs to be done, whether by a human or a computer [2]. Incoming transitions (an incoming arrow) trigger the activity. If there are several incoming transitions, any of these can trigger the activity independent of the others. [5]

Figure 19 shows an activity diagram for preparing corn on the cob. The symbols used in the diagram are the same as those used in state diagrams with the addition of the decision symbol and the synchronization bar. The symbol for a decision is the diamond shape, with one or more incoming arrows and with two or more outgoing arrows, each labeled by a distinct guard condition. A guard is a Boolean, logical expression that evaluates to "true" or "false." All possible outcomes should appear on one of the outgoing transitions.

The synchronization bar indicates that progress cannot proceed past the bar until all activities leading up to the bar have completed (the outbound trigger occurs only when all inbound triggers have occurred). The synchronization bar allows the activity diagram to be able to be used for concurrent programs. The designer can lay out the threads and when they need to synchronize.

Additionally, activity diagrams allow for parallelism, when the order of the ensuing activities is irrelevant (they can run consecutively, simultaneously, or alternately). For example in Figure 19, after the corn is boiled and the butter is melted, two things happen in parallel (the salt and the butter are put on the corn).

In the case that there is more than one possible final states, the various final states should be labeled with a name.

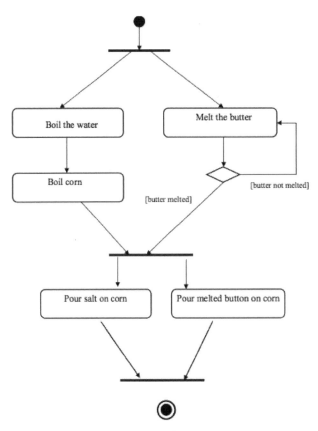

**Figure 20: An activity diagram explaining how to prepare corn on the cob**

We can use swimlanes in activity diagrams to specify "who" does what (where the "who" could be a particular role or a particular class). To use swimlanes, you must arrange your activity diagrams into vertical zones separated by dashed lines, as shown in Figure 20. The swimlanes indicate that "corn operator" is in charge of preparing the corn and putting the salt on. "Butter expert" melts the butter and pours it on the corn. Swimlanes are good in that they combine the activity diagram's depiction of logic and assign responsibility, as does the sequence diagram.

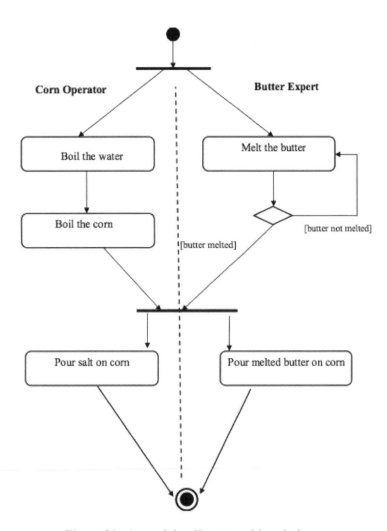

**Figure 21: An activity diagram with swimlanes**

## References

[1]    B. Bruegge and A. H. Dutoit, *Object-Oriented Software Engineering: Conquering Complex and Changing Systems*. Upper Saddle River, NJ: Prentice Hall, 2000.

[2]    M. Fowler, *UML Distilled*. Reading, Massachusetts: Addison Wesley, 2000.

[3]    D. Harel, "Statecharts: A visual formalism for complex systems," *Science of Computer Programming*, no., pp. 231-274, 1987.

[4]    I. Jacobson, M. Christerson, P. Jonsson, and G. Övergaard, *Object-Oriented Software Engineering: A Use Case Driven Approach*. Wokingham, England: Addison-Wesley, 1992.

[5]    B. Oestereich, *Developing Software with UML: Object-Oriented Analysis and Design in Practice*. London: Person Education, 2001.

[6]    D. Rosenberg and K. Scott, *Use Case Driven Object Modeling with UML: A Practical Approach*. Reading, Massachusetts: Addison-Wesley, 1999.

[7]    J. Rumbaugh, I. Jacobson, and G. Booch, *The Unified Modeling Language Reference*

*Manual.* Reading: Addison Wesley, 1999.

[8]    K. Scott, *UML Explained.* Boston, Massachusetts: Addison-Wesley, 2001.

# Glossary of Terms

| Word | Definition | Source |
|---|---|---|
| acceptance testing | formal testing conducted to determine whether or not a system satisfies its acceptance criteria (the criteria the system must satisfy to be accepted by a customer) and to enable the customer to determine whether or not to accept the system | (IEEE 1990) |
| accidental reuse | the developers of a new product "accidentally" realize that a previously developed product can be reused in the new product | (Schach 2002) |
| actor | An abstraction for entities outside a system, subsystem, or class that interact directly with the system. An actor participates in a use case or coherent set of use cases to accomplish an overall purpose. | (Rumbaugh, Jacobson et al. 1999) |
| adaptive maintenance | software maintenance performed to make a computer program usable in a changed environment | (IEEE 1990) |
| benchmark | (1) A standard against which measurements or comparisons can be made; (2) a procedure problem, or test that can be used to compare systems or components to each other or to a standard as in (1). | (IEEE 1990) |

| | | |
|---|---|---|
| best practice | a software development practice that, through experience and research, has proven to reliably lead to a desired result and is considered to be prudent and advisable to do in a variety of contexts | (Hovemeyer and Pugh 2004) |
| black box testing (also called functional testing or behavioral testing) | testing that ignores the internal mechanism of a system or component and focuses solely on the outputs generated in response to selected inputs and execution conditions | (IEEE 1990) |
| bottleneck | the location in software or hardware where the performance is lower than that in other parts of the system and thereby limits the overall throughput | |
| boundary value | data value that corresponds to a minimum or maximum input, internal, or output value specified for a system or component | (IEEE 1990) |
| branch coverage | a measure of the percentage of the decision points (Boolean expressions) of the program have been evaluated as both true and false in test cases | |
| bug pattern | a code idiom that is likely to be an error; occurrences of bug patterns are places where code does not follow usual correct practice in the use of a language feature | (Hovemeyer and Pugh 2004) |

| | | |
|---|---|---|
| change control board (also called configuration control board) | group of people responsible for evaluating and approving or disapproving proposed changes to configuration items, and for ensuring implementation of approved changes | (IEEE 1990) |
| computer science | A discipline that involves the understanding and design of computers and computational processes. In its most general form it is concerned with the understanding of information transfer and transformation. Particular interest is placed on making processes efficient and endowing them with some form of intelligence | (CSAB 1997) |
| condition coverage | a measure of the percentage of Boolean sub-expressions of the program that have been evaluated as both true or false outcome in test cases [applies to compound predicate]. | |
| constraints | a type of non-functional requirement that is imposed by the client that restricts the implementation of the system or the development process | |
| corrective maintenance | maintenance performed to correct faults in hardware or software | (IEEE 1990) |
| data flow testing | Testing that selects paths through the program's control flow in order to explore sequences of events related to the status of data objects. | (Beizer 1990) |
| defensive testing | Testing which includes tests under both normal and abnormal conditions | (Copeland 2004) |

| deliberate reuse | when a software component is constructed specifically for possible reuse | (Schach 2002) |
|---|---|---|
| driver | software module used to invoke a module under test and, often, provide test inputs, control and monitor execution, and report test results | (IEEE 1990) |
| dynamic analysis | The process of evaluating a system or component based on it behavior during execution. | (IEEE 1990) |
| emergency maintenance | unscheduled corrective maintenance performed to keep a system operational | (IEEE 1998) |
| engineering | the systematic and regular application of scientific and mathematical knowledge to the design, construction, and operation of machines, systems, and so on of practical use and, hence, of economic value.  Particular characteristic of engineers is that they take seriously their responsibility for correctness, suitability, and safety of the results of their efforts.  In this regard they consider themselves to be responsible to their customer (including their employers where relevant), to the users of their machines and systems, and to the public at large. | (Baber 1997) |
| error | the difference between a computed, observed, or measured value or condition and the true, specified, or theoretically correct value or condition | (IEEE 1990) |

| failure | the inability of a system or component to perform its required function within the specified performance requirement | (IEEE 1990) |
|---|---|---|
| failure path | a test case that intentionally forces an error condition to occur | |
| false positive | A test incorrectly reports that it has found a positive result where none really exists. | (Wikipedia) |
| fault | an incorrect step, process, or data definition in a program | (IEEE 1990) |
| feature | a small, client-valued function expressed in the form <action.><result><object> (e.g. calculate the total of a sale) | (Palmer and Felsing 2002) |
| functional requirement | requirements that specify a function that a system or system component must be able to perform | (IEEE 1990) |
| impact analysis | identification of all systems and system products affected by a change request and the development of an estimate of the resources needed to accomplish the change | (Riel 1996) |
| inspection | A static analysis technique that relies on visual examination of development products to detect errors, violations of development standards, and other problems | (IEEE 1990) |
| integration testing | testing in which software components, hardware components, or both are combined and tested to evaluate the interaction between them | (IEEE 1990) |

| latency | The time interval between the instant at which an instruction control unit issues a call for data and the instant at which the transfer of data has started; the delay between request and completion of an operation | (IEEE 1990) (Denaro, Polini et al. 2004) |
|---|---|---|
| load driver | a software program that takes the workload information as input, and generates requests that mimic the user behavior. | (Smith and Williams 2002) |
| maintainability | the ease with which a software system or component can be modified to correct faults, improve performance or other attributes, or adapt to changed environment | (IEEE 1990) |
| mean-time-to-repair (or downtime) | expected or observed time required to repair a system or component and return it to normal operation | (IEEE 1990) |
| method coverage | a measure of the percentage of methods that have been executed by test cases. | |
| mistake | human action that produces an incorrect result | (IEEE 1990) |
| mock object | debug replacement for a real-world object | (Hunt and Thomas 2003) |
| monitor | A program that observes, supervises, or controls the activities of other programs. | (Wikipedia) |
| non-functional requirements | requirements which are not specifically concerned with the functionality of a system but place restrictions on the product being developed | (Kotonya and Sommerville 1998) |
| object code | Computer instructions and data definitions in a form output by an assembler or compiler. | (IEEE 1990) |

| | | |
|---|---|---|
| pair programming | a style of programming in which *two* programmers work side-by-side at *one* computer, continuously collaborating on the same design, algorithm, code, or test. | (Williams and Kessler 2003) |
| perfective maintenance | software maintenance performed to improve the performance, maintainability, or other attributes of a computer program | (IEEE 1990) |
| performance | Degree to which a system or component accomplishes its designated functions within given constraints, such as speed, accuracy, or memory usage | (IEEE 1990) |
| performance requirement | Requirement that imposes conditions on a functional requirement; for example a requirements that specifies the speed, accuracy, or memory usage with which a given functionality must be performed | (IEEE 1990) |
| performance testing | testing conducted to evaluate the compliance of a system or component with specified performance requirements | (IEEE 1990) |
| preventative maintenance | maintenance preformed for the purpose of preventing problems before they occur | (IEEE 1990) |
| profiler | a type of performance monitor that provides code-level measurement, including timing, memory usage, and so on | (Smith and Williams 2002) |
| regression fault | faults injected when fixing other problems | |

| regression testing | selective retesting of a system or component to verify that modifications have not | (IEEE 1990) |
|---|---|---|
| | caused unintended effects and that the system or component still complies with its specified requirements | |
| requirement | (1) a condition or capability needed by a user to solve a problem or achieve an objective; (2) a condition or capability that must be met or possessed by a system or system component to satisfy a contract, standard, specification, or other formally imposed document. | (IEEE 1990) |
| requirements analysis | The process of studying user needs to arrive at a definition of system, hardware, or software requirements. | (IEEE 1990) |
| requirements engineering | a systematic way of developing requirements through an iterative process of analyzing a problem, documenting the resulting observations, and checking the accuracy of the understanding gained | (Loucopoulos and Champion April 1989) |
| requirements review | A process or meeting during which the requirements for a system, hardware item, or software item are presented to project personnel, managers, users, customers, or other interested parties for comment or approval. | (IEEE 1990) |
| requirements specification | A document that specifies the requirements for a system or component. | (IEEE 1990) |

| requirements volatility | the amount of change in the software requirements between the beginning and end of a software development project | (Boehm 1981) |
|---|---|---|
| resource consumption | the amount of memory or disk space consumed by the application | (Nixon 1998) |
| review | A process or meeting during which a work product, or set of work products, is presented to project personnel, managers, users, customers, or other interested parties for comment or approval.  Types include code review, design review, formal qualification review, requirements review, test readiness review | (IEEE 1990) |
| risk | potential future harm that may arise from some present action | (Wikipedia) |
| risk exposure | the product of the probability of a risk occurring multiplied by the magnitude of the loss if the risk did occur | (Boehm 1989) |
| risk leverage | the quotient of the difference of the risk exposure before risk reduction minus the risk exposure after risk reduction, divided by the cost of risk reduction | (Pfleeger 1998). |
| risk management | series of steps whose objectives are to identify, address, and eliminate software risk items before they become either threats to successful software operation or a major source of expensive rework | (Boehm 1989) |

| robustness testing | Testing whereby test cases are chosen outside the domain to test robustness to unexpected, erroneous input | (Bertolino May 2001) |
|---|---|---|
| scaffolding code | computer programs and data files built to support software development and testing but not intended to be included in the final product | (IEEE 1990) |
| scenario | A sequence of actions that illustrates behavior. A scenario may be used to illustrate an interaction or the execution of a use case instance. | (Rumbaugh, Jacobson et al. 1999) |
| smoke tests | group of test cases that establish that the system is stable and all major functionality is present and works under "normal" conditions | (Craig and Jaskiel 2002) |
| software development practice (or technique) | Software development practice (or technique) | (IEEE 1990) |
| software development process (or methodology) | The process by which user needs are translated into a software product. The process involves translating user needs into software requirements, transforming the software requirements into design, implementing the design in code, testing the code, and sometimes installing and checking out the software for operational use. Note: these activities might overlap or be performed iteratively. | (IEEE 1990) |

| software engineering | the application of a systematic, disciplined, quantifiable approach to the development, operation, and maintenance of software; that is, the application of engineering to software | (IEEE 1990) |
|---|---|---|
| software maintenance | The process of modifying a software system or component after delivery to correct faults, improve performance or other attributes, or adapt to a changed environment. | (IEEE 1990) |
| software process model | simplified, abstracted description of a software development process | |
| source code | Computer instructions and data definitions expressed in a form suitable for input to an assembler, compiler or other translator. | (IEEE 1990) |
| specification | A document that specifies in a complete, precise, verifiable manner, the requirements, design, behavior, or other characteristic of a system or component, and often the procedures for determining whether these provisions have been satisfied | (IEEE 1990) |
| stakeholder | key representative of the groups who have a vested interest in your system and direct or indirect influence on its requirements | |
| static analysis | the process of evaluating a system or component based on its form, structure, content, or documentation | (IEEE 1990) |

| statement coverage | a measure of the percentage of statements that have been executed by test cases. | |
|---|---|---|
| stereotype | A new kind of model element defined within the model based on an existing kind of model element. Stereotypes may extend the semantics but not the structure of pre-existing metamodel classes. | (Rumbaugh, Jacobson et al. 1999) |
| stress testing | testing conducted to evaluate a system or component at or beyond the limits of its specification or requirement | (IEEE 1990) |
| stubs | computer program statement substituting for the body of a software module that is or will be defined elsewhere | (IEEE 1990) |
| success path | a test case that execute some desirable functionality (something the customer wants to work) without any error conditions | This text |
| system testing | testing conducted on a complete, integrated system to evaluate the system compliance with its specified requirements | (IEEE 1990) |
| test case | set of test inputs, execution conditions, and expected results developed for a particular objective, such as to exercise a particular program path or to verify compliance with a specific requirement | (IEEE 1990) |

| test driver | software module used to involve a module under test and often, provide test inputs, controls, and monitor execution and report test results | (IEEE 1990) |
|---|---|---|
| test plan | document describing the scope, approach, resources, and schedule of intended test activities. It identifies test items, the features to be tested, the testing tasks, who will do each task, and any risks requiring contingency plans | (IEEE 1990) |
| testing | The process of analyzing a software item to detect the differences between existing and required conditions (that is, bugs) and to evaluate the features of the software item. | (IEEE 1990) |
| throughput | The amount of work that can be performed by a computer system or component in a given period of time; for example the number of jobs in a day | (IEEE 1990) |
| tuning | The process of transforming code that does not meet the performance requirements into code that meets the expected performance level without changing the behavior of the code. | (Smith and Williams 2002) |
| unit | a software component that cannot be subdivided into other components | (IEEE 1990) |
| unit testing | testing of individual hardware or software units or groups of related units | (IEEE 1990) |

| | | |
|---|---|---|
| usability testing | testing conducted to evaluate the extent to which a user can learn to operate, prepare inputs for, and interpret outputs of a system or component | (IEEE 1990) |
| use case | The specification of sequences of actions, including variant sequences and error sequences, that a system, subsystem, or class can perform by interacting with outside actors. | (Rumbaugh, Jacobson et al. 1999) |
| user story | a feature customers want in the software | (Beck and Fowler 2001) |
| validation | the process of evaluating a system or component during or at the end of the development process to determine whether it satisfies specified requirements | (IEEE 1990) |
| verification | the process of evaluating a system or component to determine whether the products of a given development phase satisfy the conditions imposed at the start of that phase | (IEEE 1990) |
| walkthrough | A static analysis technique in which a designer or programmer leads members of the development team and other interested parties through a segment of documentation or code, and the participants ask questions and make comments about possible errors, violations of development standards, and other problems. | (IEEE 1990) |

| white box testing | testing that takes into account the internal mechanism of a system or component | (IEEE 1990) |
|---|---|---|

## References

Baber, R. L. (1997). "Comparison of Electrical "Engineering" of Heaviside's Times and Software "Engineering" of our Times." IEEE Annals of the History of Computing 19(4): 5-17.

Beck, K. and M. Fowler (2001). Planning Extreme Programming. Reading, Massachusetts, Addison Wesley.

Beizer, B. (1990). Software Testing Techniques. London, International Thompson Computer Press.

Bertolino, A. (May 2001). Chapter 5: Software Testing. IEEE SWEBOK Trial Version 1.00.

Boehm, B. (1989). Software Risk Management. Washington, DC, IEEE Computer Society Press.

Boehm, B. W. (1981). Software Engineering Economics. Englewood Cliffs, NJ, Prentice-Hall, Inc.

Copeland, L. (2004). A Practitioner's Guide to Software Test Design. Boston, Artech House Publishers.

Craig, R. D. and S. P. Jaskiel (2002). Systematic Software Testing. Norwood, MA, Artech House Publishers.

CSAB (1997). "Defining the Computing Sciences Professions." http://www.csab.org/comp_sci_profession.html.

Denaro, G., A. Polini, et al. (2004). Early Performance Testing of Distributed Software Applications. Workshop on Software and Performance, Redwood Shores, California.

Hovemeyer, D. and W. Pugh (2004). Finding Bugs is Easy. Conference on Object Oriented Programming Systems Languages and Applications (OOSPLA) Companion, Vancouver, BC.

Hunt, A. and D. Thomas (2003). Pragmatic Unit Testing in Java with JUnit. Raleigh, NC, The Pragmatic Bookshelf.

IEEE (1990). IEEE Standard 610.12-1990, IEEE Standard Glossary of Software Engineering Terminology.

IEEE (1998). "IEEE Standard for Software Maintenance 1219-1998."

Kotonya, G. and I. Sommerville (1998). Requirements Engineering: Processes and Techniques. Chichester, John Wiley and Sons.

Loucopoulos, P. and R. Champion (April 1989). "Knowledge-Based Support for Requirements Engineering." Information and Software Technology 31(3): 123-135.

Nixon, B. A. (1998). Managing Performance Requirements for Information Systems. the 1st International Workshop on Software and Performance, Santa Fe, NM.

Palmer, S. R. and J. M. Felsing (2002). A Practical Guide to Feature-Driven Development. Upper Saddle River, NJ, Prentice Hall PTR.

Pfleeger, S. L. (1998). Software Engineering: Theory and Practice. Upper Saddle River, NJ, Prentice Hall.

Riel, A. J. (1996). <u>Object Oriented Design Heuristics</u>. Reading, Massachusetts, Addison Wesley.

Rumbaugh, J., I. Jacobson, et al. (1999). <u>The Unified Modeling Language Reference Manual</u>. Reading, Addison Wesley.

Schach, S. R. (2002). <u>Object-Oriented and Classical Software Engineering</u>. Boston, McGraw-Hill.

Smith, C. U. and L. G. Williams (2002). <u>Performance Solutions: A Practical Guide to Creating Responsive, Scalable Software</u>. Boston, MA, Addison-Wesley.

Wikipedia "http://www.wikipedia.org/."

Williams, L. and R. Kessler (2003). <u>Pair Programming Illuminated</u>. Reading, Massachusetts, Addison Wesley.

---

[1] An early use of this term was the 1972 Turing Award speech by Edsger W. Dijkstra (http://www.cs.utexas.edu/users/EWD/transcriptions/EWD03xx/EWD340.html).

[2] ACM (http://www.acm.org/) is the world's largest educational and scientific computing society, delivers resources that advance computing as a science and a profession.

[3] http://www.ieee.org

[4] http://www.realvnc.com/

[5] http://www.microsoft.com/windows/products/windowsvista/features/details/meetingspace.mspx

[6] http://xpairtise.sourceforge.net/

[7] JUnit is available at http://junit.org/index.htm. At this website, there are also many resources and articles written by JUnit users around the world.

[8] To be honest, we did not know `ArrayList` has such a method. We were planning to do a linear search through the `ArrayList`. That was why we had this test. If we had known this method before we wrote the test, we would not have written the test.

[9] http://httpunit.sourceforge.net/

[10] 1.    http://findbugs.sourceforge.net/

[11] Personal Software Process, PSP, Team Software Process, and TSP are all service marks of Carnegie Mellon University. Rational Unified Process and RUP are registered trademarks of IBM, Corp.

[12] The Software Engineering Institute (http://www.sei.cmu.edu/) is a federally funded research and development center sponsored by the U.S. Department of Defense. The SEI's core purpose is to help others make measured improvements in their software engineering capabilities.

[13] See http://www.ipd.uka.de/PSP/ for helpful PSP information and links to available PSP tools.

[14] Believe it or not, IEEE has a definition for *mistake*: a human action that produces an incorrect result.

[15] IEEE defines *failure* as the inability of a system or component to perform its required function within specified performance requirements. IEEE distinguishes between a human action (a *mistake*), the results of that mistake (a software *fault* that may or may not be noticed), and the noticeable result of the fault (a *failure*).

[16] In the lose-lose strategy, everyone gives something up, in the sense that neither side gets what they want, but everyone can live with the decision.

[17] For more information on the OMG, see http://www.omg.org

Made in the USA
Middletown, DE
27 August 2015